PRAISE FOR *20 SOMETHING MANIFESTO*

"*20 Something Manifesto* gives voice to the aspirations, expectations, confusion, and self-doubt of a generation. Christine Hassler goes deeper than the quick fix. She pushes, prods, nudges, and guides her readers to create their own road map. Offering information and inspiration in equal measure, Hassler provides tools for twenty somethings to chart an effective, fulfilling, and meaningful life journey all their own."

— Willow Bay, senior editor of the Huffington Post and author of *Talking to Your Kids in Tough Times*

"*20 Something Manifesto* is a great read for twenty somethings seeking honest answers to life's challenging questions. Christine approaches this journey of self-discovery and personal awareness in a way that is inspiring, comforting, and actionable. She brings to life emotions and feelings that will strike a chord with twenty somethings from all backgrounds. I strongly recommend this book."

— Jason Ryan Dorsey, Gen Y consultant and author of *My Reality Check Bounced!*

"The stories in *20 Something Manifesto* are inspiring, helpful, and deeply genuine. Christine Hassler is the perfect tour guide to take readers through the ups and downs of twenty-something life. She provides support, companionship, and tangible tools readers can use to create their own road map for a productive, fulfilling, and meaningful adult life. I wish I had Christine as a resource when I was in my twenties!"

— Lindsey Pollak, author of *Getting from College to Career: 90 Things to Do Before You Join the Real World*

"In her successful career as an author and life coach, Christine Hassler demonstrates a true gift — the ability to inspire twenty somethings to take stock of where they are and take the steps to become the people they want to be. Reading *20 Something Manifesto* feels warm and intimate, like sitting around a fire late at night and chatting with your closest friends."

— Alexandra Levit, author of *They Don't Teach Corporate in College* and *How'd You Score That Gig?*

"A great exploration into what it means to have one foot in childhood and one in so-called adulthood. As the average life span increases, technology advances, and the world spins ever faster, finding one's voice is a bigger challenge amid the cacophony of advertising, the internet, and reality TV. Christine Hassler 'gets it' that identity is a multifaceted, evolving process. With irreverent humor, heartfelt honesty, and deep poignancy, *20 Something Manifesto* is a wonderful guide for the quarter-lifers who ask at every turn 'Who am I now?' and 'Who am I becoming?'"

— Courtney A. Walsh, author of *Lipstick and Thongs in the Loony Bin*

20 SOMETHING
MANIFESTO

20 SOMETHING MANIFESTO

Quarter-Lifers Speak Out about Who They Are,
What They Want, and How to Get It

CHRISTINE HASSLER

New World Library
Novato, California

New World Library
14 Pamaron Way
Novato, California 94949

Copyright © 2008 by Christine Hassler

Expectation Hangover™ is a registered trademark of Christine Hassler.

The material in this book is intended for educational purposes only. No expressed or implied guarantee as to the effects of the use of the recommendations can be given nor liability taken.

Text design by Tona Pearce Myers

Library of Congress Cataloging-in-Publication Data
Hassler, Christine.
Twenty-something manifesto : quarter-lifers speak out about who they are, what they want, and how to get it / [compiled and edited by] Christine Hassler.
      p.   cm.
Includes index.
ISBN 978-1-57731-595-7 (pbk. : alk. paper)
1. Young adults—Conduct of life. 2. Young adults—Life skills guides.
I. Title.
HQ799.5.H37 2008
646.70084'2—dc22   2007044159

First printing, February 2008
ISBN: 978-1-57731-595-7
Printed in Canada on 100% postconsumer-waste recycled paper

New World Library is a proud member of the Green Press Initiative.

10   9   8   7   6   5   4   3   2   1

This manifesto is dedicated to everyone on their twenty-something journey.
May your path be blessed with self-discovery, insight, and joy.

CONTENTS

List of Exercises   xiii
Preface   xv
Introduction   xix

PART ONE
TWENTY SOMETHING IS TWENTY EVERYTHING   2

Chapter One. Your Twenty-Something Journey   3

"Confusion and Anxiousness" by Kaitlin   4
"Follow the Yellow Brick Road" by Jennifer   9
"The Blessed Miserable Generation" by Julie   15
"Where's My Corner Office?" by Patrick   20
"Bubble of Invincibility" by Diane   22
"Cruise Control" by Paul   25
"Complacency" by Luke   28

Chapter Two. Expectation Hangovers   31

"Compare, Regret, and Panic!" by Erin   40
"Detour" by Lisa   44

"Recovering from a Hangover" by Aurora   50

"Getting More Than I Gave" by Lauren   53

PART TWO

WHO AM I?: THE SELF-AWARENESS CONTINUUM 58

Chapter Three. Basic Self-Awareness   63

"Stranger in the Mirror" by Phil   66

"My Love/Hate Relationship with Me" by Kimberly   70

Chapter Four. Investigative Self-Awareness   73

"My Grown-Up Life" by Noelle   79

"Headiness" by Alexandra   84

"At Trust's Doorstep" by Gretchen   86

Chapter Five. Integrated Self-Awareness   89

"My Job Is Not My Identity" by Liz   93

"Seeing My Mom and Dad for Who They Are" by Victoria 97

"My Spiritual Growth" by Elissa   100

PART THREE

NAVIGATING THE TWENTIES TRIANGLE   106

Chapter Six. What Do I Want?   107

"Confessions of a Straight-A Slacker" by Caitlin   111

"Sweet Uncertainty" by Ann   117

"Job Jumper" by Steve   123

"Musings on Not Being a Pediatrician" by Kristin   126

"Choosing My Own Adventure" by Lindsey   130

"They Don't Teach Self-Discovery in College" by Natalie 133

Chapter Seven. How Do I Get What I Want?   139

"Listening to Myself" by Jess   142
"The Self-Sufficiency Standard" by Lucy   148
"Stuck in Quicksand" by R.J.   150

PART FOUR
THE TWENTY-SOMETHING PUZZLE   156

Chapter Eight. Friends and Family: Your Network   159

"Ruined by a Roommate" by Amanda   164
"Superfriend" by Kelly   167
"Friend Me" by Justin   170
"Thousand-Piece Jigsaw Puzzle" by Jessica   173
"Sometimes It Just Doesn't Make Any Sense" by Anne   178

Chapter Nine. Love   183

"Falling in Love with Me" by Eileen   186
"Let's Not Just Be Friends" by Eddie   192
"Dive In" by Jeff   195
"Always the Bridesmaid" by Chrissy   200
"Cautious Courage" by Jen   207
"Putting Me Back Together" by Sarah   209
"Whatever Happens, I'll Be Okay" by Tabatha   214
"He Said: We Don't Have to Fight or Flight" by Tim   218
"She Said: I Was Taking Love for Granted" by Michelle   219
"My Happy Ending" by Jonathan   228

Chapter Ten. Work and Career   231

"I Hated My Job" by Justin   237
"Paying My Dues" by Jeannette   244

"Solid Ground" by Jon   248
"I Love What I Do, but I Can't Pay My Bills" by Christina   258

PART FIVE
SURVIVING AND THRIVING   270

Chapter Eleven. Tough Stuff   271

"I Don't Get It!" by Giscelle   273
"My Soap-Opera Life as a Second Wife" by Angela   278
"My Lesson, in the Form of a Hurricane" by Brianne   280
"Honoring a Vow to Myself" by Josie   284
"Deportation to Restoration" by Jacqueline   286

Chapter Twelve. Body, Mind, and Money   291

"My Body Image Crisis" by Ashley   295
"Numbing the Pain" by Kurt   298
"From Euphoria to the Psych Ward" by Carla   301
"Charge It" by Aaron   308

Chapter Thirteen. Shift Happens   315

"Divorce — Take Two" by Heather   316
"This Too Shall Pass" by Jenna   323
"Everything Happens for a Reason" by Kim   324
"I've Done More Than Survive — I've Started to Thrive" by Denelle   326
"Dance Naked" by Tamara   330

Afterword: Share Your Twenty-Something Story   333
Acknowledgments   335
List of Contributors   337
Index   341
About the Author   353

EXERCISES

Part One

Get Inspired	12
What's Your Twenty?	29
Clarifying Goals	36
Expectation Implants	39
Commitment Contract	49
Expectation Hangover Treatment and Prevention Plan	54

Part Two

Grat-I-tude	78
Qual-YOU-ty Time	82
I Am Who I Am!	92
The Self-Awareness Continuum Counselor	104

Part Three

Smart-Slacking Game Plan	115
The Right-Answer Reflex Game	119

Past-Performance Review   122
Do-It-Yourself Personality Tests   132

Part Four

Identifying Toxic Relationships   162
Identifying Triggers and Corner Pieces   176
Finding Your Keys   191
Graduating from Singlehood   194
Manifest Your Soul Match   205
Relationship 101   222
"I Hate My Job" Survival Kit   239
Mission Vision Overview   258
Quarter Plan Overview   266

Part Five

The Acceptance Process   276
Walking in a Bully's Shoes   283
Give Your Label a Name   305
Throw a Money Party   311
Create a Vision Board   321

PREFACE

If you are looking for a book that gives you all the answers to make your twenty-something woes disappear, this is not it. If you are looking for someone else to tell you what decisions to make about your life, I'm not that person. If you want to read stories that talk about material achievements, this is not the manifesto you want. And if you are looking for a motivational book that is simply going to tell you things like, "Follow your dreams and anything is possible," or "You are in the prime of your life and it is supposed to be great" — sorry. However, if you are looking for a book full of *real* stories of personal struggles and successes, this is your manifesto. If you want to learn how to find your *own* answers, I'll share with you how that is possible. And if you are ready to look beyond inspirational anecdotes and take a hard look at yourself so that you are empowered and inspired, then you picked up the right book.

How many times have you been told to "simply follow your passion, and money, love, and success will follow?" I've read my fair share of motivational books and went to many seminars in my twenties looking for the key to getting out of my own quarter-life crisis. They would leave me inspired for about a week and then I'd fade right back into my funk. So this book really isn't about getting you pumped up or solving all your problems — you have to do more than just read a book for that. It's about inspiring you to accept where you are and take action to move forward to where you want to be. This manifesto is about supporting you as you navigate through the questions of what I call the "Twenties Triangle": Who am I? What do I want? How do I get it?

The twenty-something years are a confusing, scary, frustrating *and* exciting, stimulating, and transformational time. Unfortunately, a high school or college diploma does not come with instructions for the "real world." You have to believe in and truly get to know yourself in order to have clarity about your dreams and goals as well as insights about how to reach them. But that is no easy task, especially in a society that is so externally focused and driven by expectations.

Somehow this decade has gotten the reputation for being a time when you are supposed to figure out your entire life while having the time of your life. My purpose in writing this manifesto is to change this expectation. The twenty-something years are a rather messy rite of passage without any fancy ceremonies or parties to mark that you are through it. Sometimes it's a fun play-in-the-mud-during-a-rainstorm kind of messy — other times it's a your-car-is-stuck-in-the-mud-and-it's-all-over-your-new-suit kind of messy. If you are struggling to find balance and direction, welcome to *really* being twenty something! It's okay — once you remove this intense pressure to do, be, and have so much on the outside, and shift your focus inside, you will see that *you* get to decide what your twenty-something years are really about. You are the expert, you have the answers, and you will be your own greatest motivator.

But I bet you don't feel like an expert. . . . In fact you are probably craving expert advice from someone. Like some kind of sign from the heavens that will tell you what to do or reassure you that what you are doing is "right." Perhaps you are confused over the life you are "supposed" to be living versus the life you are actually living. Twenty-something life is not like an episode of *Friends*, but for some reason we think it should be. This has left a lot of twenty somethings stressed out on the inside while trying to be something they think they're supposed to be on the outside. No more. Welcome to the *Twenty-Something Manifesto*.

This is a book about one of the most important journeys of your life, the twenty-something journey. As you travel thru this manifesto, you'll hear from people who are just packing their bags for the trip and people who are at the end of the journey reflecting on what they saw, experienced, and learned along the way. Hopefully, the information and stories shared in this book, along with some nudging and support from me, will encourage you to give in to the ride of your twenty-something experiences. As you do, your dreams will unfold and answers to your questions will become clearer. All the twists and turns, unknowns, and Expectation Hangovers™ that come with this decade will make sense eventually. I promise. You just need to give it some investigation and time. So let go of the safety bar, toss your hands in the air, let out a scream, and enjoy the ride. . . .

> "The most difficult thing about being a twenty something is trying to sort out where I fit in life. Am I an adult or am I still a child in many ways? What am I going to do with my life? I feel confused and overwhelmed in general. That is what I find difficult about being a twenty something. I wish I came equipped with a manual."
>
> *Sales associate, 25, separated, Ohio*

INTRODUCTION

Since writing *Twenty Something, Twenty Everything*, I have seen firsthand the immense need for guidance that twenty somethings have and their thirst to feel "not alone." I have received thousands of emails and letters from twenty-something women and men (as well as from their parents) asking for more information, advice, and feedback. At the end of almost every email is the question, "Am I alone in feeling this way?" or, "Am I the only one going through this?" To anyone faced with uncertainty, sadness, or disillusionment, I can unequivocally tell you — you are not alone.

When I finished my first book, I was twenty-seven years old and I thought I knew a lot. Sitting here at thirty writing this manifesto, I realize that there was a lot I didn't know that I didn't even know I didn't know. The point is that each moment of life, each experience, each breath provides another opportunity for learning and growth. There is no such thing as knowing it all. Wisdom continuously evolves. Each person we come in contact with, whether for years or minutes, has something to share with us. I have been blessed with a life rich with people sharing their most profound experiences and have had many of my own; however, I do not know it all.

> "The twenties are about not knowing anything, but thinking that you do. It's realizing the mistakes you've made and figuring out how you are going to fix them inside your soul. It's about knowing you're going to be okay, even though it doesn't feel that way."
>
> Consultant, 27, married with two stepchildren, Virginia

What I do know is that we all have a purpose in life, and this purpose evolves as time ticks on and experience shapes and teaches us. At this point in my life, part of my purpose is to be a voice of encouragement and support for those experiencing a twenty-something crisis. Over the past five years, I've become a sort of "twenty-something expert," and here's what I've learned: The twenty-something crisis is a melting pot of issues; one topic or issue never stands alone. Twenty somethings desperately want to know *how* and *what* other twenty somethings are doing or did to get through their issues. And just talking about the issues is not enough; a practical manual is required that covers how to deal with all the real-life stuff not learned in college or from parents. I call it "twenty-something self-enlightenment." I like the word "self-enlightenment" much better than "self-help" or "self-improvement," which imply something is wrong with you — and there isn't!

WELCOME TO THE
TWENTY SOMETHING MANIFESTO

"Manifesto" is defined by *Merriam-Webster's Dictionary* as a "statement declaring publicly the intentions, motives, or views of its issuer." Let me just say this book is not only my manifesto — it is yours, the collective voice of twenty somethings. It's a place for twenty somethings to throw off the reputation and stereotypes society places on them and describe their lives the way they actually live them. It's a place for twenty somethings to voice what they are really going through and feeling. Not just job angst, not just relationship drama — but the nitty-gritty stuff that no one talks about. Even those who constantly write about their lives on blogs or MySpace, telling every intimate detail, may find them-

> "The hardest thing about being a twenty something is not knowing if you missed the boat on getting to where you want to be in ten or twenty years. I just feel like I missed something someone said during college, and everyone else heard it but me."
>
> Marketer, 26,
> serious boyfriend, Colorado

selves lost — asking questions but not coming up with answers. Twenty somethings need a road map, one that shows a path through their own troubled ground.

This book is meant to help you create your road map. To do so, you will have to learn about yourself along the way, and this takes time, patience, and experience. I know: you want answers now! I can't promise that, but I've filled this manifesto with the stories of twenty somethings, and in their struggles you may find the answers and lessons you need. The suggestions, advice, and exercises in this book are inspired from my own life, from the lives of my clients, from an online survey I conducted involving over a thousand twenty somethings, and from the twenty somethings who were inspired to write a personal story for this manifesto. These stories appear throughout and include a "Declaration" in which the person encapsulates the predominate take-aways from his or her story. Quotes by twenty somethings reflecting on their lives appear on nearly every page, and these include each person's "stats": profession, age, relationship status, number of children, and place of residence. The status of these "stats" preoccupies the thoughts of most twenty somethings I know.

This manifesto is a collection of puzzle pieces that each person will assemble in his or her own way. We begin by emptying the box and identifying all the pieces that make up our own twenty-something puzzles. We then identify where we are in our journeys and discover ways for making them a smoother ride. As we assemble our ideal picture, we'll see if certain puzzle pieces are missing, or if some do not fit, and decide what to do about them. Finally, we will celebrate the completion of our puzzles with stories of surviving and thriving.

> "One of the hardest parts of being a twenty something is feeling that you need to achieve it all — whatever 'all' may be. It's a feeling of urgency, like you need to achieve in every area of 'life' — career, marriage, family, money. All the while being happy and content. It's a feeling of great pressure — that if you don't work it all out now, you are setting yourself up for a fall in your thirties."
>
> Teacher, 27, married, Australia

You can read this manifesto from beginning to end or jump in at any place. Grab it when you need a pick-me-up or a swift but gentle kick in the right direction. Dog-ear the stories that move you or make you go "aha." Commit to doing the exercises and answering the questions. I encourage you to keep a journal in a notebook or on your laptop to capture your insights and ideas along the way.

WE ARE MORE ALIKE THAN WE ARE DIFFERENT

We really are more alike than we are different. This can be hard to remember, or even believe, since we live in a culture that focuses on what we look like, what we do, who we are with, what we have, and all the things that make us feel unique. But when we focus our attention inward, we begin to feel more connected to one another. We all cry, laugh, hurt, grow, worry, fear, think, make mistakes, obsess, dream, and love. As Alissa, twenty-seven, shared with me, "At this stage in my life, I'm always looking for people to latch on to who have felt the same, to see how they dealt with things and how I can get myself out of this suffocating black hole." We all have felt like we were in a black hole from time to time, but we must trust that, when we reach out to others, we'll find an experience, a person, or an intuitive connection that will shed light on our paths.

As you read, pay attention to the stories that really resonate with you, evoke an emotional reaction, or inspire you. There is a bit of you in every story — though we connect more deeply with some than others. Remember how certain films completely moved you? Reading or experiencing other people's stories creates an emotional impact and an opportunity for learning at a heightened level because it's not personal. When it's not *about* you, it's easier to see yourself. I've experienced this in my coaching practice; even as I counsel others, I learn about myself from my clients. They force me, unknowingly, to stay on top of my "stuff." They inspire me to keep investigating, to keep understanding myself, and to keep moving toward joy and wisdom.

YOUR TWENTY-SOMETHING TOUR GUIDE

If this is your manifesto, then think of me as the tour guide. I selected each story because I believed there was a lesson to learn or an insight to share. As the narrator who is reading between the lines, I offer suggestions on how to learn from your fellow twenty somethings. I hope you will be inspired and that their experiences will move you to tears, laughter, and action. This manifesto is a compass — it may point you in the right direction, but it's up to you to follow it.

You may notice that I use a lot of analogies — it has become part of my coaching and writing style. Why? Well, it actually has to do with the way the brain works. The left side of the brain focuses on rational thought, logic, and intellect, while the right side has a little more fun and operates our creativity and emotions. We need to use both to solve our problems. When reading a book, our left brain does most of the thinking. The problem is that we usually pick up self-enlightenment books when we have roadblocks in our lives that we can't logically think our way past. Even when our left brain understands the problem — in its very literal, black-and-white language — we may not solve it without the emotional and creative involvement of our right brain. Analogies evoke the pictures we need to "turn on" our right brain, which supports us in solving problems and dealing with emotions. And hey, if you are going to take the time to delve into this book, you might as well get the full-brain-experience guarantee.

Since the beginning of my own quarter-life crisis more than eight years ago, both sides of my brain have been a sponge soaking up information. What I have learned I share with you, and it comes from a potpourri of teachers and sources. But as I say above, this book is a map, not the gospel. It's a "manifesto" — a declaration of "intentions, motives, and views" — not the answer. Only you know what is right for you. If something resonates and raises questions I don't address, I encourage you to pursue your own answers in whatever way is personal and relevant to you. As one of the many tour guides you will have along your journey, I'm honored and excited to share this manifesto with you.

> "It seems like every decision you make in your twenties is the most important decision of your life. It's like you're standing at *many* crossroads, and they're all beckoning you to take a risk."
>
> Writer, 26, serious relationship, Texas

CREATING A
TWENTY-SOMETHING COMMUNITY

My hope is that you connect with this book and then want to connect with one another. For that reason, certain contributors' names are listed on pages 337–39. Others have stayed anonymous;

however, if you read a story by someone you feel a deep need to connect with, please email me (christine@christinehassler.com) and I will seek permission to get you in touch with him or her.

There is also a Twenty-Something Manifesto website that you can access at www.20somethingmanifesto.com to share your thoughts, comments, stories, and insights. I know that I have not covered every topic, so I encourage you to share the stories, perspectives, and issues that are missing! The manifesto does not end with the last page of this book; twenty somethings continue to write it each and every day.

PART 1

TWENTY SOMETHING
IS TWENTY EVERYTHING

"The most difficult thing about being twenty something is that this is the time when you build your foundation for all aspects of life, including job, love life, family, and finance. It takes time to see the results, it's difficult to focus on the 'now,' and sometimes I want to give up because I start doubting that what I am doing is for me."

Recruiter, 25, serious relationship, Virginia

You have arrived at an in-between stage of life: your twenties. This is a time between being a kid and being a real, full-fledged grown-up. It is a a time of firsts, decisions, changes, surprises, and — for the most part — a pretty good time. But then there are those other times that aren't so good. When those not-so-good times pile up until you feel like they fill your whole life, you know you are having a twenty-something, or quarter-life, crisis.

An in-between stage of life is by definition full of transition, and many common twenty-something transitions naturally put you at unfamiliar crossroads or dead ends. In this part of the book, we'll look at the common behaviors, feelings, and challenges that mark these transitional times. We'll also look at the disappointments that often come with the twenty-something experience and investigate ways to deal with Expectation Hangovers. You'll discover that the key to dealing with struggles and stresses is learning to see your twenties for what they are rather than trying to make them something you think they should be. Pack up your brain power, experience, gut feelings, and courage — you'll need them all as you embark on the twenty-something journey.

1. YOUR TWENTY-SOMETHING JOURNEY

"Being a twenty something is a time when everything in life is uncertain. I feel like the rug is constantly being pulled out from under me. The overwhelming guilt for not being happy for what I have in my life combined with constantly feeling like there is more to achieve and not enough time is exhausting. I wonder, is this as good as it gets?"

Executive administrator, 24, single, Minnesota

Remember puberty? Would you rather not? For many, those memories aren't exactly fond ones — acne, voice cracking, mood swings, and uncomfortable awkwardness. Yet we all expected it and made our way through it. How come we don't call adolescence a "crisis"? Because it's a normal part of our development. A twenty-something crisis is just as normal as our puberty "crisis," but that's not how most people treat it. Twenty somethings can get caught up in a tremendous amount of judgment — thinking they are alone, that there is something wrong with them, or that they should have it all figured out by now.

In this chapter we'll canvas the main reasons that twenty-something transitions come to feel like crises and the "syndromes"

> "As a twenty something, I feel like I have the world at my fingertips, but I don't know what to do with it all or any part of it."
>
> *Consumer analyst,*
> *23, dating, North Dakota*

that result. Many times it boils down to expectations. Where do you find yourself in the kaleidoscope of experiences and stories below? Where are you in your journey? I can guarantee that for every story here, there are thousands of other twenty somethings who can relate.

CHECKLISTERS AND PLANNERS

Do you live your life by a checklist? Have you developed a master plan that you pressure yourself to stick to? First high school, then college, then job, maybe grad school, then promotion, then relationship, then marriage, then buy a house, then have kids, then make X dollars by twenty-eight, and so on? A life goals checklist seems to come with an iPod these days — everyone has one. It doesn't take a rocket scientist to figure out why these checklists exist: expectations and uncertainty. Checklists and plans help us feel more secure and in control. But as a failed checklister, believe me, a checklist is not the recipe for success. In fact, it is more likely to whip up doubt and worry.

"CONFUSION AND ANXIOUSNESS" by Kaitlin, 21

DECLARATION: *By trying to convince myself that my hard work will result in a successful life in the future, I'm afraid that I am truly missing out on my life right now.*

I will be graduating from college this fall, and I am doing everything that was on my checklist to prepare me for a career. I have worked relentlessly to maintain my high GPA, take a full load of courses every semester, learn the necessary professional skills at my twenty-hour-a-week public relations internship, and work at a restaurant on the weekends. The word "exhaustion" might come to mind, but I continue to tell myself that it will all pay off in the years to come — this is what I am "supposed" to do. But what if it doesn't? What if after graduation, I get the job that I think I want, yet face the disappointment of feeling unhappy with my career choice when I thought I had it all figured out in college? I have these great expectations to be a successful public relations executive in a big city, with the corner office and spectacular view, have great friends, and maybe even a boyfriend. But how do I know what I really want?

I cannot help but feel like by putting all of my focus on my professional goals, I will one day regret not experiencing other aspects of life. I could reflect on my college experience as a time of fleeting independence, or I could choose to see the reality of my situation and look back on four years without a solid relationship, very few nights out with my girlfriends, and all-nighters spent studying for a morning exam.

My stress is perpetuated by my checklist of long-term goals and aspirations, and the pressure I exert upon myself to achieve them all. In what seems like a pretty early start for a twenty-something crisis, I can only hope to persevere by holding on to my ambition and being confident that my life will be all that I hope it will be.

Take Anxiety and Regret and Shove It . . . into the Present!

Anxiety (anticipation about something yet to happen) lives in the future; depression (sadness over things that you did or didn't do) signs a lease in the past. That is why, if you are a checklister, you probably suffer from a mixed bag of anxiety and depression. Checklisters and planners are consumed with worry about achieving everything on their list and then heavy with regret as they think about things they are missing out on.

"Having it all" is a common desire for checklisters. We grow up hearing that if we apply ourselves, we can get anything we want. So we put everything we want into our life goals list. I believe having it all at once is a myth — but you can have it all at different times in your life. The problem is, twenty somethings get so obsessed about the future that they overextend themselves and burn out by trying to accomplish all their goals right now.

If you are an anxious and confused checklister, get into the present! Be proud of your accomplishments and also have some fun. Go out with friends, have a social life, and take some pressure off. Consider this statement from a twenty-one-year-old about to graduate from college, "College should be a time of self-discovery; the years that shape who you are and who you want to be in life." Do you agree? I do, but I would add that self-discovery is a curriculum for life, not just college. It's true that college shapes you, but it provides just some of the clay you will mold into your life. Don't worry if college does not answer "who I am and what I want to be"; it probably won't, not completely and forever. Take college for what it is, a piece of the ongoing puzzle of who you are.

Living by a checklist and planning is actually a lot easier in college when the goal line is clearer and the timeline is shorter — graduate, get a job, find a place to live, and so on. But after college, and as your twenties continue, not only do the goals get bigger and more complicated, but you may find you don't even know what to plan for. A twenty-one-year-old confesses, "Being a planner and one who has always 'known' what I would do with my life,

> "The most difficult thing about being a twenty something is that even with all your plans, there are no guarantees. You are not guaranteed a job after college, you are not guaranteed friends if you move to a new place, you are not guaranteed a passionate career, you are not guaranteed a loving partner. You have to go out and create all this or at least hold the thought that it will all happen."
>
> *Program developer,*
> *28, engaged, California*

the deep sense of not knowing what is ahead for me is so hard to deal with. It's not that I don't think I could accomplish my goals; it's that I am not sure if I am willing to work toward something I'm not sure is even what I really want." This quandary is incredibly difficult for planners. We love to plan, but we don't know what to plan for. The solution? Less planning and more investigation of the questions of the Twenties Triangle (which we'll cover in part 2).

THE CHEESECAKE FACTORY PARALYSIS

Welcome to my first and perhaps most infamous analogy: "Life is like the Cheesecake Factory." If you have ever been to the Cheesecake Factory, you'll get this analogy. If you have not had the delectable dining privilege of this chain restaurant, let me explain: you sit down and the host hands you the menu, which is like a book — it has a spiral. There are 167 items to choose from and that is *not* including drinks, sides, and more than 20 types of cheesecake. Upon my first visit, I was immediately stressed out. First of all, the menu was heavy. Second, I felt like I needed an hour to read through all my options — there were too many things to decide among:

> "There are so many options open to one at this time of life. With the way the world is today, we are encouraged to be all we can be, and more. There is pressure to make decisions that will form the foundation for the rest of your life in your twenties. It's almost as if having a range of limited options would be easier."
>
> Human resources employee, 24, recovering from a breakup, Virginia

from pizzas to salads to fish to pasta to burgers, every type of food seemed to be somehow represented (and I hadn't even gotten to the cheesecakes yet). How was I supposed to pick just one dish? What was the best thing? As everyone else around me ordered, I became even more anxious — should I get what someone else was having? Would it be better than what I thought I wanted?

Finally, I did choose something — after asking the waiter an incessant series of questions about menu options (how in the world do they memorize it?). As soon as the waiter walked away with my order, I immediately felt buyer's remorse. Did I pick right? As the food was delivered to the table, I looked at everyone else's choices with envy. Their decisions looked better, I wanted their entrées. What was in front of me, now that it was mine, did not seem appetizing anymore. I was lost in comparison land. What happened to my nice evening out?

The twenty-something experience is full of limitless options and choices with no guarantees. Growing up, today's young adults are exposed to an expansive world: they can leap nations and cultures in a single bound, and new forms of entertainment and technology multiply career possibilities almost infinitely. Yet as possibilities expand, contentment and a sense of direction among the twenty-something generation contracts. Being told "You can do and be anything you want" has become more of a pressure cooker of expectations than a motivational quote. And when you do make a choice about any aspect of your life, how do you know it will be both appetizing and satisfying? You don't. And living in this Cheesecake Factory world makes that reality harder to swallow.

> "I feel like the window to my future is all fogged up. Every time I wipe it in order to see it, it fogs up within seconds. I feel like I have all the options in the world — like life is one big multiple choice and I want to pick (d), all of the above."
>
> Bartender, 25, recovering from a breakup, Ontario, Canada

My solution, when I go to the Cheesecake Factory now, is that I don't take a menu. That's right — I refuse it. I have found one dish in the encyclopedia of food they call a menu that I like and I always order that. Why stress myself out with more choices? I order what I know I will enjoy and don't fret over what I am missing out on. When, if ever, I get sick of the Herbed Salmon Salad (because I know you are curious), then I may entertain the idea of taking a look at the menu to investigate a little more — but I will never try to sample everything on the menu, it's just impossible.

The same is true in life. Sometimes you just have to decide and be content with your decision, otherwise you will continue to be overwhelmed by possibilities and torn between the reality of what you have and the fantasy in your head that you think would be better. You know what is very interesting about the letters and emails I get from twenty somethings? There is always at least one complaint. Something is always wrong — and I am not being critical here, because believe me, I earned a PhD in complaining in my twenties. To me, the overfocusing on what is wrong is a direct result of the checklists and plans twenty-somethings feel pressured to create, coupled with Cheesecake Factory paralysis. It is challenging for today's twenty somethings to be content in a world of endless choices and expectations.

"FOLLOW THE YELLOW BRICK ROAD" by Jennifer, 25

DECLARATION: *My fear is the constant wonder whether or not what I'm doing with my twenty-something years is right.*

I think about where I'm going a lot as a twenty something. I wonder, what will my life look like in six months? A year? Five years? I think about the choices I'm making. I feel paralyzed by all the options I have regarding decisions I have to make. I question whether or not I'm "doing enough." I compare my life to those of others, wondering if I might be "missing something" that will help me "get somewhere" quicker or with more meaning. I wonder if I really am making valuable connections and networks that will help shape my future career.

Working for a leadership institute, I hear amazing women tell their career success stories every day. While they're inspiring and full of amazing advice, it's somewhat terrifying to think about all the things I'm supposed to be doing in order to "get somewhere" successful: "Follow your passions, live your dreams, take risks, network with the right people, find mentors, be financially responsible, volunteer, work, think about or go to grad school, fall in love, and maintain personal well-being, mental health, and nutrition." When is there time to just be and enjoy, especially when the cycle is doing, going, sleeping, eating, networking? Then there are fears that are largely irrational, and that I know I can and will overcome, but still stick inside my head. My fears come from constantly wondering whether or not what I'm doing with my twenty-something years, while okay, is really me. Maybe I'm not doing the "right" things that are leading me where I think I might want to or should go. The tricky part is quieting the fear, trusting the process in a competitive world, getting ahead, and being patient.

I liken the twenty-something years to the yellow brick road. Possibility lies ahead. There are twists and turns that can throw you backward, make you think differently, or give you insight and perspective into what it is you might really want and strive for. You never really know where the road is going to lead. You make choices that are hard to make because you never know if they are "right," but you can't turn back. And it's scary.

And so far my twenty-something years have been, well, kind of ordinary. I had some expectation that they would be more exciting, more revealing, or more inspiring. But they haven't been...so I've learned that I have to laugh at life, no matter how ordinary it is, and constantly look for opportunities to learn.

There Is No "Right" Thing

Unless you are breaking a legal or moral law, purposely hurting someone, or lying — forget about doing the "right" thing. Seriously, there is no such thing as "right" or "wrong" in terms of what you are doing in your twenty-something years. As long as we are committed to learning from our experiences, there are no mistakes! And life is like the yellow brick road — there are many surprises ahead, but eventually we do get home. When? Not when we hit thirty (trust me, I'm there). It happens when we take our last breath on this planet. If we really understand now that our entire life is about learning, we can free ourselves from having to be "right."

> "Too many options are making me indecisive. I feel that because I have been told 'you can do anything,' I must explore everything and feel pressure to make the right choices every time."
>
> *Student, 21, single, Tennessee*

Like Jennifer, perhaps you worry about "making valuable connections and networks that will help shape your future career." You know what? As long as we are interacting and engaging with other people in the world, we are making connections. Developing strong interpersonal skills and creating a network of colleagues and friends who support our growth helps us in life. Every interaction or connection does not have to have a "point" or a "result." Just because someone may not be able to help your immediate career advancement does not mean the person is not a valuable connection. Cultivating relationships is just as valuable as "networking"! When we consistently look for opportunities to learn from people and events, an "ordinary" life can indeed become extraordinary.

Do You Get Inspired and Then Feel Bad?

Another quandary twenty somethings get into is finding inspiration but then quickly becoming deflated. Jennifer admitted in her story that career success stories she hears are momentarily inspiring but then leave her feeling like she should be doing more. Inspire means "to influence, move, or guide"; it does not mean "get motivated for five minutes and then start beating yourself up for not being more like the person who just inspired you." Are you guilty of tainting inspiration with self-judgment? Inspiration is supposed to be full of light, coming from something divine. As soon as we add comparison, we make it dark, and what was at first positive becomes negative.

When we wander into comparison land, any opportunity for learning vanishes and we miss out on valuable information. Also, when we compare ourselves to people who are older and have more experience, we can forget we each need to follow our own yellow brick road. I struggled with comparing myself to my coach, Mona, who I think is brilliant, funny, and the most consistently at-peace person I've met. Thankfully, she lovingly scolded me for comparing and reminded me that we all have our own unique purpose. Now I am able to be inspired by her, which opens up my heart and mind to learn from her and allows me to be me.

GET INSPIRED

Next time you feel that wonderful feeling of inspiration — STOP! Allow yourself to truly enjoy that feeling without jumping into a cycle of self-doubt and analysis. Everyone is on his or her own unique path. If you do find yourself envious of someone else's job or life, use the person as a source of motivation and information. Ask the person specific questions that may spark insight about your own path and rescue you from comparison land. For example: "What is the most significant event or decision in your life that has gotten you to where you are today?" "What qualities do you attribute to your success?" "What have you had to sacrifice?" "What has surprised you about your job?" "What do you really enjoy?" "What challenges do you face?"

If you cannot directly communicate with the person, write down all the things you admire and respect about them that inspire you. What qualities do you notice? What specifically do you want to emulate? As you learn more about what inspires you, you will gain insight into what truly moves you, and this will help you carve your own path. Allow inspiration to be a form of investigation rather than comparison.

INSTANT-GRATIFICATION GENERATION

There is a sense of entitlement that is an epidemic among twenty somethings, and I include myself in this. At my first job I wondered where my business cards were. I mean, didn't they know I graduated from a top school with a 3.9 GPA? Turns out they didn't care — no one really did. Many twenty somethings write to me expressing frustration over not being taken seriously because of their age or about feeling underestimated. Where does this expectation come from that success, results, and recognition should appear instantly? And why is it dangerous?

> "Everything seems to be happening too slow — I want to see results in everything I do *now*."
>
> Content developer, 27, married, Korea

Of course, not every twenty something suffers from this, but I believe the feeling of wanting instant gratification is becoming more and more common. With today's media, our accessibility to the world is infinite. The internet, cell phones, and BlackBerries have made it possible to get any information we want from anywhere in the world at any time. We can share and communicate with anyone instantly. In college, we get immediate feedback and recognition for our accomplishments at the end of every semester; in our jobs, we may get a review every six months. We have fast-food restaurants and ready-made meals at grocery stores. We are not used to waiting because what we want is usually designed to be had easily and quickly.

But this instant-gratification epidemic goes deeper than drive-up windows and twenty-four-hour banking. I received the following email from a recent twenty-three-year-old college graduate that puts it well: "Very frequently my generation seems to reflect one where we have set the highest expectations for ourselves. We have all this technology; our baby-boomer parents tell us we're special and answer yes to our requests with cruise-control frequency. Study after study reveals us as the most narcissistic of any generation before us, we have become soaked in a celebrity-based culture, and we expect to become instantly success-ful, famous, rich, powerful, recognized. But these expectations have made us super-sensitive to the inevitable failures and disappointments of life, the bites of reality that have plagued every genera-tion before us. So many of us are recognizing what it's like to be brought down to Earth, like I have the last eight months."

> "It is difficult because everyone is at a different point in their life, and it's hard not to compare where you are with others (especially friends). But everyone is different. The older I get, the more I am able to understand this and can be happy with my accomplishments. I am working on not comparing my life to others — and it's a relief!"
>
> Therapist, 26,
> serious relationship, Delaware

For many, the twenties are a frustrating combination of hav-ing the world at your fingertips but not knowing how to grasp it. Twenty somethings today want and expect to have it all — and who can blame you? You've been conditioned to believe it. You've grown up in a time when "anything is possible" and "you can have it all" became bumper sticker–worthy mantras. And many times, parents encouraged this, eager to provide a life they did not have as children. Again, no matter what any of our personal situations may have been, we all soak up these beliefs from the wider culture.

It has been said that each generation stands on the shoulders of the previous. From the expectations that many twenty somethings feel from parents, authorities, and society at large, the previous generation seems to be on stilts. They

> "I believe our baby-boomers parents have very high expectations, and sometimes we feel discouraged because we haven't reached those lucrative goals. I just have to remind myself that I am only twenty-four, and I have a lifetime to live. The only expectations that are truly important are my own."
>
> *Legal administrator, 24,*
> *single, South Carolina*

have raised the bar of what there is to achieve, and twenty somethings feel the weight of those expectations. The American Dream has expanded from the simple white picket fence to an unreachable belief in "having it all."

"THE BLESSED MISERABLE GENERATION" by Julie, 23

DECLARATION: *Too much opportunity and too many options left me paralyzed. I wasn't thinking about anything but what I wanted.*

Confession: I played with Barbies until I was thirteen. Skipper was studying anthropology and having an affair with her psychology professor. Kelly was jet-setting to Paris for an unpaid internship with *Vogue* and working on her tan. Midge was writing the next great American novel, while Barbie was putting in long hours at a law firm and getting divorced. Ken, who was a successful doctor, traveled to various medical conferences around the country. Barbie and Ken were responsible; they worked hard and brought home the bacon. They encouraged Skipper,

Midge, and Kelly to be creative, and college was inevitable. They wouldn't have student loans; they would study dance and film at small liberal arts colleges in New England. They would have cars already paid for and money to fall back on. They wouldn't need part-time jobs. Their options were endless as my imagination ran wild.

Eventually, I stopped playing with Barbies, but I still believed in boundless opportunity. I still hadn't made the transition from child to adult, a transition I assumed would naturally occur during college. I was wrong. Instead of being a microcosm of the "real world," college was more like an episode of MTV's reality show. We were given so much, endless subjects to study and explore, libraries full of books to read, not to mention food, gyms, and other resources that we weren't paying for. We didn't have much responsibility, besides class and homework, yet somehow everyone I knew in college had some sort of problem. Everyone was stressed out and complained. Then of course there was the drama of parties — hook ups and the constant drunken haze that made everyone act like animals in a circus ring from Thursday until Sunday night.

We were miserable, not realizing how blessed we were. I wish I had the perspective that I do now, and that I had forced myself to take a few steps back and focus on what really mattered. It was only when someone passed away, got sick, or was in an accident that anyone in college took a moment to act like they really cared. It was the same with politics; you wouldn't hear a peep from anyone about health care, taxes, or the state of our education system until just before election week, and then all of a sudden everyone had an opinion about everything. We were a group of young people who didn't have a cause. We were so different from our parents' generation.

My parents had careers in medicine and business. They got through college on scholarships and by working. They understood that college was a means to financial security, and that money wasn't something your father deposited into an ATM. They had opinions, not because it seemed like they should, but because they knew that life outside their social circle would affect them. When they had children, they were thrilled that they could give their daughters a life full of summer camp, vacations, writing classes, and French horn lessons. My parents showed me that security, love, and opportunities were endless — so I cultivated a vivid imagination. I fell in and out of love — there was always something to plan for: the next party, the job, the apartment, and the book I wanted to write. Possibility was enough, and it kept me from growing up. I wasn't thinking about anything but what I wanted.

Sure, I felt a little guilty sometimes. When I realized I didn't know how to iron a shirt or anything about taxes. When I thought about my dad driving to work every day, and how every time I bought a new dress, he was picking up the bill. My senior year of college I felt like I was still thirteen, upstairs playing with Barbies.

When I graduated, I got a job in publishing after five unpaid magazine internships. It was perfect and glamorous. I would write, design fashion spreads, and go to photo shoots. I felt ready. Once I was on my own in New York City, the reality set in that I wasn't making enough money to cover my rent. I was adjusting to a lifestyle that was so unnatural compared to my college experience. I felt like I wasn't enjoying my life, but just going through the motions. People

> "Reaching your goals always takes longer than you expect. There's no such thing as instant gratification."
>
> Musician, 29,
> serious relationship, California

bumped into me on the subway, and I snapped at them. I stopped looking at buildings and writing poetry. Mentally, I began to feel numb, like my life, my job, and my bills were just another unpaid internship that would be over at the end of the summer or a spring break vacation gone sour — but that was not the reality.

I developed a terrible fear that my job wasn't a real career because I couldn't support myself. I was embarrassed. What did I have to show for myself? Was everyone waiting for me to stop with the publishing business and start my "real" career in business or law? It feels like life at twenty-three is just another round of make-believe. I want to pay my own taxes and cover my rent and start thinking about buying a house. And then I don't — I want to stay out until midnight singing karaoke with my girlfriends and read all day on Sunday. I want to pretend for a little while longer. I wait for a turning point, a clearing in my head. I am torn between reality and make-believe.

I am part of "the Entitlement Generation." I was encouraged to think creatively. I had so many options that I had too many. This led to a sort of plateau in my personal development. It is a double-edged sword because on the one hand I am so blessed with my experiences and endless options, but on the other hand, I still feel like a child. I feel like my job isn't real because I am not where my parents were at my age. Walking home, in the shoes my father bought me, I still feel I have yet to grow up.

CHAMPAGNE TOASTS
AND EXPECTATION HANGOVERS

There is a lot to celebrate in your twenties. You may "toast" your first job, first home, first love, first anniversary, first promotion, first child. You may boast about your graduation from college and have your first real experience of adult independence and freedom. But these celebrations are often followed by grown-up doses of disappointment and the reality of deferred gratification — something the instant-gratification generation often forgets exists. Relationships end. Jobs are harder to get. Friends fade. Money is tight. Perhaps your life as a twenty something is not living up to the picture of what you thought it would look like. You probably didn't expect twenty-something life to be this hard.

> "The most difficult thing about being a twenty something is being okay with the fact that your first job, your first apartment, your love life, your finances, your family and friends are not going to be at all what you hoped or expected, and instead of worrying about it, enjoy it."
>
> Accountant, 27, single, New York

If you can relate, you may be experiencing what I call an "Expectation Hangover," which is a term I created to help twenty somethings get a handle on what they are going through. While

I discuss how to deal with Expectation Hangovers in the next chapter, here is my dictionary-quality definition of an Expectation Hangover™: *the myriad undesirable feelings or thoughts present when a desired result is not met or an undesired, unexpected event occurs.* (Sounds pretty official, huh? If this book thing doesn't work out, perhaps I'll write for *Webster's* ...)

I've heard thousands of twenty somethings complain that life is not turning out like they thought. It sounds rather catastrophic to some to label this as a quarter-life "crisis." Instead, it is simply discontent and not knowing what to do about it, an unhappy mix of morning-after feelings and symptoms. An Expectation Hangover does not have to come from something huge to affect you greatly. For instance, think of how much a tiny little splinter bothers you. Until you get it out, it is painful and annoying — and often the process of removal is no bowl of cherries either. But if you have a good set of tweezers and a steady hand, the removal process does not have to be so bad. Like a splinter, Expectation Hangovers get worse the longer they remain — but with the right tools you can recover from them quickly, or better yet, prevent them in the first place.

> "I thought I'd be a lot 'happier' at this point. I thought I'd know what I wanted to do as a career and be doing it (but I'm not). I thought my serious boyfriend would be the type of man who had a stable job where he made good money (but he's sort of 'finding himself' too). I thought some of my friendships would never change, but they have (for the worse). I thought I'd be getting my master's degree, but I haven't because I didn't expect to be so indecisive."
>
> *Program coordinator, 27, serious relationship, California*

And sometimes you just have to accept that you'll pay some dues in your twenties. Expect that your first job, relationship, or apartment may not be 100 percent exactly what you want. Trust me, with time and patience, your life will align in a way that exceeds your expectations.

"WHERE'S MY CORNER OFFICE?" by Patrick, 22

DECLARATION: *Don't give up on your dreams,*
but don't be afraid to tweak them a bit.

They say that college is the best four to eight and a half years of your life. Whoever "they" are, they hit the nail right on the head. College was everything I could have imagined it to be and more. While a lot of aspects of campus life mirror what is portrayed in the movies, one major aspect of "movie college life" is *completely* inaccurate: When Bill McPopular gets close to graduation, job offers start coming in. And of course Mr. McPopular's job offers are for incredible amounts of money with amazing benefits, most of the time including cars, mansions, and beautiful women.

I was not naive enough to actually believe that happened in real life, but I thought that finding a job out of college would be easy. I never thought making it on my own would be this hard. I graduated with a respectable 3.3 GPA with extracurricular activities and leadership roles under my belt — I did all the right "get a good job after college" preparatory things. Heck, my sister lovingly refers to me as her "overachieving brother." I was sure that I was a shoo-in for a decent job out of college.

My opinion about my opportunities out of college was inflated by positive reinforcement from professors and advisers. Putting all those compliments together with parents who made life pretty easy, it seemed like I was completely awesome.

I haven't had horribly bad luck since graduation. I have a roof over my head, a head on my shoulders, and some money in my wallet. On the other hand, I haven't had incredibly good luck either. I just have not reached my expectation of having a respectable job that's rewarding both financially and personally. That makes the exciting dating life I expected out of college unaffordable and thus unattainable as well. I am building up the all-important experience factor that will hopefully land me the great job soon, but I am still the lowly, dateless, broke intern.

I may have been an all-star during college, but now that I am in the big leagues, I am just another rookie who has to pay his dues with a résumé that looks like everybody else's. Now I see that the encouragement I received from mentors was supposed to be used as a spark to get my fire going after college, instead of using it as the wind in my sail. Instead of having it motivate me to get where I wanted to go, I used it as the fuel that would take me there without much effort. It took a month or two of getting kicked in the butt to figure it out, but now I am back on track.

While it is frustrating to not get instant gratification for all the hard work that I have put into the grand investment that is my life, I think that it will be much more meaningful once I do reach success.

BLINDED BY SELF-FOCUS

Growing up in the instant-gratification generation with a backpack full of expectations, it's hard to avoid becoming overly self-focused. Not all twenty somethings are. But even those who commit to making a difference in the world — who fight this tendency by passionately working for political, social, and environmental change, by volunteering, or by simply making themselves aware of what is going on in the world — can, to put it bluntly, still be very self-absorbed. In fact, I think it is hard not to be given the conditioning of society. Moreover, many twenty somethings had "helicopter parents" (parents who were overinvolved in their child's life). They were overscheduled, overstimulated, overanalyzed, and often overprotected. With all this "overing" and "hovering," it's no wonder that they may feel a bit separated from the rest of the world. And if you did not have parents who made you the center of their world, you are still

> "I am consumed by the societal and self-inflicted pressures to accomplish 'life milestones,' especially on a given timeline. It's all I can think about."
>
> Student, 21, on a break, Arizona

> "A twenty something is someone who is constantly evaluating and analyzing his or her life and continually coming up with the answer 'I don't know.'"
>
> *Product manager, 26, recovering from a breakup, California*

influenced by the "me" mentality of today's culture.

Twenty-something life today can be isolating — it's not like in college where our best friends were delivered in residence halls and classrooms. There really isn't a sense of community anymore. Do we even know our neighbors? Twenty somethings are living in a very competitive, externally driven "real world." I believe this puts an enormous amount of pressure on young adults and often drives them into self-sabotaging, fairly careless, and often rebellious behavior. One twenty-five-year-old shares, "As a star athlete in high school striving toward a law degree at twenty, I assumed that everything would fall into place. My world revolved around me. My need for perfection, 'to be the best,' led me to try cocaine and fall into addiction. Today, I am clean from cocaine, but will always be an addict. That is something I never expected." Self-focus can be dangerous and destructive. Being blinded by our own goals and desires can cloud our judgment. Youth tempts risky behavior, but it does make us invincible.

"BUBBLE OF INVINCIBILITY" by Diane, 24

DECLARATION: *We are so focused on being and doing that we are losing sight of the big picture.*

I come from a generation where our parents told us that the world was at our feet, that we could do and be anything we wanted to be, but they forget to mention that there is more to life than that: the rest of the world.

My generation believes that it is invincible. Somewhere along the way we lost focus of the big picture and only focused on being and doing what we want, without worrying about the consequences. Invincible — incapable of being conquered, defeated, or subdued. We will get what we want and be who we want without anyone or anything defeating us. But obviously that is not real life; no one is invincible or immune to everything, yet we lead reckless and careless lives thinking that we are. We drink too much, drive too fast, have unprotected sex with numerous partners, lose touch with old friends in hopes of finding *better* ones, all the while thinking that when it comes to the consequences "that can't happen to me."

And regardless of what we see in the news every day (car accidents, alcohol poisoning, teen pregnancies and abortions, the rise in sexually transmitted diseases), we still continue to think, "It can't happen to me. It *won't* happen to me." We look at those people and think that we are better and that things like that don't happen to people like us. Until it does. Until you get the phone call bringing bad news of someone you care about … or until it is too late and someone is making that phone call about you.

In my experience, college and the few years after it seems to be the place where most of my generation lives in this bubble of "invincibility." I know I did. My college years were filled with partying all night long and running around all day. Sleep didn't matter. I will never forget my moment of "defeat" when I woke up in a hospital after a night of partying. In that moment, I suddenly realized that I was not invincible. I would be lying if I said that I did not, in some ways, go back to my old lifestyle. I still partied a lot and slept very little, but I did become more aware of what I was doing to myself. Aware of the fact that I am not invincible. But what happens after you realize you are not invincible? Eventually, twenty-something life will kick in again and the behaviors that brought us defeat will be pushed to a dark corner in our mind. Suddenly, we are invincible again … claiming to have learned … and go back to leading our lives with reckless abandon.

Is this way of life something that we ever grow out of? I mean right now we are in our carefree twenties. When we hit thirty years old, will we grow up? Will we face the fact that no one is invincible to life, or will we continue in our wild ways, not worrying about how it will affect those we love?

THE PETER PAN SYNDROME

For some, the twenty-something experience really is like Neverland — a place outside of time where you get the freedoms of adulthood without all of the adult responsibilities of mortgages, spouses, children, aging parents, and all the other things that make eternal childhood seem so appealing! Not every twenty something is having a crisis. Some are having the time of their lives, partying hard and living fast. I liken it to the "Peter Pan Syndrome," which is not limited to guys. It's a form of escapism, denial, and delayed adulthood, and it's accomplished by a lot of play, feelings of invincibility, and self-obsession.

On the surface, the Peter Pan Syndrome sounds attractive, just the kind of fun twenty-something experience we are supposed to be having. But don't get too green with envy — every Peter Pan eventually wakes up. In fact, underneath, these Peter Pans feel a twinge of fear and long for a sense of purpose. Living a fast-paced life while racking up debt is basically a way to avoid growing up and making choices by covering up the underlying questions about the lack of direction they feel. It's important to have fun in your twenties, but if your kind of fun is irresponsible and distracts you from

> "I feel like I'm stuck between floors in an elevator, trapped in this limbo between being an adolescent and being an adult. I still want to have fun, but I'm supposed to be a 'grown-up.' I've graduated from college, I have a full-time job, and yet I still live at home. I feel like life is on warp speed sometimes, but then when I realize where I am at, I feel like I'm crawling along."
>
> *Assistant editor,*
> *24, serious relationship, Illinois*

responsibilities or unresolved issues, just remember that eventually you are going to wake up. Balance your trips to never-never land with reality checks.

"CRUISE CONTROL" by Paul, 25

DECLARATION: *Despite my unknown future,
I will keep working to find change, driving to be successful,
and most important, having fun and enjoying life
to the fullest as my direction takes its time to unfold.*

Life as a twenty-five-year-old guy is pretty simple. I really have three primary focuses the minute I get out of bed — girls, having fun with my buddies, and trying to earn a lot of money so I don't have to work as hard in a job I'm really not that passionate about. And yes, it's pretty much in that order.

I'll admit that while there is a level of attitude that comes with this package, on many levels there is a total lack of direction and security. I believe that my life will eventually have more substance, but for now I'm happy and choose to ignore having to grow up and be somewhat responsible. My direction is more driven by group mentality for now. I guess all this comes out of fear of being bored and average.

My days consist of going to the gym, going to work, and going out. My job also gives me the amazing opportunity to live (and I mean live it up right) months at a time in travel to foreign countries like Argentina, Venezuela, Mexico, Hong Kong, and Taiwan. With nearly thirty-five countries under my belt, I'm trying to put that old sailor adage to work — having a girl in every port, as my mom likes to say with a smirk of judgment and a twinge of guilt laced in it. At work, I pass the time wondering where our next blowout event will be by chatting profusely with my own tier-two rat pack via IM.

I still have to work hard for my next hot date, as I drive a Nissan,

I have a roommate who is my best friend, and I make under $50K. Yes, the not-so-fancy ride and less-than-fancy apartment is the root of insecurity. There is always a more handsome guy with a better job, more money, and nicer things. I compare, I judge, and I keep trying to keep up. I continue to hope there is a purposed-filled light at the end of this directionless tunnel.

For now, I continue to just move ahead and learn what it is I don't want to do. I do not have a girlfriend, and while it would be nice to have one, in reality I can't be bothered. Having one will just pose the dilemma of my potentially missing that next big party with more hot girls or another trip I'm planning with my buddies. The grass-is-greener mentality runs deep.

> "We should be keeping it light and not get bogged down with anything. We're too young to worry about the big picture yet. I say learn to live happy now and that will take you through your entire life."
>
> Nonprofit administrator,
> 27, married, Texas

And, yes, I am overstretched in debt up to my ears and not so worried about how and when I'll pay it off. I figure I'm smart enough, with a college education and a crazy work ethic, which will always bail me out. My friends are somewhat better off though. They all make more than me for working less. I get jealous; we're a competitive group. It's a healthy competition on the surface, but it pains me sometimes as I just wish things could come easier.

My life always has to have an activity. I guess I don't fully feel comfortable with just being by myself. I mean I like myself, but I need stimulus; too much time alone sparks too many unwanted, racing thoughts about how boring life can be without a girl, money, and a set career path. A mild case of depression sets in. For me it's a sign of weakness, and so I push through. Burying any notion of having a weakness is all too common. It just doesn't fit into my schedule at the mature age of twenty-five.

I know there is probably a bigger, more substantive life out there for me, whatever my purpose is supposed to be. For now, though, the purpose seems to be about highs. I'm an adrenaline junkie. Perhaps the anticipation of my next fun-filled activity is causing me to forget about the actual ride and preventing me from appreciating all that's around me? I think that could be part of it. Still, something is telling me that this is my course for now and that a more meaningful one will unfold.

Whatever the life lessons that come my way, I try not to overthink it, but I do reflect on it. The grass won't always be greener, or at least I will finally realize that this is really a cliché. The good thing that I keep telling myself is that at least I'm getting it out of my system so when the time is right to grow up, I may actually do so willingly.

STUCK IN NEVER-NEVER LAND

The dilemmas and questions of the twenty-something years can lead to another common and completely opposite reaction: rather than racing around in a fun-filled frenzy to avoid self-reflection, we allow our lack of direction to stop us completely. Where once we moved with purpose and excitement, now we hardly move at all.

Common estimates are that approximately 48 percent of students who graduate from college move back into their parents' home either right after school or several years afterward. This group of twenty-something "boomerangers" often get stuck in a never-never land made very comfortable by their parents. Though it looks different than the Peter Pan Syndrome, I think this is the same type of reaction to the overwhelming pressures and expectations twenty somethings feel, particularly among those who were overachievers in high school and college. Many twenty somethings run out of steam, feel overwhelmed by financial burdens, develop a defeatist attitude, and get stuck — hiding from the responsibilities, choices, and disappointments adulthood brings.

> "I thought I'd be at a different place by now. I'm twenty-seven, I'm broke, still living with my parents, and still working at the same job I had in college."
>
> *Bookstore employee, 27, single, Ohio*

"COMPLACENCY" by Luke, 23

DECLARATION: *I tell myself that I still have plenty of time to change my life and figure out what I want to do, but I lack the desire to start that process.*

I don't really feel all that stressed as a twenty something. I used to, but now I am kind of indifferent. It's a little strange, I guess, seeing that I live with my parents and I don't know what I want to do with my life. I guess I am most worried over what I ultimately will do, but after thinking about it for two years, I still don't feel I have any direction. Yet somehow none of that gets to me too much; I've just gotten comfortable with where I am. Or maybe I've just gotten complacent.

My twenty-something life is not turning out like I expected. I slacked off too much in college and had to transfer to a small school close to home and move in with my parents. Also, for reasons I don't really understand, my commitment to getting a good job is gone. I just don't have a great work ethic when it comes to really getting out there and networking or job hunting, even though I was a total overachiever in high school. Maybe I just burned out.

I tell myself that I still have plenty of time to change my life and figure out what I want to do. I wish I knew three years ago what I know now, because if I did, things may have been different. I would not have taken things for granted. When I look at what I could afford on my blue-collar-job salary, my parents' four-bedroom house in the suburbs is a lot nicer. Maybe my problem is my life is too easy, and I've accepted it the way it is.

"Being a twenty something is like being a fish in a fishbowl. Everyone around you is looking in, and they assume you know what you are doing and you are following the guidelines of what it is to be a fish."

Teacher, 29, serious relationship, Texas

A common trend I see in twenty somethings today, especially among those with parents who are "friends" with their children, is the tendency to lean on their parents a little too much. This makes it hard to have your own life, relationships, opinions, and independence. If you are financially or emotionally dependent on your parents, recognize it's time to grow up and become your own parent. It's understandable if you need to live at home; just make it temporary. Create an "exit strategy." Start by paying rent for your room, and set a move out date. Then create a plan and budget for living on your own. Roommates, second jobs, and fewer shopping sprees may be the not-so-fun price for independence, but they are also great motivators for improving your situation. Living at home

> "I truly think one of the best things I did for myself and my sanity was move out of my mom and dad's house. It has allowed me to get to know myself better and not be so afraid of being alone with myself. My parents were not supportive, but I did what I needed to and we are all the better for it, especially me."
>
> *Administrative assistant,*
> *26, single, North Dakota*

may be easy, but it's not your home. Get out of never-never land — reality may sometimes bite, but you can't stay a kid forever.

WHAT'S YOUR TWENTY?

Where are you in your twenty-something journey? Are you busy creating lists to check off? Are you obsessively planning the future? Do you sit staring at your Cheesecake Factory menu? Are you a member of the instant-gratification generation? Are you celebrating with champagne toasts only to suffer Expectation Hangovers? Do you think about "me-me-me" all the time? Are you flying through your twenties like Peter Pan? Are you stuck in never-never land? Whatever your experience, remember that you are not alone and you won't be where you are forever.

Right now, take some time to write down a few insights in your journal about what your journey has been like so far. I suggest making two columns — one for things that have happened, and one for things you have learned. In the first column, reflect on your twenty-something experience so far by taking an inventory of your major life events, those you have "toasted" and those that may have resulted in an Expectation Hangover. In the second column, consider the lessons and insights you have gained from your experiences. When making your lists, ask yourself questions like: What has surprised me? What have I learned? What have I proved to myself? What have I gotten through that at first appeared insurmountable? What do I know to be true?

Next, on a new page, respond to this question, "What are the goals that I am aspiring to in my twenties?" Be specific. Write down anything you hope to put in motion or accomplish during this decade. If questions arise regarding the specifics of how you will go about achieving your goals, write those down as well. Keep those questions in mind as you continue to journey through this manifesto.

2. EXPECTATION HANGOVERS

"An Expectation Hangover is just like a dark storm cloud that continues to loom overhead. Nothing really ever comes of it — it just makes your day dark and dreary, and you walk around all the time waiting for the bottom to fall out. You know it's there, even when you're not looking up at it, because you can feel it. And most of all, it brings your entire mood down just by virtue of the fact that it is *there*, lurking."

Accounts coordinator, 25, single, Nebraska

Can you relate to any of the following? You are often in a funk that you can't get out of. You have low energy and trouble focusing on things. TiVo has become your most fulfilling relationship. You obsess about things in the past or to come in the future like it's your favorite hobby. You are losing hope that you will ever figure out what you want and actually get it. Something turned out different than what you wanted and planned, so you gave up trying. Something unexpected and undesirable occurred, and you can't get over it. If you answered yes to any of the above, you are likely suffering from an Expectation Hangover.

The symptoms that accompany Expectation Hangovers are as miserable as those from a hangover from alcohol. You feel lethargic, down in the dumps, and regretful. You wish you could turn back time and would do anything to end your suffering. Your level of performance at work may suffer, your creativity is stifled, you may withdraw from your social life, and your self-esteem plummets.

One twenty-eight-year-old woman describes her Expectation Hangovers: "It feels like a dull pain in my chest. It's the terrible disappointment I've felt when faced with the results of my decisions and has led to some depression, much anxiety, and a lot of introspection. I would say during these Hangovers I am motivated toward change — but the scary part is seeing how to make the change and also seeing the obstacles in the way, mainly being the opinion of family and loved ones. These obstacles can make what seems to be a simple fix a much more complicated process. It can be quite daunting to try to change my life in a way I see fit when I feel like no one is supporting it or even trying to simply accept it."

In college, when you nursed a hangover from too much drinking, what did you do? Took some aspirin, ate some greasy food, and stayed inside with the lights low for a day until it wore off. But an Expectation Hangover can last for days, weeks, and even months because time is no cure — instead, it just hands us more expectations. Expectation Hangovers have become an epidemic, and this chapter presents twenty somethings with a treatment and prevention plan. For the quick overview, see page 54.

THIS IS MY LIFE?

Only 20 percent of twenty somethings in my online survey said they are where they expected to be in life. The rest — *80 percent* — reported suffering from an Expectation Hangover. Expectation Hangovers arise when things don't go as expected, when we are unable to match our expectations for ourselves, or when something unexpected (and undesirable) happens. When our expectations are met, we feel great; if it's something we've accomplished, we usually receive praise. But if we don't succeed or meet the standards set for us (or that we set for ourselves), the incessant judgment begins. The majority of disappointment stems from career, relationship, and money issues. Here are some of the answers I received to the following question on the Manifesto Survey: "What are some things that you expected to happen that either have not happened or didn't turn out like you expected them to?":

> "I expected to be involved in a job with people I feel comfortable with and in a steady relationship, live near my family, spend a lot of time in the sun, and have a dog. I live three thousand miles away in an apartment that does not allow pets and spend most of my hours in an office without a window."
>
> *Art director,*
> *26, single and hate it, New York*

"I thought I'd be comfortably and confidently on a path with a clear vision about what I want."

"I thought I'd be married by now."

"I thought I'd be happy after I lost 120 pounds, but I'm still as empty as before."

"I thought I'd be financially stable."

"I never thought I'd move for a man."

"I thought it would be easy to find a life mate and not hard to slip into a career that I love."

"I thought I would graduate sooner than I did."

"I thought things would work out with my ex."

"I thought the money I invested in my education would lead to a higher paying job than the one I have."

"I thought I'd be further along in my career."

"I thought it would be easier to meet people and make friends."

"I thought I'd feel like an adult."

"I thought I'd be helping more people than I am."

"I thought career success and marriage would bring more happiness than what I have."

Can you relate to any of these? If you are not where you want to be in your life and you feel like there is nothing you can do about it, let me remind you that *this is your life*. It's not a dress rehearsal, and you don't get a twenty-something do-over. If you want to be happier, more focused, more decisive — you have that choice. Remember, you cannot completely control your external world, but you do have power over your thoughts. As Victor Frankl says in *Man's Search for Meaning*, "The last of one's freedoms is to choose one's attitude in any given circumstance."

In the midst of an Expectation Hangover, simple choices can feel very challenging. While it's impossible to avoid them entirely, it is possible to reduce the severity and frequency of Expectation Hangovers — as long as you take responsibility for what you drink. Accept that you have the choice to put down that cup full of expectations, to walk away from that shot of disappointment. The key to overcoming an Expectation Hangover is to change the way you respond to Hangovers and eventually free yourself from expectations.

> "My Expectation Hangover left me short-changed, burdened, and just plain stunted for a couple of years. It is a difficult time finding a new path, but it does happen if one chooses to do more than just exist."
>
> Dental assistant, 27, divorced but found love again, Washington

GOALS VERSUS EXPECTATIONS

Let's return to the twenty-something goals list that you created at the end of the "What's Your Twenty?" exercise. What did you write down? Marriage, kids, a certain income, a profession? These are the things you want and plan to achieve in life. Your expectation is that as you succeed at certain goals, predictable results will follow that lead to everything you want. For example, graduating with honors from a good college leads to getting a good job, which leads to making more money, which leads to being able to support a family, which leads to having it all, which leads to happiness and success — or so we hope.

But what if we don't get into that good college or make the grades we hoped, or we find that in real life our chosen profession is dull and boring —

> "It is harder for me to figure out what I really want in life because I feel so desensitized from the Hangover — from the results and goals that didn't turn out how I expected."
>
> Business analyst,
> 29, on and off dating, New York

does that doom us to unhappiness and failure? Of course not. The first step in minimizing an Expectation Hangover is to distinguish a goal from an expectation. First, let's turn to the dictionary. A goal is defined as "the end to which effort is directed," while to expect is defined as "to anticipate or look forward to." Notice that the definition of a goal involves action intended to achieve a tangible outcome. Whereas expectation is more of an emotion, one that waits to be fulfilled. Or, to put it another way, goals refer to things we can do, while expectations refer to what we desire or hope for. By working toward a goal, we engage in thoughtful, planned action, which often leads to success even if our ultimate goal (or desire) changes. However, to sit in expectation is to live inside our heads, waiting; we are stuck until our expectations are met, and when they aren't, we feel more pressure and disappointment as time goes by. We identify goals whenever we say, "I want to," while expectations are often prefaced by "I have to," "I should," or "I expect to."

I find that twenty somethings are often not sure of what they really want, so they focus on what they believe is expected. Then

> "I am seeing that expecting too unrealistic goals and not being more specific or breaking big goals into smaller pieces in order to really conquer them contributed to the Hangover I experienced."
>
> Student, 20, engaged, Arkansas

they despair because these expectations, disguised as life goals and ambitions, seem so out of reach, so impossible. To move away from expectations, practice creating specific short-term goals. Keep in mind, even when our goals are reasonable, the devil's in the details, in the steps to reach them.

CLARIFYING GOALS

A good way to create clarity between goals and expectations, and between lifelong ambitions and goals to focus on right now, is to write out a long list of everything you want to achieve without thinking about whether they are expectations or goals. Next, go through the list and circle anything that does not involve a specific, clear action step that you know how to realistically execute. For instance, "apply to law school" is a goal you have 100 percent control over reaching. "Get into law school" or "become a successful lawyer" are expectations. Similarly, "ask X for a date" or "put a profile on an internet dating site" are attainable goals right now. "Get married by twenty-eight" is an expectation. Anything you don't circle can go on your short-term goals list.

Next, identify which of the items you circled on your list are expectations, and amend them into goals. Then, working backward, take any long-term life goals and create one action for each that you can accomplish and put it on your short-term goals list. For example, if you have an expectation to be wealthy, an attainable short-term goal you could create would be to open a savings account now.

Remember, short-term goals can be very simple — there is nothing wrong with that. Creating an action plan of things you can do right now is empowering and gets you out of thinking in terms of expectations. In fact, setting attainable goals throughout your life will probably make you more successful, as they are self-driven and self-fulfilling. Stop playing the disempowering waiting game!

YOUR EXPECTATION OR MINE?

An important step in identifying and treating Expectation Hangovers is to understand whose expectations are creating pressure or confusion in your life. Are you suffering because you've disappointed yourself or someone else? Part of maturing is discerning the expectations of others from the goals you set for yourself. This is one of the main challenges for twenty somethings, and it's the cause of much of the unhappiness they report.

As a twenty-seven-year-old shares: "I have lived the past several years fulfilling expectations (like getting married) I felt were being placed on me by my family. Their wishes and needs superseded my own, but now I feel trapped in this life that I half-willingly created for myself. All I want to do is make my own life what I want it to be, without other people weighing in with their disapproval or opinions. I am independent and wish to remain so, but ironically I conformed to what my family and others around me expected. Now, I'm struggling to get out of a life I don't want and that is turning out to be harder than I thought it would be."

I see many twenty somethings exhausting themselves trying to create a life that someone else — especially parents — wants for them. Living your life according to your own plan is part of becoming an adult. No matter how challenging it seems, you do have the courage and strength to take a stand for who you are and what you want — or against who you do *not* want to be and what you *don't* want. Remember, this is your life.

In addition, members of the instant-gratification generation are likely to spend a large part of their twenties striving for external gratification, expecting that it will make them feel happy and successful. A hot car, a gorgeous date, a nice income: that's what life is all about, right? But even when they gather all the necessary comforts to live the "expected" life, they can wake up with a huge Hangover because they never stopped to question whether these were things they really wanted. Plus, when emotional gratification is consistently attached to external things and a lifestyle, when do you learn how to generate satisfaction from within?

Another twenty-seven-year-old says, "Upon graduating from college I began working for the company I wanted and moved into my own one-bedroom apartment. I started dating a doctor who drove me everywhere in his BMW. I had a great social life, going to all the hottest clubs, eating at some of the best restaurants, and I shopped for new clothes every week. I had fulfilled all my expectations. From the outside my life seemed grand, but I was not truly happy. I felt empty, unfulfilled, unsatisfied, and I couldn't figure out why for the life of me."

> "I learned that the most stressful thing in my life was my tenacity at holding on to all of the 'shoulds' in my life. Shoulds only matter if you're considering other people's standards and milestones. I decided it was important to live by my own timeline and gave myself permission to go at my own speed. Life is a wonderful, mysterious process, and my only expectation these days is that everything will unfold as it should. My job is to be true to myself and work at the things I know will make me happy. Everything else will work out around me."
>
> *Web developer and life coach, 29, married, Colorado*

This type of "I did everything I was supposed to do, so what gives?" Hangover is extremely common, since our consumer culture consistently sells and validates the importance of stuff.

Expectations about the stuff we should own have replaced our "dreams" about who we should be. It's hard to even know what our dreams are when our lives are so focused on fulfilling expectations. In part 2, we'll dig into the question of our dreams and desires even more. But first, here's a way to help distinguish your own expectations from those of others, whether they are presented by relatives, friends, or society.

EXPECTATION IMPLANTS

Write a list of every expectation you can think of: all the things that are expected of you by others, that you expect from life, or that you expect yourself to achieve. After you write the list, circle anything that may be an "expectation implant" — meaning that it reflects a belief that you don't agree with or that does not belong to you. It may be something someone else wants or something you bought into based on messages from parents, peers, or society. Also circle any expectations of a desired feeling from a desired result. For example, circle any sentence like "I expect to feel more peaceful once I'm married."

Next, look at all the expectations you circled: what are you doing (or torturing yourself thinking you *should* be doing) based on these expectation implants? Is this serving you? If you removed these expectations from your life, how would you feel? Would you do anything differently? Write down a list of these differences, and use it to take a stand for what is true for you — even if someone may be disappointed! Then look at all the expectations you did not circle, the nonimplants. What action steps can you take to transform those expectations into goals? See the "Clarifying Goals" exercise (page 36), and create a list of achievable actions. As you start to bring more awareness and energy toward your internal, authentic desires and goals, it will become easier to move away from external expectations.

"COMPARE, REGRET, AND PANIC!" by Erin, 27

DECLARATION: *At my age I feel*
I should be doing a lot more with my life.

When I was twenty-five, I tried to move to New York to pursue my dream of becoming a dancer. I lasted six weeks and came home broke and disheartened to my Midwestern town. Since returning home and living with my parents to pay off the debt, I've been crying a lot — depressed about money and that I failed at my "dream." Major Expectation Hangover.

About a year ago, everything was beginning to look up. I started a job teaching dance and even started performing. I made a budget and actually lived by it, which made it possible for me to start to save again. But I still get hit with this sense of failure that I'm almost thirty and what have I done? My answer to myself is "not that much." I'm sick of having crappy jobs that don't leave me time or energy to pursue my passion.

I don't have a boyfriend. I date casually and don't feel like getting attached because I want to move out of the state to pursue dance, but then I get sad when I don't "have someone." I don't know if I want kids because of the kind of lifestyle I want to have with dance, but then again, I don't want to miss out on being a mom.

I am not where I thought I'd be. I compare myself to my friends who are getting promoted, planning weddings, having kids, and buying houses. All this really hit me hard when my twenty-two-year-old brother said to me during one of my Hangover moments, "You're twenty-seven. I hope for your sake you start doing something with yourself and soon." Now there's a confidence booster — even he expects me to do more with my life. I feel like a loser and like everyone is looking at me thinking, "When is she gonna get the show on the road?"

How do I stop feeling so regretful and like I failed and start making solid decisions to follow my dreams? How do I stop comparing myself to everyone else around me?

"HOW" IS NOT AS HARD AS YOU THINK

I have an answer to Erin's question: "How do I stop feeling so regretful and like I failed?" It's very profound, so brace yourself and grab a notebook. Ready? Just stop. Stop feeling regretful and start feeling more positive. Okay — I realize "just stop" may not seem like a very helpful answer, but it is the *only* answer. The reason twenty somethings get so frustrated and despairing is that they haven't yet learned *how* to just stop an Expectation Hangover.

Reading Erin's story, it seems like she is putting her energy into beating herself up and creating more anxiety for herself, rather than focusing on pragmatic actions. For instance, is she being fair with herself to write off her time in New York as a failure? If she puts aside her self-criticism, she may discover that she actually did learn a few things while she was there. She has more of an idea of how much money it takes and what kind of jobs are available. She can treat her past experience as a "rehearsal" and set goals for her next "performance." Erin can examine her feelings of success as a teacher and perhaps fine-tune her goals for a dance career, while taking manageable small steps toward them. When we focus on actions rather than on our emotions, and when we learn from our experience rather than constantly measuring it against our expectations, we can avoid major Hangovers and keep moving forward.

Picture this: You are at the bottom of a staircase, and you really want to get to the second floor. How do you do it? Do you take a running leap and jump straight for the top? Of course not! You take one step at a time, trusting that the next step will be there and you will eventually ascend to the next floor. The emotional quicksand so many twenty somethings get trapped in is that they wait for one big thing to happen that will set them where they want to be instead of taking small steps in the direction of their dream. Clarify your short-term goals!

> "If you asked me when I was six where I'd be at almost twenty-six, I would have told you that I would be a graduate of medical school, with a home, a husband, 2.5 kids, and a dog. So far, only the dog part has worked out."
>
> Support supervisor, 25, serious relationship, Virginia

I DON'T, I HAVEN'T, THEREFORE I WON'T

If you consistently focus on what you don't have or what you think can't be done, you are impairing your ability to arrive at what you want. The present is the result of the past, not a predictor of the future. Erin is quick to discount her efforts and achievements (calling herself a "loser") in the face of all she hasn't yet done, and she uses both her own expectations and those of others to beat herself up. I see this negative thinking in many of my clients.

I'm sure you can guess my answer to Erin's other question — "How do I stop comparing myself to everyone else around me?" Again, just give it up. There will always be people more successful, prettier, smarter, richer, more in love, and so on. Count on it for the rest of your life. It's self-defeating and counterproductive to compare yourself to others; it yields only envy and feelings of inferiority. Break the comparison habit now, and I promise you that you will have more peace in your life. There is enough abundance in the world to go around, so keep your attention on your own life. Redirect your focus to all the things you have done and you do have.

My recommendation for those who continually get trapped comparing themselves to others is to keep a gratitude journal — you can do it in your head, but it is more useful and effective to write things down. For example, if you have $10 in your savings account, focus on and celebrate how awesome it is to have that $10, rather than think about the $10,000 you don't have.

> "I've been too busy living life to focus on what I should have or how I measure up to others. The expectations I do have are to be generally happy, feel good about my work, have health insurance, and stay in touch with old friends. The rest of it is just whining."
>
> *Project manager,*
> *24, serious relationship, Washington*

If You Are Going to Take Yourself to Trial, At Least Have a Case!

I've found that many twenty somethings are experts at worrying about and beating themselves up for problems and concerns that do not even exist yet. It's a symptom of living in the "what ifs" of the future, which drain the enjoyment and chance for success in the now. In Erin's case, she seems emotionally paralyzed in classic twenty-something domino fashion: pursing dance means moving, which means she can't pursue a serious romance, and a dancing life also seems to threaten any chance at future motherhood. These are serious issues, but they are not issues she is facing, or can do anything about, at the current moment.

Besides, who says what's possible or impossible? What if Erin met a local guy with big-city dreams as well? Don't professional dancers have children? Anything is possible and creative solutions can be found — as long as you stay out of the court of imaginary worry.

"Our culture really focuses on youth and success, and many of us feel that we have to be fabulously successful by age thirty or we're failures. I think we forget that lives don't have to follow a single path. . . . Many people don't become truly successful until they're older, which makes a lot of sense."

Graduate student, 25, dating, New Jersey

In our twenties, we become hyperfocused on our futures while we are still trying to figure out who we are (based mainly on our childhoods), all the while obsessively comparing our progress to others. Twenty somethings spend less time in the present than an atheist spends at church. Would you like to avoid an Expectation Hangover? Live in the moment, focus on your own short-term goals, and trust that life does have a way of working itself out.

EXPECTATION HANGOVER R$_X$

No matter how well we manage our expectations, one day we will still wake up with a Hangover. The advice to "just let go of expectations and be happy with who you are and what you have" is cold comfort on those dreary mornings. If it were that easy, we would not see countless commercials for antidepressants on television. Being human means experiencing letdowns as well as joy. But there are ways to shorten the severity of Hangovers and ease our suffering. Don't panic if you've mistakenly taken the road to Doomsville; you also have the ability to find your way out of town.

"DETOUR" by Lisa, 27

DECLARATION: *My twenty-something years have turned out to be a huge realization that I'm not who or where I had pictured myself to be...and that's okay.*

I'm a twenty-seven-year-old woman who still feels like a lost teenager. I had a great family life and no real angst growing up besides the typical teenage string of heartaches and tribulations. After completing my degree, I have worked "successfully" in my industry for the last four years. But to me, it feels like I haven't found satisfaction, and I don't personally see myself as successful.

After an unexpected breakup with my boyfriend of three years, I went hardcore into the partying scene. I was always upset and started drinking and eating way too much. This combo helped to distract me so I wouldn't have to think about the decisions or feelings I faced at the time. I've gained fifteen pounds with emotional eating and have lost my drive for the gym. This past year has been full of many mistakes, humiliating regrets, and then the overanalyzing of those mistakes and regrets.

I need to make some major changes, and I need to find my passion for life again — in all aspects. But as a self-confessed anxiety junkie consumed with every idiotic action no matter how small it may be, change is a bit daunting. It's funny how long you can continue to be unhappy and maintain patterns you hate because change seems so much more difficult.

I realize I can't continue to have reckless partying nights, which lead to wasted days and anxiety, and I can no longer eat like there's a trough set up in my living room. I'm learning not to dwell on the many mistakes I've made and truly use them as learning tools (so very, very hard to do). I've learned that toxic people no longer have a place in my life and that sometimes friendships die without a dramatic ending — people just grow apart. I'm learning the art of saying no, though I still feel like I'm letting people down. I know the biggest thing I want is a peaceful mind instead of the negative internal dialogue.

I am beginning to feel a little more upbeat about getting my life

> "During my Expectation Hangover, every day it seemed like something would go wrong or not work out for me. It would seem that my needs where not being met. In actuality it was me not accepting the position that life had put me in. I was fighting the present and trying to regain the past, which only made everyone around me suffer — including me."
>
> *Teacher, 25,*
> *serious relationship, Illinois*

on track after four or five months of wallowing. What a waste of time, eh? I'm not who or where I had pictured myself to be, and that's okay (I'm slowly learning to accept this). Things don't magically fall into place after university. I have hit some rough patches. I may continue to make some wrong decisions, and I *will* continue to have some really embarrassing moments I wish I could erase — but that's life. Maybe these moments are here to remind me that I've made a major detour and it's time to refocus.

Don't Hang Out in Your Hangover

Like Lisa, we may find that our Expectation Hangover leads to real hangovers — and to overeating, laziness, overwork, and any number of emotional avoidance and self-medicating strategies. It's very easy to beat ourselves up, belabor our mistakes, and throw a pity party when symptoms of a Hangover flare up, but that only perpetuates our symptoms. Practice healthy behavior instead. Eliminate or drastically reduce the amount you drink. Alcohol is a depressant that may temporarily make us feel better, but the next day we will feel even more down than before — and it takes a good three days for the toxins to leave our bodies. Some respond to emotional stress by taking recreational drugs, binge eating, going on shopping sprees, or slacking off at work, while others do the opposite: burying themselves in work, becoming hyper-productive. Yet all of these behaviors are merely temporary Band-Aids. As soon as we stop, our undesirable feelings return.

A better rehab program, as Lisa is discovering, is to commit to living a healthier lifestyle — physically, mentally, and fiscally. Exercise is a wonderful way to release endorphins (the "feel-good" hormone) and combat Hangover symptoms. Take care of your body by eating healthy, which provides a sense of empowerment over your own physical domain when everything else may seem out of control. Maintain a healthy work/life balance. When you are at work, be present. Don't spend time IM'ing your friends about your Expectation Hangover. Focus on what you are paid to do, and at the end of the day, leave your work at work. Fill your personal life with nourishing social and creative activities. Keep your home neat and organized so that you have a sanctuary to return to. And finally, stick to a budget so that you are conscious about where you are spending your money. Debt is a common unpleasant side effect of many Expectation Hangovers.

When feelings are overwhelming and thoughts are unclear, journaling is an excellent remedy. Don't leave your concerns and feelings bottled up inside. Talk to your friends, mentors, or a counselor about the stress and disappointment you are feeling. Holding unhappiness inside is like trying to submerge a beach ball underwater — eventually it will erupt, and the deeper it's held, the bigger the splash. Decision making is stressful during an Expectation Hangover, so put off major decisions if you can, until you have strengthened your resolve and clarified your emotions by making healthier choices about your body, mind, and spirit.

> "An Expectation Hangover about my job and relationships led to a short temper and some physical manifestations of my stress. Not wanting to be too angry at work or the people I love, I internalized the anger and it lead to insomnia, constant heartburn, and a depressed immune system that left me constantly sick. I spent a year worrying about why I wasn't where I was 'supposed' to be and frantically trying to get there."
>
> *Policy analyst,*
> *26, dating, Washington, D.C.*

Be Proactive Rather Than Reactive

In *The Seven Habits of Highly Effective People*, Stephen Covey explains that one of the fundamental qualities of being an effective person is being proactive, which he associates with being responsible for your own life. Covey breaks down the word "responsibility" into "response-ability." He asserts that highly proactive people "do not blame circumstances, conditions, or conditioning for their behavior." In other words, no matter what cards life deals us, we are all responsible for how we choose to respond.

Remember the "90/10" rule when dealing with an Expectation Hangover. Only 10 percent of our symptoms are dictated by what actually happened; 90 percent of how we feel is determined by how we react to what happened. Treating an Expectation Hangover begins with accountability: accepting that how we feel about our situations is up to us. If we allow ourselves to be merely reactive — complaining about our situations, texting our friends about it, blaming someone else for it, or throwing ourselves a lively pity party — that's our choice.

However, it's not enough just to *know* we are being reactive. Many twenty somethings will acknowledge that they know their Hangover behavior isn't serving their highest good. We have to become proactive; we have to *do* something differently. And what you do does not have to create a dramatic change. Simple shifts can make twenty-something travel a lot smoother. In fact, the final destination of the proactive train is a peaceful mind. When we free ourselves from negative thinking, it's easy to see what action to take. But in order to do this, we need to stop beating ourselves up for mistakes and instead learn from them. Uncover the "aha" in any regret. Mistakes are valuable lessons that we do not have to repeat if we uncover what they are meant to teach us.

To begin to untangle our knot of reactive behaviors, all we need to do is choose one proactive step and commit to doing it. In the past, how did you react to Expectation Hangovers — by drinking too much? Resolve, this time, not to drink. By eating out of emotion rather than hunger? Stick to a diet. By wallowing alone in a dark room? Go outside; meet friends. By disappearing into your job? Take a few days off instead. As important as what you do is that you commit to doing it and follow through. It doesn't even matter if what you choose isn't entirely successful. Commitment to an action itself may be the beginning of your cure.

COMMITMENT CONTRACT

A commitment to your goals is much more powerful than an expectation to achieve them. It's important that your focus be on your *intention*, not the *outcome*. For instance, commit to an exercise program and make your goal sticking to it rather than how much weight you may lose. Committing to altering your thoughts and behaviors is something you can do *right now* and will immediately alleviate your Hangover symptoms.

Break away from expectations and commit to your action steps. Commit to becoming more aware of your internal dialogue and refocus it in a more positive direction. Commit to specific thoughts and behaviors that move you away from expectations. Examples of commitments you could make are:

- I commit to finding one thing about my job each day to appreciate.
- Each time I am feeling regretful about a mistake, I commit to reminding myself what I learned from that mistake.
- I commit to having only one drink per week.
- I commit to exercising at least five times per week for a minimum of forty minutes.
- I commit to journaling about my feelings when they begin to feel overwhelming.

Create a commitment contract with yourself right now. Make it official by printing the contract on a thick embossed-style paper (like the kind diplomas are printed on) and design some kind of personal seal or graphic. Type out each commitment and begin each one with "I, [*your name*], commit to [*xyz*]." Sign and date your contract. Display it where you can see it — especially when you feel an Expectation Hangover coming on.

"RECOVERING FROM A HANGOVER" by Aurora, 23

DECLARATION: *Overcoming Expectation Hangovers is all about finding balance as well as making an effort to recognize all the positives in your life and being grateful for them.*

I hit a big Expectation Hangover right out of college and am recovering slowly and steadily. Everything after college happens at a much slower pace than I ever expected. I got used to living life in the four-month sections of semesters — now everything feels so long term and overwhelming. I was disappointed when I realized how unexciting a corporate job was compared to going to college. It takes up more time in your day, making less time for personal hobbies and socializing. And it's not always going to be exciting! It takes a lot of patience and learning before management is going to trust you to do the more exciting work.

Also, at work I expected people to recognize me and give me feedback, probably because I got so used to being graded and evaluated all throughout school (and at home for that matter). I took no recognition and feedback as meaning I wasn't any good at what I was doing or there was something wrong with me, when really it's just how things work in the post-college "real world." Now I realize that I've always done good work that people appreciate. I was just looking for some kind of more explicit "grade." I've stopped buying into my belief that work defines who I am as a person — which is emotionally freeing!

I've treated my Expectation Hangovers by changing my thoughts and surrendering to the process of my life. Also, sharing my experiences with my friends who are going through the same thing really helped me. I'm very proud that I didn't get trapped into the negative thinking and bad attitude I had toward everything. I've been able to pull through with a new perspective on life and what it's all about — learning and growing, constantly. It's just part of coming down from that college-age high of feeling on top of the world and knowing everything there is to know. Graduating from college was a very humbling experience, and I'm proud of myself for the growth I've gone through (and will continue). I love feeling like I have my whole life ahead of me, and as much as I might like to plan what it will be like, I really have no idea what life has in store for me. But I feel like if I could handle the major Expectation Hangover I went through, I can handle almost anything in life and walk away from it feeling wiser and happier — and that's worth celebrating!

Practice Gratitude; Be of Service

What are the quickest, most effective ways to treat an Expectation Hangover? Practice gratitude and selflessness. First, appreciate who you are, what you've learned, and everything you have. This is vastly different from being self-absorbed or selfish (which can be disguised as "ambitious"). During an Expectation Hangover, we focus on ourselves and all we don't have or didn't get. But our Hangovers disappear whenever we focus on what we are grateful for and then shift our attention to the needs of others.

> "When I do things to help others and feel like I am somehow contributing to help make a difference in the world, I am filled with happiness and excitement."
>
> *Life coach and server, 27, recovering from a breakup, New Jersey*

I've learned this for myself whenever I'm involved in volunteer work. Giving to others always translates to receiving. But what motivates me is not what I get back; instead, it's the feeling inside me that emerges in the process of service. I wish I could bottle that feeling and offer it to people in lieu of antidepressants.

When you're feeling sorry for yourself, commit to finding some way to be of service to others. Get involved and donate your time (which is often more valuable than money) to a person or organization that needs help. For instance, commit to giving at least two hours a month. Being of service is part of our responsibility as human beings. However, if you are prone to "overgiving," remember that we are responsible for taking care of ourselves as well; stay balanced and don't give so much you're depleted. Even Gandhi and Mother Teresa had help.

Also, remember that service to others only helps when it's truly selfless, when we give with no expectation to receive. If we give hoping to get something back, we are setting ourselves up for an Expectation Hangover. Don't give from a place of expectation, give from your heart, and you could discover parts of yourself you may not have known were there.

> "There is no greater beauty in my eyes than that of a human being who selflessly and passionately sacrifices his- or herself for the well-being of others."
>
> Logistics analyst,
> 29, serious relationship, California

Often ways to be of service are right under our nose, and many are so simple we overlook them. We don't have to travel to an impoverished nation or a suffering city to serve. Help a friend who is moving, offer to watch your neighbor's kids, smile at a passerby, let someone in front of you in line, or call someone who you know is lonely. Everyone can help someone.

"GETTING MORE THAN I GAVE" by Lauren, 25

DECLARATION: *Life often brings unexpected lessons, and I have learned to embrace them as the most important lessons of all.*

My life has always been ordered and scheduled and rather predictable. I went to college, married my high school sweetheart, and began graduate school. I do not mean to downplay the things that I have experienced in my life. I just recognize that none of it was ever really unexpected or out of the ordinary. This remained true until March 2006 when I had the opportunity to be a part of one of the greatest life-changing events.

As a graduate student, I felt compelled to give back, so I helped plan a Katrina Relief trip as an alternative spring break for college students. I felt a surge of positive energy as I worked with an amazing group of people tirelessly organizing a huge undertaking. I poured myself into this trip to Biloxi, Mississippi, and loved being part of something so important and meaningful.

When spring break arrived, I could not wait to get on my bus and start a week of rebuilding and reinvigorating a community. Seven buses carrying 405 college students, administrators, faculty, and community members left the parking lot on a mission. Never in my life have I been so proud.

I spent my week making sure that everyone involved in our trip had a task. I talked with citizens who needed work done to their homes, yards, and other properties in the community. As I met community members, I had the chance to see firsthand some of the devastation. I was astounded to know that so much of the Gulf Coast looked the same as it did when Hurricane Katrina first hit almost eight months prior. My heart broke knowing so many residents could do nothing but wait for volunteers.

By the time our week was over, I knew that I had changed. This effort helped me to put my life into perspective. Helping others through such a difficult time allowed me to see the changes I needed to make in my own life. The people of the Gulf Coast taught me that life lays down unexpected roadblocks, and the only thing people can do to survive is to find a positive and meaningful way to make it through.

> "An Expectation Hangover is like giving the bullies at school a reaction to their behavior. Once they realize that you get upset, they continue to do it over and over again. When you finally realize that they will leave you alone when you don't react, the situation doesn't seem so bad and you gain confidence, friends, and you move on."
>
> *Marketer, 25,*
> *serious relationship, Colorado*

When I returned home, I stopped controlling the things that were truly out of my hands. I couldn't make people understand things or act a certain way. I found freedom in letting go of the small things instead of getting angry and upset. I also stopped controlling my feelings. I began to let them out and work through them instead of bottling them up and being mad at myself for feeling a certain way.

Since my trip to the Gulf Coast, I decide each and every day to take time and slow down. My life is not a race. I don't have to have it all ordered and figured out every minute. I still work on reminding myself of the importance of this. Sometimes I am not so optimistic that things will work out, but when I think about the victims of Katrina, I am reminded of how good I have it. And you know what? Each day gets better and better!

EXPECTATION HANGOVER TREATMENT AND PREVENTION PLAN

There is no pill for an Expectation Hangover, but here's the next best thing: a quick summary of this chapter's healing advice and preventative medicine. Bookmark this page. Not only will it support you in curing Hangovers and assist you during a quarter-life crisis, but it's a handy reference for enhancing a twenty-something life.

PREVENTATIVE MAINTENANCE:

- Uncover expectations. Come clean about what you expect of yourself and life, and recognize the expectations you've taken on from others.
- Define your goals. Keep an ongoing list of immediate, *attainable* short-term goals; focus on this, not expected outcomes or desires.
- Take steps rather than leaps. Each day, take a small step forward — don't try to have it all or do it all at once.
- Leave comparison land. Quit "more, better, different" thinking. Pay attention to your own progress, not that of others.
- Expect nothing from anyone else. Speak your mind; don't expect others to read it. Be honest about what you expect from others, but be willing to let those expectations go.
- Acknowledge and appreciate yourself. Every day, express gratitude for your life and what you have. Don't wait for someone else to tell you that you are fabulous!
- Be in the PRESENT! Avoid Expectation Hangovers by living in the here and now. Focus on today, and eliminate "when/then" thinking.

TREATMENT PLAN:

- Accept where you are. When you have a Hangover, accept it; don't resist it or regret it (which only makes it worse).
- Find the "aha." Put your emotions aside and learn from

any mistakes. What is life teaching you? There is a reason for everything.

- Do a reality check. Make a list of other unpleasant outcomes or expectations that have not manifested, and consider all the ways things have actually turned out for the better.
- Stay healthy. Combat depression with exercise and a healthy diet; avoid alcohol, overeating, overcaffeinating, sugar highs, oversleeping, and moping in front of the TV.
- Break up the pity party. Accept a Hangover, don't wallow in it. Plan something nice to do to help snap out of it.
- Be proactive. Be responsible for your feelings and take action to change them. Enact a plan for healthier behaviors and commit to it. Focus on what you *could* do differently rather than overthinking the past.
- Get to gratitude. Making a list of all the things in your life you are grateful for can be an immediate source of relief.
- Be selfless. It's simple. Do for others and you'll stop obsessing about yourself.

PART

2

WHO AM I?

The Self-Awareness Continuum

"Navigating the questions of the Twenties Triangle is complicated because you have no clue where you have been, where you are headed, what your goals are, what you want to be, and where you want to be. Up until now, I've been living according to other people's instructions, and now I feel like I don't know anything! I've realized I've made mistakes I need to fix inside my soul . . . and I trust that I'll be okay even though I don't always feel that way."

Consultant, 24, dating, Louisiana

Anyone who's had the fun of dealing with an Expectation Hangover knows that the twenty-something experience is laced with uncertainty. In parts 2 and 3, we will get to the heart of this twenty-something confusion as we tackle the three questions that make up what I call the "Twenties Triangle": Who am I? What do I want? and How do I get it?

THE TWENTIES TRIANGLE

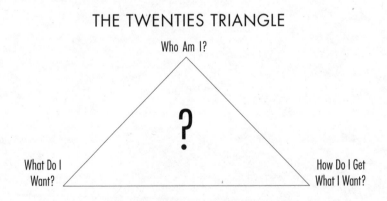

right to the second and third questions, but I encourage you to fully investigate the first question, "Who am I?" As our self-awareness evolves, we are more likely to make the choices that lead to the results we actually want, thus avoiding those dreaded Expectation Hangovers.

Who am I? The answers to this question evolve throughout our lifetime — they begin in childhood, and then shift into teen angst over where and how we fit in. Yet this question slaps us in the face the hardest in our twenties, when so many grown-up, real-world, this-is-your-life questions arrive at our doorstep. Until our twenties, we didn't know how good we had it. Remember when prom was stressful? Ah, the good old days...

We are not the roles we play in life or who other people want us to be. We are not our jobs, our relationships, our bodies, our accomplishments, or our bank accounts. The answer to "Who am I?" comes from inside — it's what makes each of us a unique individual. What makes us tick? What drives us? Who do we allow to come out when no one else is looking? In this part, we will begin searching out our most authentic selves. Getting to this form of "I" is like peeling back layers of an onion. The layers of your "identity onion" are likely to include who you have been told to be, who you believe you should be, and personas you've developed to handle certain situations or people — whether to get something, impress someone, or escape an uncomfortable situation.

The peeling of this identity onion is not easy because we are rarely taught how. Instructions for soul-searching questioning are usually not shared around the family dinner table or outlined on the blackboard at school. Plus, becoming clear on who we are

> "I've learned the importance of figuring out just exactly who you are. Not who other people want you to be. Not who you thought you were by virtue of the way you were raised. But who you truly are."
>
> *Legal secretary, 29, single and love it and hate it, Maine*

is an ongoing process, not a single event. It's like a class that never ends, and just like when we peel an onion, there are often tears. I am still peeling my own onion and probably will be for the rest of my life.

> "I expected that at twenty-five I would at least know who I am and who I want to be. I thought the hell of adolescence was the price we paid to figure it out. I'll soon be closing in on thirty and the fact that I still haven't had my day, week, month, or year of epiphany leaves me disheartened."
>
> Accountant, 25,
> single and love it, Washington

In my own experience, and in my research and coaching practice, I've noticed three common developmental stages that twenty somethings evolve through as they investigate the question, "Who Am I?" I call this evolution the "Self-Awareness Continuum," and it's the process by which we understand, assess, and develop our identities. I call the three phases of the Self-Awareness Continuum (which we will cover in the next three chapters): Basic, Investigative, and Integrated (see the diagram on page 61).

While the phases are distinct, there is no particular age or experience that marks each stage; rather, our building awareness moves us from one phase into the next.

> "These have been years of self-discovery through the good, the bad . . . and the ugly."
>
> Student and legal assistant,
> 25, dating, Pennsylvania

Also, the transition between phases can be faster in some areas of our lives and slower in others. For instance, we may move to a more integrated awareness in our careers before we have done this in our romantic relationships. It takes many years to truly integrate all the pieces of our identities so that they come together and we become more consistent in who we are in all aspects of our lives.

"WHO AM I?" — AWARENESS CONTINUUM

Basic
Approximate ages: 20–24

- Identifies self by interests, desires, roles
- Experiences duality thinking, confusion, and inconsistent levels of self-esteem
- Relies on and regurgitates external feedback
- Measures self via comparison
- Feels driven to meet external expectations
- Lacks strong sense of self

Investigative
Approximate ages: 24–27

- Engages in internal questioning and evaluation
- Questions decisions and life choices; experiences quarter-life-crisis feelings
- Engages in private thoughts and judgments
- Assesses and discerns true values and desires
- Becomes more assertive and self-sufficient
- Recognizes the purpose of self-evaluation
- Begins to construct sense of self

Integrated
Approximate ages: 27–30

- Lives by personal values, ethics, and personalized version of success
- Handles challenges without loss of self; feels less concerned about what others think
- Forges deeper connections and spiritual awareness
- Experiences sense of discovery and "aha" moments
- Understands own role in self-perception
- Secures and continually evaluates sense of self

3. BASIC SELF-AWARENESS

"The hardest thing for me about being twenty something was the pain of figuring out who I really was. After I graduated from college and met the biggest goal in my life, I felt lost. I had a severe 'What now?' crisis."

Web developer, 30, married, Colorado

For many of us, we are finally thrust into the real world after college graduation, when for the first time we have to figure out who we are outside the walls of a school and our parents' home, and sometimes far away from our familiar hometown. Adjusting to being on our own for the first time is stressful. Do we maintain the roles we've developed up to now? Do we try to live up to the expectations and hopes others have for us? Who are we, anyway? And, as if this identity crisis wasn't enough — we have to juggle all the unfamiliar, practical problems of surviving independently.

For me, graduation led to a time of tremendous confusion over who I was. Without the well-defined "good student" identity and structure of college, I was lost. I knew who I was in the land of academia, but I struggled to know who I was as an adult on my own. I needed a new identity, so like many other twenty somethings in the Basic stage, I sought out a career and a relationship. I thought these would answer the question, "Who am I?" And yet, at twenty-three, though I was on a successful career track and dating a Hollywood guy who was exposing me to the good life, I was sad, empty, and didn't really know what to do about it.

In the Basic stage on the Self-Awareness Continuum, twenty somethings often report feeling fear, anxiety, confusion, sadness, and even depression. They frequently feel they have trouble keeping up and adjusting to the responsibility of carving out their own lives. Some say they exhaust themselves trying to live up to everyone's expectations, burning out as they push their bodies and minds past their limits. Others are overwhelmed with loss and sadness: they miss college life, both the status they enjoyed and the community, and they feel like small, lost fish in a very big pond.

In the Basic stage, we often cling to our roles and use them to define ourselves: "I am a nursing student, a son, a waitress, an engineer, an alumnus, a girlfriend, an athlete." We also frequently identify ourselves by our characteristics and desires, by our likes and dislikes: "I play soccer, I love music, I'm a redhead, I care about the environment." This is natural. For two decades others have labeled us and identified us in these ways, and we are only just figuring out what we think of ourselves.

> "I feel like I am at an in-between place; I have broken off from my family and my close-knit community in college, and I'm on my own in the real world. What is my role? I'm not a student; I'm not a spouse; I'm not a parent. . . . I'm just whoever I make myself to be. This is both freeing and frightening."
>
> *Industrial engineer, 25, single and hate it, Minnesota*

PARDON MY DUST: UNDER CONSTRUCTION

Growing up, we are classified and distinguished by our gender, hobbies, academic interests, socioeconomic status, and so on. From elementary school onward, our abilities and activities are the stuff of dinner conversations, and our characteristics and interests often collect into an easily recognized type or "brand." Perhaps you were the funny hyperactive performer, or the easygoing athletic friend, or the introverted grade-A student. In the Basic stage, our labels are usually still stuck to us; although we may begin to feel the urge to pull them off, we aren't quite sure how yet.

> "It's hard to separate myself from my parents' reassurance of who I am. Even though I am independent, I still seek their approval and opinion."
>
> *Medical school student, 24, serious relationship, Michigan*

We've come to rely on our "brand," no matter how badly it may seem to fit or how much we dislike it. It's the basis for the approval and feedback we've always gotten from our parents, teachers, and peers. When we describe ourselves, we may continue to regurgitate this external feedback, reinforcing it at the very same time that we may want to undo it. Growing up, intelligence was my most externally reinforced characteristic, so I was always either "smart" (positive) or "a goody-goody/nerd" (negative).

During the Basic stage, it's common to experience a lot of confusion and self-doubt. We tend to engage in a lot of comparison with others, and more than ever our self-worth or confidence may rise or fall based on what others think. We pursue compliments like candy, while criticism is hard to handle, making us defensive on the outside and very upset on the inside. It can be hard to distinguish our authentic self from our "brand," and to reconcile our "good" attributes (those that earn praise) with our "bad" (those that are criticized or considered weak). Twenty somethings can get caught up in a duality of thinking that is hard to shake. In some contexts, "smart" is good, but in others it's bad — and so we end up loving and hating being "smart" at the same time. Society doesn't help. For instance, when job hunting, we are constantly being asked, "What are your strengths and weaknesses? Tell me about your accomplishments." Since we are supposed to "accentuate the positive," we hide, judge, and shame the things we don't like about ourselves, hoping we can either change them, hide them, or eventually grow out of them.

"STRANGER IN THE MIRROR" by Phil, 22

DECLARATION: *I'm anxious because I don't know who I am, and until I do, I don't know where I'm going.*

I stood among peers wearing suits and ties, wineglass in hand, detached from the piano music and the sputtering jokes and conversations, hand shaking. The event was my first alumni gathering only two months after my college graduation. I recognized no one, and I made no attempt to try. Instead, I went in the men's room and tried to understand who that person was I was looking at in the mirror.

I won't be ridiculous — I knew it was my face. But the face, to me, was that of quiet desperation. This desperation had no single cause, but rather it seemed to be a concentration of causes. The stress from overloaded course schedules, the self-doubt from peer criticism in the classroom, the loneliness stemming from nagging shyness, insecurity, and parents whom I could never seem to please. But most prominently, my anxiety was not only over lack of understanding of who I was but where I was going.

At eighteen I wanted to be a screenwriter-filmmaker like Oliver

Stone, so I majored in English and creative writing with a naive yearning for fame, attention, and praise. I never told my parents this dream because I doubted they would ever support me. When they found out my major, I could hear them whisper in the living room their doubts and their lack of faith in my career direction. So, with encouragement, rather insistence, from them along with my best friend, I added accounting as a second major.

The extra major didn't allow me to take a single summer off, participate in-depth with any student organizations, socialize regularly, or give me the time to practice for the driver's license my parents discouraged me from getting when I was sixteen. The workload became daunting, and I felt rushed and overloaded practically every quarter.

But in my senior year, I knew I wasn't good at accounting and I was miserable. After a horrible quarter, I switched to the manageable but no more fulfilling marketing program. My grades staggered and so did my confidence. Even worse, the extra load and switch in majors diluted my concentration on my writing. I wasn't reading novels, writing on a daily basis, or watching acclaimed films — the activities I believed made good writers and filmmakers. As a result, an inferiority complex developed. Before I knew it, I was thinking about law school as Plan B. I figured a Juris Doctor would be good enough to net me a form of the prestige, distinction, and wealth I desired.

This festive evening of mingling with strangers in the dinner hall, and me staring blankly at myself in the mirror, was also the night before I was emailed my LSAT score. But I wasn't looking forward to finding out, and I probably wasn't going to law school, because despite the six straight months of preparation, and multiple aborted attempts, I once again believed I choked under the pressure of the real thing.

> "I want to make it on my own, be independent from my family, be debt-free, happy, and successful. But I just don't think I have enough life experience yet to know who I am, and I don't think it's realistic to expect myself to have it all figured out right now. But it's hard not to compare myself to other people my age who do seem to know exactly who they are."
>
> *School secretary, 23,*
> *serious relationship, Oregon*

I am missing something anyone with a sense of direction possesses: faith and confidence in oneself. But how can I possess these when I don't know who I am?

After emerging from the restroom, I scanned the room for company. I drifted from gathering to gathering, searching for someone as confused as I was. I am lonely, sexually frustrated, insecure, shy, detached, discouraged, and fearful for the future. I have this feeling like a clock is ticking.

I don't know how long I'll feel this way about life. I've heard so many people tell me that this stage of life is just a beginning and it always works out eventually. Career counselors and parents tell me that I'm just in a phase, but oversimplifying these tangles of self-doubt and loneliness is easy for them when it's my life and not theirs. But if this is a phase, a temporary time of confusion, when does it end?

If you are still in the Basic stage on the Self-Awareness Continuum, you can probably relate to Phil's level of frustration over not knowing who he is. This ambiguous, uncertain sense of self feels like a big roadblock, and leads to frustration and panic. Trust that it is a phase that you will evolve out of — and the more self-accepting you are of exactly who and where you are, the faster this phase will end. Cultivate compassion for yourself while you are in this process of self-discovery; consider yourself "under construction." You are more than what you do or have. The emotional quagmire of this stage dissolves as you learn what makes you *you* — independent of any roles you play or labels you may have taken on.

> "All too often as a twenty something the significance of who we are recedes in the background because of the expectations of who we should be or ought to be for the culture. I've found peace by creating a counterculture inside myself that I've defined."
>
> Graduate student, 24,
> serious relationship, Missouri

MORE, BETTER, DIFFERENT

In the Basic stage, we live our lives under a microscope of self-evaluation, but at first our focus is almost constantly looking for ways to be "more, better, different." We don't know who we are, which is bad enough, but what we do know about ourselves we often don't like. We're desperate for change and self-improvement.

However, comparing ourselves to others, and trying to emulate them, is not a successful strategy. After all, there will *always* be someone who has more or seems to be doing things better. As the cliché goes, "The grass is always greener on the other side." But really, it only *seems* greener. Since you are looking from the outside, you have no way of knowing what struggles the other person is going through inside. When we are unhappy with ourselves, another "yard" is always going to look more appealing, but we must focus our attention on watering our own lawn and making our grass as green as possible.

Aim to enrich your life, not improve yourself by changing, adding, or deleting. In other words, stop trying to be a certain kind of person, and simply do the things that you enjoy. For example, if you like to create things, join a painting class. If you want to express more kindness in your life, find opportunities to volunteer. If you simply want to play, maybe it's time for a trip to the batting cages. Bring out the parts of you that you know are there, instead of struggling to mold yourself into what you think you need to be. Become more accepting of who you are.

As we begin to shed old externally given labels and identities, and as we realize we not only have a choice but the ability to create who we are, that is when we shift from the Basic to the Investigative stage on the Self-Awareness Continuum.

"MY LOVE/HATE RELATIONSHIP WITH ME" by Kimberly, 21

DECLARATION: *I'm not doing things anymore to be more or better or different; I'm doing them to improve the parts of my life that are okay the way they are.*

I've never been completely satisfied with myself. My thighs are too wide and my belly's too soft. My one eyebrow arches slightly higher than the other (an asymmetry exaggerated with a few margaritas). I'm beautiful but not by society's standards. I'm impatient, fidgety, melodramatic, emotional, and tend to read over, under, and in between lines that don't exist. At times I say the worst thing at the most inopportune time.

This is me, though. I've made all sorts of promises to myself to be "more, better, or different." From losing weight and eating the correct daily servings of fruits and veggies, to going out more while trying to save money, to working harder at finding the perfect job.

I grew up as a ballet dancer, gymnast, and straight-A student who spent eight years in Catholic school. I was a perfectionist and total type-A personality. I had to be the best so that others would like me. But it takes a lot of energy to try to be perfect, and I completely neglected any internal growth.

At about halfway into my degree, I was thoroughly confused. I threw myself into work so I didn't have to think or worry about anything else. I had good friends, a good studio apartment, and a good amount in the bank. I even met a great guy and fell in love. As crazy as it sounds, my hectic schedule facilitated our relationship; I didn't have any time to overanalyze and freak out about it. So I was set, but only on the material level — not the emotional.

I got an internship at a big NBC morning show, and when it was over, I couldn't figure out why I felt like I failed. Why did I leave that internship feeling worse off than before? My self-doubt returned with my free time. I started asking my best friends and my boyfriend, "What do you like about me? Why do you even bother spending time with me?" I had held my disdain for myself so deep inside myself that it ate up all my self-confidence. The answers I got from the people I respected were honest and straightforward: I'm smart. I'm funny. I'm beautiful. I'm happy. But it didn't sound like they were talking about me.

That's when I started realizing that the reasons they liked me were the same reasons I liked them — and I would be appalled if they ever doubted their own worth. I started to think, "Maybe he's telling me the truth. Maybe he just loves me for me." Radical, I know. I resolved to try — try to stay this happy and find more. I realized my life didn't need any drastic changes.

I am going to try to stop smoking, try to save money, try to think before speaking, try to eat better, and try to feel confident with my body every day. Granted, I'm writing this story with an ashtray of cigarette butts, but I am trying to do better. And I'm doing pretty darn well. I'm not resolved to an actual finish line; I'm just resolved to try to get somewhere. I'm not doing these things to be more or better or different. I'm doing them to improve the parts of my life that are okay the way they are.

> "People always say, 'Just be true to yourself.' But in my early twenties, I didn't feel like I knew myself very well, so I didn't know what made me happy. One of my favorite things about getting older is growing more comfortable with who I am and knowing what really makes me happy."
>
> *Engineer, 26, engaged, Oklahoma*

4. INVESTIGATIVE SELF-AWARENESS

I call this next stage of self-awareness "investigative" because it is when we are constantly questioning ourselves, our lives, and the things and people in it. However, our investigations lead to few "open and shut cases." Instead, our investigations are long and vast in scope. As we step out of the familiar, we may feel increasingly uncomfortable. On the outside, our lives during this stage may not change much, but on the inside we feel it. There are more private thoughts about ourselves and our lives. We are considering, weighing, and evaluating — trying to get beneath or beyond the roles, characteristics, and desires we began to grow frustrated with during the Basic stage. In the Investigative stage, we are extremely determined to get to the bottom of the question, "Who am I?"

> "I am faced with making decisions based on my narrow amount of experience. Although I wish someone would tell me what to do, because it would be easier, I know I need to begin trusting my judgment and believe in my ability to decide for myself what is best for me."
>
> *Marketing assistant, 23, single and love it, Nevada*

because we realize the answer has a domino effect on other decisions. When people declare they are having a "quarter-life crisis," they are usually at this level of self-awareness. This stage is often marked by questions like: Why am I like this? Why is everything bugging me? Why can't I be happy? Why don't I know what I want to do?

NOTHING IS DREADFULLY WRONG, YET NOTHING FEELS RIGHT

Twenty-six-year-old Nicole expresses well the uneasy angst that often accompanies the Investigative stage:

"Almost everything in my life is in order, no real big drama or major crisis, but nothing seems right in my life. Despite all the things I have accomplished, I feel very sad most of the time; I feel alone. I have drifted away from most of my girlfriends due to misunderstandings, moving, or simply isolating myself. I don't know what I want from my life, career, relationships, friends, and most of all I have completely lost a sense of direction. I have become very anxious, always afraid to take chances and starting to sweat the small stuff, which is affecting my mental state on a daily basis. What is wrong with me? How can I get myself together?"

The reason Nicole can't "get herself together" is because she is in the Investigative stage, which involves picking ourselves apart in order to gain understanding and insight about ourselves. It can feel very discombobulating. Our life may be going perfectly fine but we feel disconnected from it and start questioning everything. During this time, things that used to make us happy, like an accomplishment, do not have the same resonance. We may drift away from people we used to be close with. We may question our values, our relationships, our decisions, and our beliefs. Nothing is wrong; it's just the puberty of adulthood! As with actual puberty, we are changing, evolving — and often feel like our sense of direction is lost as we head down roads that have not been MapQuested for us. We may long to stop and ask for directions, but no one can help us. We may also wish to bust a U-turn and head back to our old, familiar road, but I encourage you to stay the course.

In other words, we are becoming more assertive, independent, and starting to fight for our own self-worth (we are ready to create our own road map), but we are still looking to things outside of ourselves for validation (we'd love to MapQuest it). As we learn more about ourselves and what we really like and don't like — this feedback is often surprising. It was in this stage of my own self-awareness that I realized I really did not want to work in Hollywood, that I was in a relationship I was not sure of deep down, and realized I had some issues I had not dealt with yet. I was still trying to please others on the outside, but on the inside I was starting to understand that was not in my best interest.

> "I feel like every decision I make — which jobs to apply to, which job to accept, where to move, where to live once I move there, and even things as small as whether or not to go out on a given night or if I should buy a dress I probably can't afford — has a domino effect and impacts my life. I wish someone would make all of these decisions for me because I don't have a clue as to what I am doing!"
>
> Book publishing assistant, 26, single and hate it, Washington, D.C.

This stage is also marked by extreme discomfort and conflict regarding other people's perceptions of us. We still want to be "known" and "liked," but our own sense of what we want to be known and liked for is shifting. Remember, your opinion of yourself is the most important. A twenty-seven-year-old writes, "I wish I would have understood earlier that I don't have to have all the answers, or even any answers right now. I didn't allow myself the opportunity to explore and live without huge expectations on myself, which was a burden to my growth as an individual. My life was directed by the expectations that I felt other people in my life and society created for me. Now I'm trying to discover who I really am. It may disappoint a few people, but I have to stop disappointing myself." Family, romantic, friend, and work relationships may become a little more tenuous as this process of self-exploration unfolds and who you are becoming begins to separate from who you've been for others in the past.

> "The most difficult thing about being a twenty something is filtering expectations that others put out, from my parents, my friends, and society in general. It's hard for me to find the balance to be strong enough to stand out against expectations that do not nourish and enrich my soul, while finding grace and humility to listen to the counsel of those who have more life experience."
>
> *Substitute teacher, 26, married, California*

Of course, since we are tackling big questions, quick and easy answers are few, and this stage can produce a lot of anxiety. Pay attention to how you cope with anxiety — self-evaluation is often not something we can do completely alone. You may find yourself frequenting the self-help aisles of bookstores or seeking out a counselor or therapist. It can be very helpful to find an objective third party who can reflect our questions and understandings back to us, to aid our self-evaluation. This stage can feel very scary, lonely, and disruptive. Breakups, career shifts, and family fights are common during this time — but these things may be unavoidable and even necessary. However, treat everything as a learning opportunity. Instead of asking yourself, "Why is this happening to me?" ask, "What am I learning about me as this is happening?"

I've noticed that a lot of control issues arise in this phase as we attempt to offset all the uncertainty and change. Some respond by trying to control their bodies (obsessing about size, even developing eating disorders), some by self-medicating with substances (food, alcohol, prescription drugs), and some by trying to change or control others (through codependent relationships and so on). In this stage we feel like we are on a roller-coaster ride, and we may grasp for something or someone to steady us. However, true steadiness only comes from within. As one twenty-seven-year-old woman writes: "Early in my twenties, I was uber-focused on my education, body, dating, ambition, and drive to have a 'full' and busy life. As the return on that effort did not meet my expectations, I stopped striving so much. In my mid-twenties, I have celebrated my own femininity, luxuriating in the natural world and all its wonders, my deep thoughts and desire for spiritual understanding, and my willingness to connect with my girlfriends and mother on a more graceful, compassionate, supportive, and nurturing level."

KILL YOURSELF WITH KINDNESS

The Investigative stage can be a bit bumpy, and we tend to dwell on criticisms and critiques of ourselves. It's a good idea to practice self-encouragement to balance this out. Make a conscious effort to praise and appreciate yourself. This means not only being grateful for what we *have* — health, family, a roof over our head, money, and so on — but also appreciating solely who we *are*. Remember, it's so important to like yourself — you have to spend the rest of your life with you, so you might as well start liking your permanent companion.

Spread some love, particularly to all those parts that are neglected, shut down, or just not celebrated nearly enough. At the very least, you can always praise your efforts, even when the results have not yet manifested. Thank yourself for having the courage to look for a new job, being open to falling in love, showing compassion to your friends, practicing frugality to achieve more financial balance, demonstrating enthusiasm by going to the gym, expressing creativity, or caring about yourself enough to break a bad habit.

Then, lighten up about the things you are not that fond of about yourself. For example, I am not a very patient person and criticize myself for that. But I can bring light and gratitude to this quality simply by shifting my awareness and saying, "I am grateful that I am aware of my impatience and am practicing slowing down. I am grateful my impatience makes me extremely prompt!" I can work on accepting this quality about myself instead of beating myself up over it; I can focus on what I am grateful for instead. Employing this process will help you feel better about yourself — exactly as you are right now in this moment, not as you want to be *someday*.

> "I am finally getting comfortable with who I am in general. For a long time I felt I really had to change things about my personality because other people didn't like them, but over the past year I really began to appreciate my strengths and my weaknesses. I realized I couldn't have one without the other. I've tried to stop viewing my 'weaknesses' as something I had to fix immediately and started to see them as a part of who I am and to just cut myself some slack."
>
> *Graduate student, 25, dating, Tennessee*

This is an extremely important practice for all you guys out there. Men are rarely encouraged to practice self-appreciation. They may get a few "atta boy"s for their accomplishments, but they are rarely praised for who they are.

GRAT-I-TUDE

In order to practice self-gratitude — to appreciate every piece of what makes you *you* — it helps to write down your own grat-I-tude list. Gratitude increases your awareness of your own self-perception and accelerates your growth in this Investigative stage. On your grat-i-tude list, acknowledge yourself, your accomplishments, your characteristics, and what you have learned. Put the self-appreciating "I am" into your gratitude practice. Take out the "I have." Self-appreciation and recognition not only feels good, it creates a more positive energy field around you — thereby attracting more of the things that are in line with who you really are.

GROWN-UP GROWING PAINS

The Investigative stage is also marked by the increasing awareness that you are a grown-up doing grown-up things. Many twenty somethings get married, buy homes, get promoted to more important jobs, start their own businesses, and become parents. Every now and then, you look around for an adult in the room and discover that it's you. You become more aware, and even proud, of the increasing responsibilities of your various roles: as an employee or a boss, as a husband or a wife, as a parent, homeowner, community member, and so on.

"MY GROWN-UP LIFE" by Noelle, 26

DECLARATION: *I am waiting for some sort of a finale to this dizzying journey where I declare, "I have officially finished growing up. I know exactly who I am!"*

I am twenty-six years old, and most days that sounds about right. But there have been days, more than I'd like to admit, that twenty-six sounds unfathomable. How is it possible that I am twenty-six already?

It's not that I feel old; I am just shocked that the transition from kid to adult happened so quickly. On the days when the real word and real life is just too much for me to handle, I feel far from being a grown-up.

At twenty-six, I have a teaching job in a great district, my husband and I are crazy about each other, and I love being half of our "we." We have stuff, grown-up stuff, like a mortgage and a lawn mower. We do grown-up things, like attend our friends' children's birthday parties, send Christmas cards, and go on fancy vacations. I go grocery shopping once a week, and my husband pays the bills. I do laundry, I clean, I cook dinner, and I complain when I can't keep up. I am often tired, stressed, and brought to tears for no reason at all. Some days I look around and get the feeling that I am playing house and my head starts to spin.

> "Two moments define feeling grown-up: having to actually demonstrate competence rather than just promise it, and realizing that your parents are getting old and that you are now the responsible adult."
>
> Financial salesperson, 24, single, Texas

As a new grown-up, I have screwed up my fair share of dinners, felt completely overwhelmed at work, and forcibly declared, more than once, that I was unable to go on! This transition has been surprisingly challenging, but I know I am evolving and learning, all the while clutching to that feeling hiding somewhere between hope and fear.

I can't help wondering if the girl I was at twenty would even recognize the woman I am now at twenty-six. I am so different in so many ways; but on the other hand, sometimes I feel like exactly the same person I was then and way too young! I still call my mom while I am at the grocery store because I don't know which kind of onion goes in soup. I look at my paycheck and think that it's a ton of money, when in reality it's not even enough for our mortgage. Right before my first year of teaching, despite my fine education, I felt completely clueless as I walked into my classroom for the first time. I longed for the days when I myself was in second grade.

Sometimes I can take a step back and see my younger self actually taking over. The other day my husband and I were out with a group and one of the women was really making an effort to get to know me better and deepen our friendship. Later, when we got in the car I told my husband that I think she really likes me. He looked at me with a puzzled expression and said, "Of course she does, why wouldn't she?" As I informed him that I am sometimes surprised when people enjoy my company and think that I am cool, I practically choked on the insecure teenage expressions and insecurities coming out of my mouth that are still part of my self-identity.

As Noelle makes clear, sometimes we still feel like kids who are only playing at being "grown-up," and sometimes we want to run as far from the "adult" world as possible. Trust that these growing pains are normal. They are part of the process of discovering who we are and getting comfortable in our new skin — resist the temptation to see every slip and slide in and out of adulthood as a failure. Even as we outgrow some of our childhood or teenage insecurities, others may linger. There will be moments when our inner and outer selves seem perfectly aligned in a vision of our ideal selves. Treasure and remember these moments! Because more often (though less so with time), we may struggle to act the way we'd like, or feel what we think we should feel. Even when teasing classmates, critical parents, or other judgmental authority figures have been left behind, the "kid" in us can still take over and react in the same old ways.

> "It's a struggle between wanting grown-up things and having to worry about the future, while still wanting to go out and be crazy and irresponsible."
>
> Graduate student, 26, dating, Illinois

When this happens, investigate! Ask yourself: "Why am I feeling this way? What belief system or memory is this hitting? Who can I get feedback from about this situation?" Remember, this is the Investigative stage. It's all about asking questions. The answers you get may at first feel incomplete or uncertain, but they will eventually become clear. For now, just keep asking.

During my Investigative stage, I remember thinking that if anyone could hear what I was actually thinking inside my head, they would think I was some dysfunctional version of the seven dwarfs: bitchy, crazy, whiny, fearful, tearful, critical, and pitiful. But on the outside, I somehow held it together. Yet the people closest to me could see the struggle. My ex-fiancé broke up with me during this phase of my "Who am I?" awareness — and quite frankly, I don't blame him. Being with me and my seven dwarfs was unpredictable, depressing, and a serious buzz kill. I am not saying that a breakup is part of this stage for everyone. You see, at first I approached this stage with a defeatist attitude. I really didn't understand exactly what I was going through; I just knew I didn't like it and wondered when that "someday" would come. To try to fix the internal tornado that was going on inside me, I opted to take antidepressants, to search for my "passion," to try to change the person I was with, and to obsess over my body. It really took hitting rock bottom for me to start to look within rather than out — in other words, *in*vestigate rather than *out*vestigate.

> "There is a limited life experience that comes with being in my twenties. I recognize that I have not lived long enough to make certain educated decisions or know how to deal with certain things about myself. But I do know the person that knows me the best and what is best for me is most likely me!"
>
> *Teacher, 25, dating, Georgia*

QUAL-YOU-TY TIME

It takes time to figure yourself out. You can't rush it. But you can help yourself by making time for it. Life doesn't wait while we get our act together; it rushes on, and if we're not careful, we rush right with it and never quite get around to all the investigative thinking we need to do. So commit to spending some quality time with yourself. For those who can, I recommend solo travel — even taking a week or a weekend on your own, outside of normal work and obligations, can do wonders. If you can, consider taking more time and getting a real taste of the world, and of yourself, before settling down into a career or graduate school.

This kind of "road-trip" discovery is not financially or linguistically possible for all twenty somethings. If you are firmly planted in a career, relationship, or situation, nothing prevents you from internal travel. Set aside one day or afternoon a week, or carve out fifteen minutes a day, to do something just for you — listen to your favorite music, read a great book, go for a walk. Whatever you do, do it alone and away from your traditional daily duties; treat it like a small vacation. Insight and clarity are much more likely to come when you invite them, and create space for them, by setting aside quality time for yourself.

LEARNING TO TRUST

It's no wonder that, as we get caught up examining and questioning most (if not all) aspects of our life, we have moments of pure freakout when we scream at ourself and the world: "How did I get here?" and "Why am I like this?" Instead of wisely using these moments as opportunities for learning and understanding, we often just have a self-defeating meltdown. Then, at some point, something magical happens — with nothing and no one else to rely on, we have no choice but to trust ourself. And when, to our relief, the world does not end, we start to realize that trusting ourselves — our own intuition and authentic sense of self — is the key that unlocks real change.

"HEADINESS" by Alexandra, 24

DECLARATION: *I've learned that self-trust is all about living a vibrant life and strengthening a relationship with myself.*

I am a horrible shopper. When I go, it does not take long before I am tired, hungry, and bored. If clothing does make it out of the store with me, it typically stays in the bag, in my car, ready to go back. It could be perfectionism, indecision, or commitment issues, but I think a friend said it best when he diagnosed me as being "heady."

I am very familiar with an explosive potion to concoct headiness. Here are the ingredients: a lot of analyzing, nail biting, eye glazing, and brow furrowing, too many excuses and opportunities to drink, asking opinions of too many people, and wanting to divide myself into ten mini-mes and try out each life path I am considering. The intake of this potion stirs up low energy, a bitter attitude, weird work dreams, the urge to give up, and some tears.

> "Traveling to other countries and studying sociology gave me the opportunity to learn about myself and others. It opened my mind to be aware of who I am, where I came from, and what it means. It was my own journey; I did not study what my mom wanted me to. I did it for me."
>
> *Mobile phone salesperson, 26, serious relationship, Louisiana*

Never have I been more plagued by these heady traits than in the past year when I graduated from college and moved across the country to pursue acting. The move was bold and my whole heart was behind it, but boy did I get heady! That same annoying shopping tendency extended into my daily life. Asking the salesperson, "Can I return this shirt?" and explaining, "Oh no, it's a nice shirt, I just don't think I'll wear it enough," translated into asking myself, "Can I return this life?" and explaining, "It was a good idea to follow a dream, but I just don't think this one's the right one for me."

So what might be the garlic at the door to ward off this headiness potion? I am beginning to realize it has something to do with trusting myself. Faith in my decisions. Committing to myself. But how?

I've learned that self-trust is all about living a vibrant life and strengthening a relationship with myself. It is a form of love, a virtue, and a creation. Here are some ingredients I've added to my self-trust potion. They are best when fresh, so I try and renew them every day. First, get self-aware. Learn about yourself. There is so much that the physical body communicates. I go for the experiences that give me butterflies, energy, and laughter — not lethargy, a sinking feeling, and a frown.

Second, ask questions of yourself. Here are some of mine: What are the things I doubt and why? When do I get negative, and what triggers it? What scares me? I spent time alone answering these questions, which allowed me to realize I had committed to something I really believed in, yet I was going about it weakly. I was terrified to commit to my new life because I did not want to fail.

> "I'm finally accepting that being a twenty something is a learning process — and I am wading through each experience, noticing how it impacts me as a person and paves the way for my ever-evolving personality. With each experience, my view and reaction to myself and the world changes."
>
> *Reporter, 27, dating, Georgia*

Third, add some self-acceptance. As I learn more about myself, of course I see some things I don't like, but I accept them and work with them. For example, instead of judging my restlessness, I am trying to work with it and understand that sometimes it is a royal headache; other times it's the reason behind new hobbies. What I'm finally starting to see is the truth about where I am: at best, forging a healthy commitment to pursuing my dreams; at worst, feeling that at least I've tried. I found my healthy balance by defining what it would take for me to like the process a little more and setting limits around when I would feel I had given my dream the space it needed to grow. I also realized that trusting myself and my decision was way less heady.

Finally, pour on self-reliance and take ownership of your life. I recall the times in my life when I already made good choices without the help of others. From that place, I start setting new goals. Self-trust is huge here. Setting mini (realistic) goals of going on auditions and studying my craft rather than major (fantastical) goals, like landing a role, immediately pulled me out of my self-doubt and inability to commit. I remind myself that success in adult life is far more independent and probably takes years and years of work — and won't come packaged in a pretty little blue box with a white silk ribbon on it. And if it did, I'd probably return it anyway.

I want to reiterate Alexandra's recipe for trust: combine self-awareness, self-reflection, self-acceptance, setting realistic goals, and self-reliance. All of these ingredients are integral, but you can play with the measurements to suit your taste. They do not have to be exact or perfect, and neither do you. As the next story makes clear, getting to know who you are is a process, not an event. Keep mixing, keep walking, and it will come together.

"AT TRUST'S DOORSTEP" by Gretchen, 28

DECLARATION: *Trust that everything you experience is for a reason. Though you may feel completely disconnected from the rest of the world, keep walking, for you will get to the other side of the road.*

At twenty-eight, I'm still looking for the right job that feeds my passion and purpose. I now know what I do *not* want from the varied experiences I've had. I'm holding on to the faith that I can have what I want — a flexible schedule, a job I am excited to go to on Monday morning, and a career that empowers and inspires individuals, that contributes to the greater good, *and* that pays! I want to travel the world, I wish to experience other diverse cultures, and I do want to make a difference in my own way, somehow. But right now it feels like I am still searching.

After graduating from college, I took a leap of faith and decided to head west, with little in my pocket but a dream in my heart and a

vision in my head. I eventually settled into
a job and tucked away my dreams…but
dreams we tuck away are not forgotten.
They resurface like a broken heart, reminding us of who we really are.

I know I make my own destiny, so
what am I creating in this life that is in
alignment with my goals and desires? I
don't see it. So I continue on my search.

What I've found is I have to trust the

> "While others may become stagnant or be-
> come resigned to what's not working, I
> have continued to pursue the happiness
> and joy I believe we all can have if we are
> really honest with ourselves."
>
> *Human resources manager, 28,*
> *serious relationship, Minnesota*

process. Trust myself. Trust the Universe. Trust my experiences — for
every experience holds a gift. Experiences are my guides through life
— a point of reference, if you will, to gauge my decisions. Therefore, I
have to investigate my memories, my feelings, and my emotions, for I
am seeing they are what will lead me to my own truth. I have to trust
in myself most of all.

There was a time when I believed just "going with the flow" and
"faking it till you make it" was the way to experience life. But now I am
starting to understand the tremendous power of trusting myself. I continue on my path, listening to my heart. Even though I may not know exactly what my path is or where exactly I am going, I continue walking.

I love the awareness that both Alexandra and Gretchen have gotten to in their twenty-something journeys. They trust that they are
exactly where they are supposed to be — and this trust is what will
carry them both into the next phase of awareness. Each day of your
life is part of your story. Trust that yesterday shaped today, and today creates tomorrow. Many twenty somethings often admit to
feeling like they are faking it — acting more confident, happy, or
grown up than they actually are. But there's no faking it inside. Only
when we learn to truly trust ourselves will we come to discover our
authentic self and who we want to be and what we want to do.

When you get to the point in your Investigative stage where you trust your process and the way your life is unfolding — so that you are living your story, however chaotic it may seem, and not one that someone else has scripted for you — then your intuition, intellect, and imagination will lead you into the next phase of self-awareness: Integration.

5. INTEGRATED SELF-AWARENESS

As the name implies, the Integrated stage is where all the questioning done during the Investigative stage creates an opening for assimilation and the answers to the question, "Who am I?" start to come together. We come to understand ourselves, and with increasing confidence we integrate this understanding into our daily lives, as it is reflected in our decisions, actions, relationships, and feelings. The development and integration of self-awareness really never ends — it just evolves as we achieve new levels of understanding through our entire lifetimes. I love this stage because it's full of "aha" moments — those times when we suddenly connect the dots and understanding blossoms in an instant. Our quarter-life-crisis moments have revealed valuable information and we don't feel so stuck.

During this stage, a couple of significant shifts occur. One involves our parents: we begin to separate ourselves from the parent-child relationship we've known and relate to these people we grew up with as independent adults. Many times, this process of separation leads to another shift: we may feel a growing desire to cultivate our spiritual lives, to develop our own spiritual paths.

But before these occur, we usually must finish the process of shedding our old roles and identities and fully assimilating our new sense of ourselves. In my Integrated stage, I realized "smart and successful" does not resonate with me because it does not capture the heart of what I have learned about myself from my journey so far. "Compassionate and creative" is truly more of who I am. True integration also involves accepting those parts of ourselves we don't always like and moving beyond the dualities of the past, in which we got caught up searching for approval by being the "good" kind of smart and not the "bad" kind of smart. Integrated self-awareness means acknowledging and owning all parts of ourselves — even those we wouldn't dare put on a résumé or Match.com profile.

EMBRACING YOUR BAD SELF

Deconstructing the duality of beliefs that ruled our self-perception during the Basic stage of self-awareness is a critical (and fun!) part of our development. Open awareness means that we stop running from or hiding our perceived weaknesses and instead regard them without judgment or shame. When we do this, we discover that these aspects of ourselves are really not weaknesses at all — they are learned reactions that served us at one time in perhaps important ways, but which no longer serve us today. In fact, the Integrative stage involves assessing all our so-called strengths and weaknesses and understanding how each can benefit or hinder us. The trick is learning to use all aspects of ourselves consciously and appropriately in the right situation.

For instance, I mentioned that I viewed impatience as one of my weaknesses or qualities that I disliked about myself. I always judged myself harshly for being impatient. During my Investigative stage, I learned to accept that impatience was part of me, and to be grateful that I'd become aware of it — but I didn't embrace it or know how to change it. Why? Because I had not moved into integration. I was still hoping to *separate* myself from my impatience rather than try to *integrate* this quality into my definition of who I am.

But finally I stopped and asked myself, "Why is this impatience here and how does it serve me?" What I discovered was that I had learned a pattern of impatience from my dad (who is a sweetheart and has gotten so much more patient over the years thanks to his own awareness). Impatience had also become one of my most effective defense mechanisms. If I moved fast, then I could somehow get ahead in the world. I grew up feeling alone and behind everyone else (I was a late bloomer, a nerd, and often socially ostracized), so I developed impatience to try and "catch up." To my impatience, I say thank you. Through impatience, I've learned to be extremely efficient and prompt, and I am unafraid to be assertive when I need to be. I don't want to rid myself of my impatience, but rather transform that once-defensive impulse into more positive behaviors.

"I am proud that I am taking responsibility for my life, my actions, my emotions, and my future. I am very proud of my decision to seek out help to discover myself, to take the initiative to do what I want, and not what someone else expects of me, and to put myself first."

Student and tutor, 28, dating, Maine

I AM WHO I AM!

Most of us are all too aware of the qualities we don't like about ourselves. But admitting or acknowledging these things isn't enough to change them. We must understand why these qualities exist and transform them into useful, helpful attributes.

Take a piece of paper and write down a list of what you perceive as your worst qualities, characteristics, and habits. List all the things you don't like about yourself that you want to change. (Go on, it's fun, so long as you don't use it as an opportunity to beat yourself up!) Then consider each one in turn; in a journal, write out why it is there and how it has served you or protected you in some way. For example, if you wrote "too shy," perhaps that shyness developed as a childhood protection from being teased; it was your way of making sure you were safe before speaking.

Now, write down all the ways that this "negative" reaction has actually benefited you — perhaps because of shyness you have become a good listener and friends feel safe confiding in you. "Shy" is not who you are — it's a label for a way you can choose to act or not, depending on the situation. Finally, write out all the ways in which you feel the characteristics of shyness can continue to serve you and all the ways and places it doesn't. Before you know it, you will be confidently deciding when to speak out and when to remain reserved depending on your needs in the moment, not out of habit.

Remember, at our essence we are all "neutral" — neither good nor bad, and free from judgment. "Bad" qualities are only bad because of the way we perceive them. Reframe these things so that they are integrated into your authentic self in a way that serves you today.

To successfully evaluate and construct a newly integrated version of yourself, the most critical thing is to be aware of judgment and to rid yourself of it as much as possible. And that means all types of judgment — judging yourself, judging others, and accepting others' judgments of you. This is not easy, but the more you practice, the more successful you'll become. As you practice, you'll experience a number of very positive results: you'll learn to investigate the input and feedback from others before you assimilate them into your own beliefs, and thus experience fewer "hurt feelings."

"I was always a socially anxious person, but as I am discovering my natural talents, my confidence and self-esteem have gotten a boost and have made me a stronger person — which, I think, is what your twenties are about: discovering who you are, becoming secure in that self."

Special education aide, 24, single, Massachusetts

You will begin to live from your own personal values and ethics. You'll become more dispassionate about challenges and conflicts, and able to handle them without taking things personally or becoming too emotionally involved. You will become less dependent on others for validation and security (both emotional and financial). And you will understand (and appreciate) that you and you alone are responsible for your self-esteem.

"MY JOB IS NOT MY IDENTITY" by Liz, 28

DECLARATION: *I am in charge of the actual qualities that make my life worth living.*

As the frivolous festivities of my early twenties began to wane, I started thinking more about the things associated with "maturity" and "adulthood" — financial security, a stable income, the possibility of home ownership, and eventually the ultimate plunge into marriage and family. I spent the next year and more thinking about those goals, but also fearing them at the same time. What if I am forever stuck in my first job out of college? What if I never make enough money to live comfortably without relying on my generous but aging parents? And more important — what if I'm not capable of these orthodox, traditional things?

After much soul searching and hundreds of yoga classes (my religion of choice), I realized that the only roadblock to these goals was me. I was stuck in my first job post-college because I was afraid to leave — even though the pay sucked and it was going nowhere. I was a newspaper reporter, which was always a fun thing to say at dinner parties. I loved telling stories about interviewing the likes of Katie Holmes and Michael Phelps. It was more than a job; it was my identity. An identity I had to say good-bye to as it was no longer aligned with my true nature.

> "I am most proud of the way I have grown in the past year. Baby steps are what it takes. I see myself progressing, and sometimes I take a step back, but I eventually find myself back on track and ahead."
>
> *Flight attendant and mayor's assistant, 24, single and hate it, California*

So I began job hunting, a humbling experience. The emphasis was not on fun but on more grown-up issues, like job security, marketable skills, a sturdy 401(k) program, salary, and room to grow or room to down-size once my future children came along.

I finally landed a job in marketing with the salary I wanted and plenty of opportunity to gain new skills and develop as a professional. You would think these sensible, "safe" decisions would put a serious damper on my inner party girl. Quite the contrary. The beauty of it is I have never felt more in control of my own destiny.

Sure it may not be as "fun" or "exciting" as my job as a reporter was, but I realized this very crucial thing. *Life* is fun and exciting if you make it that way — I was always depending on a job to create passion and fulfillment for me, but as soon as I realized that a job is not responsible for that, I felt empowered. I realized a job gives me a quality of life in terms of stability, but I am in charge of the actual qualities that make my life worth living.

Personalized Success

Perhaps one of the most enlightening and liberating things that occurs for many twenty somethings during this stage is that they realize they can set their own terms for success and happiness. What you do is *not* who you are! Integrating all aspects of yourself creates tremendous opportunities to redefine your life — your purpose and goals. As your priorities shift and align in a more authentic way, you realize your ability to define and create the quality of life that is most satisfying for you.

Here is a wonderful story I want to share from Damon, about how his terms for success shifted during this stage as his circumstances and awareness changed: "The pressures I feel as a twenty-nine-year-old man are different than those I felt as a twenty-one-year-old man, a twenty-five-year-old man, or even a twenty-eight-year-old man. Age and experience change the pressures, as do internal and external expectations. In my early twenty-something years, I believed money was a measure of success and self-worth. By the time I was in law school and had created a successful business, I believed that money was an indication of security and future success. Then I changed again. Today, as a self-employed twenty-something man who has dabbled in a few different fields, money enables me to pursue my personal goals and does not serve to define me or indicate my future success.

"When I had no money, my definition of success was making money. Then, when I started making money, my definition of success was being important. Now my definition of success is to be able to feed my two dogs; build solid, self-sustaining businesses; and create a compelling future, as well as find a lovely wife and create a strong family. I see success as something that I can create by staying true to the things I truly value in life. Rather than being motivated by a desire to make money, to make something of myself, or to prove something, I see money as a tool, and I define myself from an internal place."

PARENTS ARE JUST PEOPLE

Of course, one of the central aspects of growing up is separating from our parents and families. Though we remain "sons" and "daughters," we become adults too. Family relationships change: just as parents come to regard their children as independent adults, most twenty somethings reach a point where they start to see their parents as fellow people — not just Mom and Dad.

> "Your parents are not perfect. They are their own people who make mistakes and can disappoint you and pleasantly surprise you as much as everyone else."
>
> TV producer, 30, engaged, California

It's an enlightening experience, and it's a necessary one in order to create a healthy self-awareness. At some point, we all need to become less emotionally, physically, and financially tied to "who we were" as children. Our understanding of ourselves is initially based almost entirely on where we have come from and who we have been raised by. In our twenties, during all the stages of self-awareness, we are shedding and evaluating these identities, and eventually this includes turning our investigative eye on our parents. One of the most effective ways to stop seeing ourselves through our parents' eyes and expectations (and view life through our own) is to see and understand "Mom and Dad" as who *they* are separate from their role as our parents.

With that awareness, we often have the clarity to see them in a whole new light. You may discover, as I have with mine, they are pretty fun to get to know! Remember, your parents have done their job — you are an official grown-up, which means your decisions about life are 100 percent up to you now.

"SEEING MY MOM AND DAD FOR WHO THEY ARE"
by Victoria, 28

DECLARATION: *Seeing my mom and dad as people, not just parents, has helped me learn about myself.*

I never considered how my family would affect the person I would become. When I think about it now, I realize that my parents influenced who I'd grow up to be, but they are no longer responsible for who I am today. Seeing my parents as financial adults with their own bills and responsibilities, as opposed to the people I went to when I needed a prom dress, has helped me learn about my own fiscal awareness and goals.

My mother is also just a woman. In no way do I mean that she is ordinary, because she is far from that. But she is a human who has dreams and fears and makes mistakes. She isn't just a mom. Through my grown-up eyes, I can see that she is a wife who has worked hard and faced huge obstacles. She, at some point in her journey, was a self-conscious teenager, a best friend, someone's crush, and a new mom. Our relationship is different now, and I can see more clearly who we both are individually. Our conversations have changed; we have more in common. I can see her as a wife and my parents as a couple in a different way than before. My role as a woman, as a wife, and as a future mother is being shaped by my new perception of her values, fears, hopes, and actions. I can see the things I have already done or will someday do just like she did. I can also see the things I have done or will do differently. These things can be as simple as taking better care of myself or as complex as balancing my relationship with my husband and children differently. My mature self would say that this is very positive and is helping me to create my own identity, while my kid self feels bad for not wanting to be "exactly like my mom." But I realize that I don't have to be just like her, or strive to be the opposite of her. I can be somewhere in the middle, which is right where I belong.

My father and I have not had a smooth journey. We don't see eye to eye on most topics. I have spent a lot of time being very angry and blaming him for a whole list of things — from how he treated me to how he dealt with his marriage. My new perceptions help me to see that there are always two sides to every story and nobody can do things right all the time. I think understanding him better has taught me to be more empathetic, and less judgmental, while strengthening my conviction in my beliefs. I've learned that people act a certain way or make a certain decision for a reason, and sometimes these reasons may not be in their conscious control. I am better at embracing the good parts of what we have, and as time goes on, the bad feelings are diminishing. I can now see and admire him as funny, passionate, naturally intelligent, well read, generous, and a fantastic storyteller.

Although it can be hard to admit, my father and I are more alike than we probably realize. Recently, I was out to dinner with my parents and they had an argument at the table. I saw how easy it was for him to go from joking around to being angry, and as that critical thought ran through my mind, I stopped dead in my tracks. More than once, my husband has pointed out this trait in me. While I seem to disagree with my dad more often than anyone I know, I am sure that the passion I have for my opinions and values comes from him.

It's normal to want to blame our parents for something we don't like about ourselves. Let's face it — it's much easier to attribute our "negative" characteristics to their parenting faux pas than to our choices. But in the Integrative stage, as we take these negative traits and embrace them in ourselves, it's easier to do what Victoria has done, which is to take a step away from our role as the child and really see without judgment who our parents are and where they came from. If they are open and willing, ask them about their past — they did have a life before you were born!

Consider the ways you are like your parents and the ways you are not. Don't worry if you see more similarities than you'd like. Remember, ultimately, you get to choose who you are — including the ways you'd like to emulate your parents and the ways you'd rather do things differently. The only catch is that you do not get the freedom of that choice until you accept who your parents are.

Blaming them creates a vicious cycle that keeps you from moving deeper into the Integrated stage of self-awareness. This may sound radical, but it does not matter how horrible your parents are. I have seen amazing changes in the lives of twenty somethings when they stop being angry and blaming people around them.

> "I'm cherishing my independence since I've been able to stop blaming my parents and really take responsibility for my own life. I'm proud that I am able to live on my own and be comfortable in my own skin (most of the time)."
>
> *Instructor, 24, serious relationship, Maryland*

SUPPORTING THE JOURNEY: FAITH AND COMMUNITY

In the end, getting to know and accept ourselves provides a tremendous sense of inner peace — but getting there and staying there is no cake walk. We cannot do it alone. As we shed and let go, where do we get the reassurance that there will be anything left of us when we're through, that things will be okay? It requires faith and trust, the two things we may feel we lack most. As a result, many twenty somethings reach to strengthen their spiritual or religious connections, to build support from within, or seek out therapists or communities who can lend sympathetic, wise counsel as they journey.

As one twenty-seven-year-old writes, "I spent most of my life so far obsessing over what I have no control over and not honoring the present moment, which made me so unproductive because I was not showing up for life or accepting life on life's terms. I was letting my ego get the best of me — and ego stands for 'easing God out.' In this space of letting go, I've been able to step back from my mind and discover a feeling of living in the heart of life. It doesn't mean life is always easy, rather that I have stopped fighting against my experience and accepted there is something 'bigger.'"

The process of becoming self-aware is often painful and difficult because we have to leave behind many belief systems and patterns that we've relied on for years. If you are having a difficult time moving into the Integrative phase, I highly recommend seeking support from an objective, loving third-party adviser, like a counselor, coach, or spiritual adviser. They cannot solve your problems or figure things out for you, but they can help keep you on your path, and they can help you develop the healthy emotional and spiritual practices you need to keep going.

> "I feel very blessed. I've learned a lot about myself and life in general and come to realize (and celebrate this realization) that you can't sweat the small stuff. Troubles of the individual are generally insignificant in the grand scheme of the perils in the universe."
>
> *Development associate,*
> *26, engaged, Florida*

"MY SPIRITUAL GROWTH" by Elissa, 29

DECLARATION: *I stopped caring as much about what others thought of me, and focused more on what I needed to make myself more comfortable.*

As I reflect on my past, I see that all of my choices have coincided with the evolution of my spiritual self. At twenty-two, I was an overachieving woman excited to be the best investment banking analyst in my class. But over time, this lifestyle only amplified my type-A personality, creating a constant high-stress environment and leading to a very poor quality of life. To make up for those uncomfortable feelings and situations, I sought out comfort in food, which led to stress-related bingeing after very long days. I internalized my emotions and eating was my release. I was too proud to admit that I was having a hard time dealing with the stress.

After my first semester of business school, I was away on a family vacation where my bingeing became noticeable and alarming to my family. At the end of the two weeks, they urged me to deal with the problem. I worked with a behavior modification doctor specifically on my stress-related eating disorder, and I started seeing Paige. Some would call Paige a therapist; she has been a spiritual adviser to me.

While I had dabbled with spirituality, meditation, and living in the "now" on and off since high school, it was not until I met Paige that I was truly able to incorporate these beliefs into my lifestyle consistently. My path had been laid out: high school, college, two-year program at an investment bank. But now I had reached a stage in my life where there wasn't a set path. I was uncomfortable with uncertainty, and I was not good at expressing myself.

Through my work with my behavior modification doctor, I was no longer using food as my crutch, but this achievement could not have been possible had I not started to find other, safer outlets for my stress and emotions. Working with Paige allowed me to understand and become comfortable with meditation, breathing, and the benefits of self-awareness. I started to recognize how my posture or breathing changed when I was stressed or uncomfortable in a situation. I was able to calm my thoughts when I was presented with unsettling news. By noticing and acknowledging these feelings and emotions, I was able to express them rather than repress them.

I was able to express my emotions and feelings to my family, rather than being irritable and short with them. My friends noticed a change in me, but not all of them liked it. I was now much more introspective and reflective. I wasn't drinking as much, either, so some thought I wasn't any fun anymore, or that I wasn't having fun. But the truth was, I was so content with myself and who I was becoming that I didn't need to get drunk to have a great night, and I didn't need to pretend I was having an amazing time.

I stopped caring as much about what others thought of me and focused more on what I needed to make myself more comfortable. I began minimizing my interactions with those that were negative or pessimistic. I stopped fighting back when someone pissed me off. I had learned to resist reacting. I also became much more emotional. I cry easily, both tears of joy and tears of sorrow. But being in touch with these emotions creates a much healthier me than the me that couldn't express myself.

> "I feel as if I need to make my relationship with God stronger. I feel like I push it aside and try to 'concentrate' on other things too much, such as schoolwork, relationships, and guys, that really don't offer me any solace."
>
> Student and waitress, 20, single, Iowa

Developing awareness was not easy work, but I'd never go back to the "easier" way of living because I realize that while it may take less energy and consciousness, it is not nurturing or comforting in the long term. And while I still don't love uncertainty, I am much more comfortable with fuzzy lines and am able to better resist reacting when I am upset by someone. Today, as a much different person than I was at twenty, I work each day at continuing to develop my spiritual self. I know I am not perfect, and I get frustrated when I hit a challenging spot in the road. But I continue to live life as it happens, not as I want it to happen.

Cultivating a Spiritual Practice

I hear many twenty somethings say, "I am not really religious, but I am spiritual." Spirituality means different things to different people. To me, spirituality is a state of being connected. Connected to what? That is for each of us to answer for ourselves. It's a very personal question, and it's incumbent on you to define what that deeper connection is, beyond the "surface," temporal things like your job, your romantic relationship, your friends and family, your income, your house, your looks, and so on.

For me, spirituality means being connected to the Self. I write Self with a capital "S" because I am referring to my higher Self. I see this higher Self as one with God, a higher power, the Universe, and the unseen energy field we are all a part of. I've cultivated my own spiritual practice through prayer, meditation, spiritual advisers, and nondenominational church services.

My faith, and the support system that came from that faith, saved my life at my lowest twenty-something moments. Consider being open to the possibility of incorporating a spiritual practice in your life. Immeasurable blessings come from a connection to your Self, God, or the Universe — semantics are not important. If you already have a religion or practice you are dedicated to, that is wonderful and I support you in deepening that connection. The twenties are a great time to reevaluate your dedication and relationship to your faith. It gives you a foundation that is more secure than anything in the material world.

I asked one of my delightful and insightful teachers, Dr. Ron Hulnick, president of the University of Santa Monica (where he teaches spiritual psychology), what he would advise twenty somethings to do to cultivate a spiritual practice. Ron said, "Start paying attention to what moves your heart and begin to shift the focus from the external world to your internal world. As you start to focus inward, you will find spirit within yourself no matter what you

> "Part of the twenty-something journey is having found a balance for one stage, then evolving from that life point and having to find a new balance, and then another, and another. The difficulty is keeping sustained stamina through each transition while having enough energy to maintain the delicate balance of moving forward and simply enjoying the moment for what it is — because in reality, that is all we have."
>
> *Nonprofit director, 27, single, Montana*

> "I love evolving. I love this confusing quarter-life crisis. It keeps me on my toes. The slight insecurity and unknown opens doors to oneself."
>
> *Manager, 26,*
> *serious relationship, Colorado*

do in the world. The focus inward is what creates change on the outside."

Ron recommends the book *Power versus Force* by David Hawkins. I concur that this is a great book to open up your mind and heart to spirituality because it is not "airy fairy." It is reasonable, clear, and direct — *and* with such a non-woo-woo title, you can even read it in public! However, whatever you do, keep reading and searching until you find the support that's right for you.

THE SELF-AWARENESS CONTINUUM COUNSELOR

The doctor is in — and it's you! In this exercise, pretend you are the counselor and reflect upon the evolution of your own self-awareness as if it were the patient. "Diagnose" yourself after reading through part 2: What phase of awareness do you think you are in? What stories or examples resonate with you? Recall the significant moments or insights in your life that transitioned you from one phase to the next (or that you anticipate will). Now, "analyze" yourself: What have you learned from the stages you have gone through thus far? What do you still need to do or learn? And finally, "treat" yourself. Come up with at least three take-aways from this chapter that you will incorporate into your life. What changes do you still need to make in your behavior and thinking to continue evolving along the self-awareness continuum?

PART 3

NAVIGATING
THE TWENTIES TRIANGLE

Wouldn't it be nice if life afforded us the time to fully evolve through the Self-Awareness Continuum before we had to figure out what we wanted? Unfortunately, life doesn't wait for self-enlightenment: it gives us responsibilities and forces us to make decisions whether we're ready or not. We have to move forward — figuring out what we want and how to get it even as we're still discovering who we are.

The remaining two questions of the Twenties Triangle — "What do I want?" and "How do I get it?" — are the focus of the next two chapters. Remove the expectation from yourself that you should have the answers to these seemingly simple questions. They are in fact very challenging. They are questions about our life's purpose and path; they are the big questions that clarify all the little questions, and they can take years or decades to answer. Tackling them is an evolving process of discovery and experience, and part 3 guides you in how to successfully begin and maintain this process. Remember, self-awareness does not come in the form of a lightning bolt, and there is no upside-down key at the end of this book that will give you the correct answers. Don't expect to ride the express train to 100 percent clarity, or else the only station you'll wind up in is Hangover town.

6. WHAT DO I WANT?

"I want to be 'somewhere,' and not knowing where that 'somewhere' is — whether it is in reference to career, relationships, or anything else — is daunting. I want to 'hurry' life up — fast-forward it to a place where I am 'settled' in a job or in a relationship."

Freelance illustrator and designer, 26, serious relationship, Arizona

There are approximately 41 million people between the ages of twenty and twenty-nine. Today's twenty somethings are savvy, committed to making the world a better place, and dedicated to being successful and innovative. But they are also confused, stressed out, and lost. Despite all the ways there are to make the world a better place and all the ways one can be successful and innovative, they struggle to know which are best or right for them. They question their life purpose and what they want from their careers, their relationships, and their families.

I get emails from twenty somethings daily who confess they are in a state of "panic" or "extreme anxiety" because they have no clue what they want to do with their lives. This is not surprising given where they are in their lives. Most have recently left very "structured" environments — their family home and school (whether high school, college, or grad school) — and set off into the unstructured real world, which doesn't dole out a weekly allowance or come with course schedules. Twenty somethings are in an "in-between" stage: in between youth and full adulthood, and transitioning between school and career and between the families they grew up in and the families they will create.

> "I hate being in this in-between stage. Waiting for my perfect man, or for the one I already have to grow up and decide he wants to marry me. Waiting for my career to take off. I want to be happy now."
>
> Paralegal, 26,
> serious relationship, New York

It's natural to want to get out of this in-between stage as fast as possible. It is by definition a time of doubt and uncertainty — and we sometimes react by reaching for and clinging to any kind of structure we can find. Many twenty somethings I talk to are hungry for a job they love that fulfills their career goals and to be involved in a significant relationship — hopefully, one that is destined for marriage. They want to sink their teeth into something, anything to escape the anxiety of not knowing what to do.

If you've been a checklister, this awkward stage is especially frustrating, since you've done everything you were "supposed" to do to figure out what you want and get it. If college was a square box on your list, you applied and enrolled, declared a major and a minor, fulfilled course work while making sure to be "well-rounded," earned credit from internships, took part-time jobs, volunteered, got involved in campus activities, scheduled time with your career counselor, spent hours perusing the career center job boards, and followed all the résumé tips thrown your way. All together now, let's sing the résumé verb song: "developed, handled, initiated, planned, implemented, facilitated, assisted, completed, lead, organized, excelled, recognized, coordinated, and supervised." You even, most likely, succeeded in getting a job.

But for most twenty somethings I talk to, this doesn't automatically vault them past this in-between stage. Various aspects of their lives remain incomplete or unfulfilled. In fact, once they've been out in the working world for a while and no longer jump out of bed every day bursting with enthusiasm, they often get a major Expectation Hangover, one that's worse precisely because they were so sure they'd figured everything out. As part of the instant-gratification generation, they then think that the cure for their Hangover is more, better, different — a better job, a different career, more money, more respect, more fulfillment, a different partner, a better relationship, more passion. They want a different and better answer to their questions, and quick!

> "Being a twenty something is wanting things you can't have yet (love, great job, kids, living somewhere) because they usually require a little luck and a lot of hard work."
>
> Clinical social worker, 27, married, California

However, there is no avoiding this rite of passage — we all just have to go through it. Despite so many seemingly critical questions and decisions hanging over you, the way to reach satisfying, lasting answers is to embrace this transitional, developmental phase. Hang on, and spend more time with the questions. When you feel the urge to rush, slow down. When you can't answer a question, let it go for now, or ask a different question. The longer you resist entering your own transition time, the longer it will take to get your sea legs.

WELCOME ABOARD: GETTING YOUR SEA LEGS

Entering adulthood is like sailing your own boat into the ocean of life, and a good chunk of your twenty-something years will be spent getting your sea legs. You may have seen the ocean, charted it, toured portions in your parent's boat, and even ventured out a bit yourself: swimming near shore or taking short trips. But now you're in deep water, out in the middle where the swells really roll, and you need time to adapt. Babies don't come out of the womb walking and talking, and teenagers don't enter their twenties with all the answers for adulthood. Every twenty something goes through a period of transition and adjustment — just as every child gradually learns to walk and talk.

Those who have been to college sometimes mistakenly think that earning a diploma prepares them for the working world and an independent adult life, only to discover that it doesn't: friends are not delivered and are harder to make, a class schedule does not prepare you for the grind of a work schedule, dating is much different (often less casual and more mysterious), and managing class registration is nothing compared to managing your taxes, health benefits, and insurance. Twenty-three-year-old Mike voices a common feeling: "I just wish that at least one of my professors would have stopped droning on about velocity or the mating behaviors of turtles and told me that college was not the key to understanding how to be an adult. Sure, the degree could be the key to a good job, but the living part — nobody taught us that."

> "The comfort of college versus the harshness of reality. College was its own little world where women, success, and opportunities were abundant. Figuring out what I want while adjusting to a new style for dating, occupation realities, and everything else is very difficult."
>
> *Public relations assistant, 23, single and hate it, Colorado*

Indeed, the champagne toast of graduation is often followed by a killer Expectation Hangover, one that isn't improved by the rolling waves and the seawater splashing over the decks. So, take two aspirin, get back on your feet, and steady the ship before plunging ahead: experience your experience; take it easy and don't move too fast; when you get to a place that feels good, don't move; and keep your attention on the important stuff.

"CONFESSIONS OF A STRAIGHT-A SLACKER" by Caitlin, 23

DECLARATION: *I was extremely motivated as a student, but when it came to planning for my future, I was paralyzed.*

I had always loved school and been pretty good at it. Something about it really agreed with my disposition. There was plenty of room for creativity and exploration, but within the confines of a structured schedule. There were tight deadlines to ward off laziness or excessive perfectionism. I took tremendous comfort in the fixed routine. College classes forced me to read things I would never have gotten through on my own. I attended meetings of campus groups and discussed the state of the nation with my peers. It was paradise.

In the months before graduation, I began to feel a vague, but persistent, sense of dread. It began when I started hearing dispatches about post-graduation life from a friend who had graduated the year before.

> "You think that you're going to know what you want by the time you graduate. But it's more like a bucket of cold water that hits you when you realize that your twenties are the most confusing stage of your life."
>
> *Secretary, 26, married, Florida*

"I don't mean to scare you," she said, "but no one is having an easy time of it. Graduating college..." She paused, searching for the right words. "Is like being pushed off a cliff and being expected to know how to fly."

As commencement rapidly approached, we all knew we were heading toward that cliff, and some of my friends began a flurry of networking, cover-letter writing, and interviewing in an attempt to nail down a job before graduation. Their efforts paid off.

Meanwhile, I worked harder than ever in school and tried to forget about the fact that graduation day was imminent. I knew I should be looking for a job, but somehow I couldn't get myself to do even a basic internet search or stop by the career resource center. It didn't help that, having majored in ethical philosophy, I had absolutely no idea what I wanted to do. And no one was saying, "Apply to six jobs by Friday or your final grade will drop."

I had the disturbing realization that without the looming prospect of missing a deadline, I was actually sort of lazy. I was, as my mother put it, a "straight-A slacker." I was motivated as a student, but when it came to planning for my future, I was paralyzed.

It was certainly tempting to apply to go to graduate school; if I went to grad school right away, I wouldn't have to jump off the cliff. But I knew that I would just be prolonging the inevitable. I was beginning to suspect that, after eighteen years of schooling, I had become addicted to school, and it was time to kick my habit.

I decided to go cold turkey and not to look for a career-track job at all. Instead, I was going to move back into my parents' apartment in New York City and try to find waitressing work. When I wasn't working, I would do what I loved most: reading and writing.

With my new plan (or lack thereof) in mind, I began to daydream about my post-graduation life. I envisioned myself getting a job at a tiny, casual but chic French bistro; the kind of place that is called "the neighborhood's best-kept secret" by local magazines. The chef would be a temperamental but lovable portly Parisian man who provided me with a constant supply of free quiche. I would work only nights, making fabulous amounts of money and having a glass of red wine when I was done with my shift.

As it happened, the casual but chic French bistro I had been eyeing wasn't hiring. I didn't have a contingency plan and I needed money, so I ended up getting a job at a trendy Manhattan bowling alley. I had to wear a fifties-style super-short magenta bowling dress, fishnet stockings, and black boots. Our manager encouraged us to put on makeup so we would look "classy and sassy." On weekends I would work eleven-hour shifts until 3:30 AM, at which point I would crawl into bed and pass out.

Even on my days off, I couldn't motivate myself to figure out what I really wanted from life. I became furious with myself; was I really so lazy that I didn't do anything — even something I loved as much as writing — unless there was a grade and a deadline?

As the months wore on and winter set in, I became so discouraged that I picked up more shifts at the bowling alley to save money, but I began to tire of serving shots of fancy tequila to young invest-ment bankers. It was hard to feel classy and sassy when I was per-petually covered in a thin coating of Bud Light and grease.

Then the holidays rolled around and I got my first look at our "hol-iday uniform": a "sexy Santa outfit" consisting of a crushed red velvet dress with white marabou trim. I balked. I knew at that moment I was ready for a change. I can't say exactly what prompted it: maybe it was the fact that the Santa suit had to be hand-washed, and the feather trim blow-dried by hand. Or maybe I couldn't bear to hear yet another drunk man yelling, "Hey, Santa's Little Helper!" at me. But whatever it was, suddenly, it wasn't as hard to get myself to look at job postings online. Given the choice between mending the holes in my fishnet stockings or formatting the margins on my résumé, I chose my résumé this time.

After writing around thirty cover letters and going on about six interviews, I landed a job I really wanted: doing strategizing and media relations for progressive nonprofit organizations. I have just started my second week. Sometimes when I peel myself out of bed at 7:00 AM, I have a pang of nostalgia for the nocturnal life of a cocktail waitress. But I like having structure in my life again. I'm doing something I care about, and I don't have to entirely motivate myself; my co-workers are de-pending on this Straight-A Slacker!

Truly Experience Your Experiences

Are you living your life fully right now? Caitlin's story is a great example of allowing yourself to become totally immersed in what you're doing, to enjoy it and get the most out of it you can, instead of letting the present be overwhelmed by obsessive dread about the future. Like any college graduate, Caitlin was anxious over what she was going to do with her life, but she didn't react abruptly or defensively. Instead, she gave herself permission to enjoy college, writing, and learning right up to graduation, and afterward she allowed herself to take a "whatever" job (but one that, she imagined, might be fun) while she figured out what she wanted to do next. To me, these choices were important for her to succeed in her last step: interviewing for and getting a job she *really* wanted.

> "I've watched my mother struggle with making ends meet and that has motivated me to get into a high-paying career... except right when I got that career I realized there is so much more to life than making money. Now, instead of trying to get a microchip to run at a faster speed, I'd like to do some work where I actually feel like I'm making a difference in the world, and that can be as small as making a difference in just one person's life."
>
> *Engineer, 24, single and love it, Texas*

If you are not fully present in the moment because you are constantly worried about what's next, you are more likely to miss the lessons of your current experience. It is just like when you're reading a book and your mind wanders — until you realize you've just read three pages without taking in a word. Then you have to go back, find the last place you remembered, and reread. Do you want to do that with your life? Of course not, but that's how many twenty somethings often feel: like they are learning the same lessons over and over. In fact, they are, because they are too distracted with worry to really take in the lessons the first time. A big part of getting your sea legs is paying attention to what you are learning, what you are doing, and what is going on around you. Each experience is a lesson that offers us information about what we want — we just have to give ourselves the permission to be aware and honest in the moment as we transition from one lesson to the next.

Smart Slacking

I applaud Caitlin for her responsible approach to life post-college. She wasn't a slacker for not jumping immediately into the résumé ring of fire. There is nothing wrong with taking time to transition, as long as you do it with responsibility and integrity (i.e., pay your bills and don't sit around in coffee shops all day longing for college while mooching off your parents). If the ocean of adulthood is making you queasy, practice "smart" slacking: put aside the "What am I going to do with my life?" questions and experience life (and yourself) a little more.

After a college life of reading Nietzsche, pondering Big Questions, doing what we enjoy, and living in a hive of our peers — what job *wouldn't* be a letdown? If we aren't even sure what kind of career we want, then there's even less chance we'll find deeply satisfying employment immediately after school. As Caitlin did, sometimes a better approach is to take a job that seems reasonably interesting and that will keep you financially afloat until motivation and clarity return. Become a bowling alley waitress and make the best of it, zipping up your magenta dress with a good attitude each day. When this stops working, you'll know it. For Caitlin, it happened when she contemplated trading her dress for a Santa suit; faced with that, suddenly she found it easy to motivate herself to finish her résumé, send it to dozens of companies, and interview for six jobs. But it became easy only because Caitlin gave herself time to transition, and in the process she got her sea legs (in fishnets!).

SMART-SLACKING GAME PLAN

"Smart slacking" won't become "slacking off" if you follow this game plan. Above all, *don't* feel guilty for giving yourself time to take it easy — doing so will most likely help you feel more focused because you've had time to adjust. It's like mountain climbing: you don't jog to the top the first day. Instead, you start out slow to give yourself time to adjust to the altitude, otherwise you'll run out of breath and never make it.

Feel free to expand or amend the following suggestions (possibly with the help of a trusted adviser or mentor) to create a smart-slacking game plan that fits you:

1. Designate the length of your transition time — I recommend six months to a year. At the end of this time, set a clear goal or action, such as to start applying for or perhaps to have gotten a career-track job.

2. Get a "noncareer" job that pays the bills and gets you out in the world, meeting people and being part of society.

3. Organize your money: set up a checking account and a savings account with interest, and consolidate your credit cards and other debt as much as you can.

4. Create a budget to live by, and stick to it! Avoid ignoring or adding debt.

5. Live on your own. Find an apartment you can afford, or if you live with your parents, pay them rent.

6. Get health insurance. Research plans and enroll in one for the length of your transition time. If you are still on your parents plan, pay them the monthly coverage fee.

7. Get out of your comfort zone: date, go out, and have fun!

8. Explore the world in new ways: volunteer, travel, surprise and challenge yourself.

9. As you see cool jobs and meet interesting people, find out more about them. Set up informational interviews. Don't worry if you pursue things that have no relation to anything you've been interested in before.

10. As you get inspired, work on your résumé; perhaps hire a résumé consultant to help you polish it.

11. Stay in the employment loop by casually "window shopping" for jobs, seeing what's out there without the pressure to have to find something. If something appeals to you, apply without expecting to be hired.

12. Exercise, breathe, and enjoy your smart slacking — take advantage of this unique time and your freedom to explore! It'll be over before you know it.

"SWEET UNCERTAINTY" by Ann, 22

DECLARATION: *What do I want? A wonderful question — however, the answers appear to be far from my grasp.*

For the greater part of my life, decisions were made for me. So when senior year of college came along, and I was asked to figure out what my next step would be, I was dumbfounded and responded with "Are you serious?" The whole cliché of spreading your wings and flying did not seem so idealistic to me anymore. There I was at twenty-two with a bachelor's degree in psychology, lavish dreams, and all I could think about was what horrible timing my newfound state of confusion had. I mean, come on Ann, you're a graduate, your family and friends are awaiting your next move, your life is ahead of you, and now you have no idea what you're doing? Get it together... and fast. I'll be honest, there were those days when I didn't want to get out of bed. Waking up meant I needed to tackle the uncertainty that had consumed my life.

My first job was working at a day-care center. Quite honestly, it was to appease my parents. It wasn't what I wanted to do, but it was a job. I struggled daily with "wandering lost." Then one day I found an ad in the paper for a position working with autistic and ADHD children. I quit my job (having no clue if the grass would be greener on the other side) and went for it. And now I can't imagine making a different choice. I get to use my psychology degree in my new job, and I feel like it is a good beginning.

Do I know what I want to do with the rest of my life? Of course not! I'm still trying to figure out exactly *who* I am and *what* I want.

> "The most difficult thing is the inner battle: one side wants to be free and curious and the other wants to be responsible and settled. My parents want me to have a great career and meet Mr. Right. I want to discover my talents in various positions and date Mr. Right Now."
>
> *Insurance representative and entertainment production assistant, 24, single, Connecticut*

But I finally had my very own twenty-something realization as I was lying in bed one sleepless night that has saved me from meltdown: "*Not knowing is okay.*" It's normal. It's acceptable.

And there are still days when I'm not so at peace. I'm anxious and frustrated. But eventually I get tired of being miserable, and I remind myself that I can either jump in and enjoy as much as I can right now amidst the chaos and uncertainty, or I can continue to be depressed, in a state of confusion, and wondering when everything's going to turn itself around. It's really about choice.

It's really easy for my parents or teachers or older friends to look at me and judge or have high expectations, but it isn't their life. So while some people may look at me as someone who is wasting away not knowing what the future holds, I'd like to think of myself as someone who is out there living her life, doing what she can with what she has and where she is in her life as a twenty something.

If It Feels Right, Don't Move

"It isn't what I want to do forever, but it feels right, right now." If you can say this, then nine times out of ten you *are* doing the right thing, and you shouldn't worry about what's next until you can't say this honestly anymore.

I see so many twenty somethings who are perfectly content but feel pressure to figure out their next move. Stop! Enjoy the moment

— as soon as you get into "what's next" thinking, you interrupt the flow of your life. If you enjoy where you are, trust that more opportunities and clarity will follow. Don't overanalyze. When what you're doing starts to feel wrong or unsatisfying, then make a move.

Warning: other people will ask you questions like, "So what's next?" or "When are you going to get a real job?" You have permission to say, "I don't know" or "We'll see." Just because someone — even a parent — asks you these questions does not mean you are obligated to know. How *do* you respond when someone asks you a question about your future? Is your automatic reflex to spout out what you think you should say or what they want to hear? And if you don't, do you feel guilty and/or incompetent? If so, then you probably suffer from a twenty-something syndrome I call the "right-answer reflex."

> "I believe our parents, the baby boomers, have very high expectations, and sometimes we feel stressed or discouraged because we haven't reached those lofty goals. I just have to remind myself that I am only twenty-four, I have a lifetime to live, and the only expectations that are truly important are my own."
>
> *Legal administrator, 24, dating, South Carolina*

THE RIGHT-ANSWER REFLEX GAME

Welcome to our game show! The contestants we have today are your fellow twenty somethings, and our host is the most fear-inducing authority figure you can imagine (perhaps a parent, a teacher, or some combination). To play, the host will pose a variety of questions about your future, and you and your fellow contestants are expected to hit the buzzer as quickly as you can with your answer. Ready? Now: What are your career goals? How many interviews have you set up? When was the last time you updated your résumé? What are you planning to do with your life? What are you doing to network? Who are you dating? What is your five-year plan?

Do the other contestants beat you to the buzzer? Do you answer fast to score points? Can you picture yourself winning this game? If so, I'm sorry to tell you that the Right-Answer Reflex Game is rigged. In fact, it's a game you can't "win," except by refusing to play. Instead, when any kind of "host" poses a question to you about your life and future plans, and you feel that temptation to hit the buzzer and say the "right" thing — stop! Don't touch that buzzer!! Resist regurgitating what you think someone else wants to hear to win their approval. Count to three, take a breath, and give yourself permission to lose this game by saying, "I don't know." Only press that buzzer when the *true* answer is going to come out of your mouth. The Right-Answer Reflex Game is always played by someone else's rules — and you need to play by your own.

Shifting Your Attention

In college and graduate school, and usually for the year or so after, *your attention is to the urgent, not necessarily the important.* What does this mean? In the structure of school, there are always finals, project due dates, and eventually, graduation. You always have something that is due and that you have to focus on. For much of the year after college, you then have to attend to urgent real-world necessities, like

> "In every situation there are things that you can't see, and what you can't see can be amazing, for if we knew what was the future, there would be nothing to look forward to!"
>
> Sales coordinator, 26, serious relationship, Kentucky

finding a place to live, moving, getting a job, setting up bank accounts, getting insurance, and so on. There is always something "urgent" that fills your immediate attention.

However, once that urgent pace slackens, we can begin to think about "important" things, like what we will do for the rest of our lives and where and with whom we will spend them. Without the distraction of urgency, our minds have the opportunity to look farther ahead. This shift of attention is what produces a lot of the overwhelming anxiety twenty somethings feel.

Have you ever been to the eye doctor and had your eyes dilated? As soon as they put those drops in, you are no longer able to see what is immediately in front of you; you can see only into the distance. Similarly, in the adjustment to twenty-something life, our minds often dilate so they focus on things we want to see in the distance and do not see clearly what is immediately in front of us. When we can't see the future clearly either, that leads to even more frustration.

But just like we deal with the discomfort of having our eyes dilated because we know it's part of the process of the examination, we have to deal with the discomfort of the here and now. Be patient with yourself and keep your mind focused on what's important, not distracted by what's urgent; let your future come into focus as it will. Soon, the adjustment period of your twenty-something experience will wear off and you will be able to *see clearly*. Tell yourself, "I don't need to stress out about this, I am just adjusting to shifting my focus."

> "I've noticed that in my twenties my indecisiveness seems to have peaked. I question every single decision that I make, sometimes to the point of exhaustion. I feel like every little decision will greatly affect the outcome of my life! If I break up with this guy, is it a mistake? Is he the one, and I'm letting him go? If I take this job over that one, will I have set myself down the wrong career path? It's exhausting, really, this obsession about the future!"
>
> *Graphic artist, 25, recovering from a breakup, Virginia*

PAST-PERFORMANCE REVIEW

A great thing to do when you are stressing over not being able to see a clear vision of the future is to review the past, particularly your experience in school. Whether you attended high school, college, or graduate school, and whether your graduation was last year or ten years ago, evaluating your past performance helps bring into focus where you want to go. Too often we think of academia narrowly, as training for a specific career. Then, if we don't follow that career, college seems a bust, and all that tuition a waste! Never fear, you learned a lot more than you think.

In a journal, answer the following questions:

- What did I learn about friendship?
- What did I learn about my emotional and physical needs?
- What did I learn about relationships?
- What did I learn about being away from home?
- What did I learn from my least favorite class? From my most favorite?
- What did I learn that I could do that surprised me?
- What did I learn that I enjoyed that never occurred to me?
- What did I learn about the way I handle stress, deadlines, and expectations?
- What else did I learn?

Now, look at what you've written, and imagine a job, career, and family situation that brings out and supports your strengths and the things you enjoy most. What would it look like? You don't have to decide anything, and it's okay if nothing specific comes to mind. For now, use this awareness about what you've learned from your past as research for decisions you are faced with concerning your future.

NOODLE THROWING

Once you've got your sea legs and have adjusted somewhat to the ocean of reality, the next phase you are likely to enter is noodle throwing. Why do I call it this? Well, when I was a little girl, my favorite meal to help my mom cook was spaghetti because I loved cooking the noodles. As they boiled, I would pick one out and toss it up against the wall to see if it stuck. If the noodle stuck, that meant the pasta was done. If it slid down the wall, I'd throw it back in the pot because it needed more cooking time.

Figuring out what we want to do with our lives can be very much like this. We try many different things and throw them against the wall — sometimes they stick, sometimes they don't. When

> "After having that first job out of college, it may be what you wanted, it may not — so begins the journey of options. Do I stay in this job I don't like? Do I try a different field? Do I go back to school? Do I just tough it out and see if it gets better? It's the journey of questions and having to actually try different things to get the answers."
>
> *Human resources manager, 28, serious relationship, Minnesota*

they don't, we toss them back in the pot and keep cooking. It does not mean we've failed. You wouldn't throw out a pot of spaghetti just because one strand was underdone. It only means the dish isn't ready yet. In time, your cooking skills will improve: you just need to keep throwing noodles, be willing to risk a bad meal occasionally, and hone your intuition. Eventually, you will find something that sticks.

"JOB JUMPER" by Steve, 26

DECLARATION: *I seem to be figuring out what I don't want to do a lot more than I am figuring out what I actually do want to do.*

I worked in a job with no direction for four years after college, always knowing I did not see a future for myself there. Why did I stay? It was easy. I could do the job in my sleep, and I got good at it. But I was bored and knew it was time to leave my comfort zone in pursuit of doing something I liked that actually challenged me. I just don't have a clue what that is.

I left the cush job and decided to start taking risks — part of it sounded exciting, I gotta admit. My first stop was the financial planning industry, for really no other reason than a lot of my friends were making money at it. I was there a few months of trying to get my business going before I walked away, as I didn't really enjoy drinking the company Kool-Aid.

> "I am having the patience to allow myself to try different jobs, and not giving in to my feelings of inadequacy and taking any old job just to feel validated as an adult."
>
> *Artist and painter, a little of this and a little of that, 24, dating, Arizona*

Stop two was getting my real estate license — seemed like a good plan. Make money, be my own boss, work with people, and again make money (can you see what my motivating factor often is?). What I learned is that the real estate market is highly competitive, as the perks are so alluring. To make a long story short, you won't see my name on a "For Sale" sign of any building.

What made these risks enticing at first only to lose my interest in a few short months? After the novelty wore off, and I realized I was not going to get rich quick, the truth was hard to ignore. Direct sales is not for me, and hunting down customers all the time wasn't the challenge I was looking for — I have enough trouble with that in my dating life!

What keeps me from beating myself up and feeling like a total failure? Well, I see these risks as opportunities to learn and explore possibilities. Call it a process of elimination, and the money spent on my risks as an investment in myself. A few months ago I decided to start a file on my computer devoted to my ideas. Whenever something comes to mind, I start to pontificate about it. Big or small, from products to businesses, I write all my ideas down, from concepts like making a documentary and opening a breakfast place to designing video games. At first I felt weird about keeping this idea log — I mean, guys are kind of just expected to get a job and start building their career. I feel a little behind my peers in that I am still trying to figure out what it is I even want to do.

So, what's next? I really don't know, and I'd be lying if I said that doesn't scare me. Right now it's day by day — I work a job to pay my bills and keep hunting.

The Process of Elimination

The process of elimination is a very important component of noodle throwing. After all, you want the first few noodles you toss against the wall to be slightly underdone to avoid overcooking the whole pot. In the same way, your list of "big ideas" for your career may not be thoroughly cooked — but you only find that out when you try one or two and see what sticks. Steve has the right attitude: he's trying things and paying close attention to what he's learning along the way.

What strikes me most about Steve's story is that his initial career decisions

> "I don't know what my passion is — I tend to know what I don't enjoy rather than what I do. Other times, I feel like I'm interested in so many things that I couldn't possibly try them all in my lifetime!"
>
> *Program coordinator, 27, serious relationship, Wisconsin*

were driven largely by a desire to make a lot of money. He was focusing on his lifestyle, on how he'd like his life to look. He pigeon-holed himself into jobs that fit an ideal of what he thought he wanted to be, rather than an actuality of who he really is. However, he sees that and is now developing a much more creative-sounding idea file, which includes filmmaker, restaurant owner, and game designer. Deep down, Steve sounds like a very creative guy, and eventually he will probably want a job that satisfies that creativity.

Eventually, of course, Steve will have to make a choice, but at first it's more important to leave your options open, listen to your heart and intuition while ignoring external expectations, and don't fixate on the "how" just yet. Simply brainstorm the "what" and keep throwing noodles. As soon as you start worrying about the "how," your rational left brain steps in and discourages you (trying to convince you that you'll never make enough money, you're not talented enough, there's no future in it, and so on).

As Steve is finding, when you're not sure what to do, eliminating possibilities is the first step to making the right choice. You need to test your ideas and desires, see how they hold up in real life, and keep fine-tuning them. Many of our likes and dislikes, our expectations and big ideas for our lives, have been hanging around since before we could legally order a beer. Are they still valid? Throw a noodle. Make sure you are throwing noodles from your own pot, not the pot someone else wants you to cook from. This applies to all aspects of your life, not just your career.

Also, stay open to the random, unexpected opportunities that come your way. Have a chance to try something you never considered? Throw a noodle. Has there always been something you wanted to experience but never have? Throw a noodle. If these things don't stick, you don't have to think about them ever again, and you have a better idea of what to try next. And if something does stick? Hmmm. Now you have something to think about.

"MUSINGS ON NOT BEING A PEDIATRICIAN" by Kristin, 24

DECLARATION: *My path toward finding the right job has been an overwhelmingly unsatisfying quest to please others and flaunt my degree.*

At my preschool graduation, each student shared the occupation that they wanted to be when they grew up. My mother instructed me to state that I wanted to be a pediatrician. Mind you, I had no idea what this job entailed (nor could I adequately pronounce it), but I dutifully declared it, much to my mother's delight and the audience's amusement. I certainly stood out from the other aspiring ballerinas, baseball players, and mommies.

Looking back, my attitude toward finding the right job has been alarmingly similar to this childhood experience — I have found myself on an overwhelmingly unsatisfying quest to please others and flaunt my degree. I grew up in a disarmingly wealthy "more is more" type neighborhood, where AP classes and SAT prep courses were a given, as was receiving a BMW on your sixteenth birthday. I certainly didn't fit into this mold nor did I agree with the majority of its beliefs, yet I somehow became molded with a need to impress others with my success stories.

The pediatrician thing was quickly out of the question. I decided to major in English. I convinced myself and my parents that such a major would provide the stepping-stone for a prestigious, not to mention lucrative, career as an attorney. The only problem was that deep within I had no interest in the law.

As graduation approached and the thought of entering law school became more and more despicable, I realized that I was in trouble — it seemed there was very little I could do with my major that would offer me both a challenge and a decent living. Making matters worse were the daily questions from annoying relatives who somehow forgot my birthday but always managed to slip in queries about my job search.

I felt as if I were under siege, questioning for the first time whether I would ever be able to achieve the lofty goals, and luxurious lifestyle, that I had been taught to equate with achievement. Seeking solace, I furiously scribbled in my journal, angry with the world and mostly myself for having foolishly ignored my parents' career suggestions.

Not wanting to become a teacher, I turned to the only job that seemed obtainable to me, that of a publicist. My sister was thriving at a beauty PR firm and seemed to be having a blast. I accepted the first offer that I received, ignoring the not-so-covert clues that this was a far cry from my dream job, to say the least. Eager to develop an impressive career, I pretended that I enjoyed it and somehow managed to trick my colleagues and employers, and I was promoted within the ranks in just one short year.

Instead of being thrilled about my promotion, I felt worse than ever, much to my parents' dismay and my boyfriend's confusion. My dissatisfaction with my job finally hit me, and at last I accepted the truth that I needed to escape this dreary, tedious nightmare of a job.

I'd love to say that I found the job of my dreams at this point, but that would make everything much too easy. However, I did find another public relations job that captivates my attention much more and is more entertaining, but it still doesn't challenge me on a constant basis and allow me to flaunt the very best of my abilities. Another wave of anguish hit as I realized this too might not be what was right for me.

But my seemingly restless mind has finally started to appreciate the fact that uncertainty and questions are what gives life its richness.

Be Willing to Make a Few Bad Dishes

In the noodle-throwing process, we are likely to have an experience (or two or twenty) that leaves a bad taste in our mouths. This is especially likely when our egos, and not our passion, take over the kitchen. I threw a lot of noodles in my twenties — assistant, agent, personal trainer, nutritionist, freelance writer, hand model (seriously!), producer — and most slid and slithered down the wall. It was a humbling process. When I was a trainer, I didn't think that was impressive enough, so I'd tell people, "I used to be a Hollywood

> "I didn't expect to switch jobs so many times. I'm twenty-eight and have worked in five different places. Ironically, those jobs (both good and bad) all led me to where I am today... which I love."
>
> PR and marketing assistant, 28, recovering from a breakup, New York

agent." What a snob! Talk about ego masking insecurity. When I got engaged the first time, I considered just giving up on a career and becoming a full-time wife and hopefully mother because I felt so hopeless and was grasping for something else to make me feel like I mattered. But I kept experimenting, and as I did, I learned to distinguish my ego from my true desires, and I worked to remove expectations and insecurities from my decisions. Trust that as you eliminate all your ego or expectation-driven possibilities, you will start to throw noodles that stick.

You know what you want, and you know what's best for you — I promise, you do. But part of embracing the process of elimination is that not everything you make is going to taste great. You are perfecting the recipe of your own unique self — and you can't follow someone else's recipe, and it must be done from scratch. Resist the temptation to discuss your decisions with everyone you know and get caught up in comparisons. It's great to talk to peers about what they are doing, but their path won't be yours, even if you're aiming for the same place! For instance, I had a client who always wanted to teach abroad; however, all her peers were landing jobs that paid serious dough, and her parents were pushing her to buckle down and get benefits. She had an offer to work at a consulting firm, but ultimately decided to go to Japan and pursue what she really wanted. A year later, she came back and was offered a job by the same consulting company — only now for more money and a better title, since the company was so impressed by her work in Asia.

You are the one who has to live your life, so pick what *you* think fits you, and always remember, nothing is written in stone. Experiment, pay attention, taste what you're cooking often, learn what flavors you like best, adjust the seasonings, and keep throwing noodles. Life is a series of adventures in which our choices dictate our destiny.

"CHOOSING MY OWN ADVENTURE" by Lindsey, 29

DECLARATION: *We can't cheat and sneak a peek
at the potential outcomes of our decisions.
We have to live our adventures one page at a time.*

As a child of the 1980s, I was a big fan of the Choose Your Own Adventure series. In these books, you read several pages of a story, then receive a choice of which destiny the characters should follow. The book continues on a certain page depending on which destiny you select, and different story lines — leading to different endings — ensue.

I've found the Choose Your Own Adventure series to be a relatively good metaphor for twenty-something life. You go along for a while, have some adventures, and then reach a crossroads. So you choose a path, and that path leads to a new set of adventures and decisions. And at certain milestone moments, you pause to reflect and perhaps choose a new book of adventures.

But, like more than a few kids who read the Choose Your Own Adventure books, I cheated. I would flip to the potential outcome of each decision to see which one looked the best, then go back to the "choice" page and make my selection based on the ending I wanted. But alas, life is not a 1980s young-adult fad novel. We can't cheat and sneak a peek at the potential outcomes of our decisions. We have to live our adventures one page at a time.

As I stop at the end of my twenty-something years to reflect, I know that my story could have turned out other ways if I had taken other paths. For instance, I could be a lawyer. In fact, according to various relatives and teachers and the Myers-Briggs personality-type indicator, I *should* be a lawyer. Because everyone thought so, I used to think so too. Let's flip back a few pages in my tale....

At some point in college, I signed up for a free practice LSAT law school entrance exam and took the test cold. No studying. "I'm smart," I rationalized. "Everyone thinks I should go to law school. Maybe I'm a natural. How hard could this be?" I never told anyone that I took the practice test. I thought the questions seemed impossible. Every answer seemed plausible. I guessed on half the choices and barely finished in the time allotted. I never picked up my scores because I was too scared of having the lowest practice LSAT score in history. But what if I had aced it? Would I be a hugely successful lawyer right now?

How about the path to a not-so-happy ending? After returning home from two and a half exciting years in Australia after college (the path I took instead of law school), I experienced a mild bout of depression. I was sad that my overseas adventure was over and undecided about where to live in the United States and what kind of jobs to pursue. I felt I had fallen behind my successful friends in America. For five months I lived at home in my old bedroom with the imitation Laura Ashley red heart wallpaper and framed photos of my bat mitzvah and high school prom. I saw a therapist and spent the first session curled up in a chair, sobbing into a wet tissue that I was washed up at twenty-four. Eventually, I made phone calls to local friends and sent around résumés, and I found a job, an apartment, and a new life in New York City. But what if I had stayed under the covers?

One day during this time, I sent one of my best friends, Derek, a long email wondering, again, if I should just go to law school like a normal overachiever. But something was hidden within these thoughts. I typed, "I think I really want to be a writer." Derek, ignoring every sentence but that one, wrote back: "I always knew you'd be a writer, you dummy. Glad you finally figured it out for yourself. Now do it!"

So, fast-forward. I am a writer, but it took all of my other adventures — good and bad — to show me that is indeed what I wanted to do. So maybe I wasn't really cheating when I read all of the possible endings in the Choose Your Own Adventure books. By reading my "unchosen" endings, the characters and challenges and outcomes of those stories became just as much a part of me as the endings I did select. And in life, the paths we don't choose (or the paths that don't choose us) don't disappear, but they accompany us on the paths we do choose and help us learn more about who we are and who we want to be.

DO-IT-YOURSELF PERSONALITY TESTS

Sometimes we get so stuck in the question "What do I want?" that it feels as if we don't even know ourselves. We take personality tests, career counseling quizzes, and scour job-hunting websites for weeks to find some focus, but we still don't know what to do. I encourage you to get creative, get active, and have some fun with yourself. You know yourself better than any prefab magazine quiz, so make up your own "test" to help answer the question "What do I want?" The following are all ways to activate your intuition and get you following your gut instincts.

- Take a field trip to an expansive magazine stand. Just look at it. Take in all the covers, particularly of magazines you've never read. What articles and pictures grab your eye? Buy a couple new or unusual (for you) magazines that capture your gaze, that you naturally gravitate toward. Read them. What part of you do they speak to? Is there anything you can discover that you are interested in that you haven't considered before?

- Take a trip down memory lane. Gather a bunch of old pictures of yourself from your childhood. Recall what you liked to do, what you liked to play, what you drew or doodled. If possible, ask your family what types of things they remember you enjoying. Is there anything you've stopped doing that you'd like to do again?

- Date as "research." Sign up for an online dating service, and be open to all offers — at least for one night. You may think you know what you want in terms of a mate, but you might not! Think of what you like about your close friends that you'd like in a date. What kind of qualities would a person need to have that would make you "click?"

- Peruse the continuing education catalog of a local college. Is there any class you always wished you'd taken in school that never seemed to fit your major or graduation requirements? Enroll in it now!

"THEY DON'T TEACH SELF-DISCOVERY IN COLLEGE"
by Natalie, 26

DECLARATION: *Now that I have found the path that truly fits me, I am inspired to keep learning, growing, and challenging myself.*

Three years after graduating from college, I still had no clue what I wanted to do. I'd had a series of administrative jobs, one after another. With no particular drive in terms of what I would do with my degree (English literature), I felt constantly in limbo.

I felt like I was going through the motions, doing both what was expected of me and what was "safe." It wasn't until I stopped to question whom I was trying to please, and honestly ask myself where I wanted to be headed, that things started to gradually come together (or apart depending on my perception). Since I had just ended a not-right-for-me relationship and was unsure of my career future, I felt I had nothing to lose in trying to find my passion.

> "I want to start really focusing on my insights and listening to what makes me 'me' in order to really get everything I want out of life. For example, I can't say I want to be a millionaire when I'm forty, and then never save a penny or care about how I spend my money now. It'll be much harder to get what I want out of my entire life if I don't start acting on my goals, desires, and passions now."
>
> *Student, 20, dating, Ohio*

Instead of incessantly researching all the career opportunities out there, my first step was to look inside myself for direction. Looking back,

I see that I was always afraid of looking within myself. I didn't know if I would discover what I needed, and I was afraid I wouldn't find anything. Thus, I depended on the approval and advice of others, which left me in a state of confusion about what I wanted in life.

In recognizing that trap, I gradually learned to step off the treadmill of trying to please others in order to have value. I began listening to my own voice and taking better care of myself. I began to have more trust in myself — I guess you could say I've started to let go, and go within.

Eventually, after my own self-investigation, I heard myself telling myself how much I enjoyed it! I decided I wanted to enter the field of counseling, specifically college counseling. Having no experience in the area, I made cold calls to local colleges and my university and asked a lot of questions. After many phone calls and even more referrals, I finally found myself volunteering at two different colleges, while taking classes to prepare me for a graduate program in counseling.

I began working toward a path I truly enjoyed, taking risks daily, moving out of my comfort zone, and making connections. I was also working the hardest I had ever worked while feeling more energized and happier than before — because I was listening to and honoring myself. I feel much more equipped to handle the inevitable challenges I will face than I did before starting this journey of self-discovery. Now the answer to the question "What do I want to do with my life?" is much more clear.

Listening to Your Intuition

Know that voice in your head, that feeling in your gut, that always seems to know the right thing to do, even when you don't know how it knows? That's your intuition, and we all have it. It's not some mystical power reserved for palm readers and psychics, and it's not gender specific. You've heard of "women's intuition," but guys have this too — they're just more likely to call it a "gut feeling."

Many twenty somethings have a hard time knowing what is right or trusting their gut. They feel their intuition is defective; they hear a confused jumble of voices in their heads and can't tell which to listen to. In fact, this is natural; as kids and students, we internalize the voices of authority in our lives, and part of growing up is identifying and separating ourselves from those voices and recognizing and listening to our own voices of inner knowing. As with noodle throwing, this is partly a process of elimination. In order to turn inward, we have to remove external expectations and advice. Developing your intuition is like building up a muscle. We make a choice independently, see what happens, evaluate, and choose again — hopefully, with more confidence and success each time.

The other reason twenty somethings have a hard time accessing their inner knowing is because they tend to spend most of their time thinking about the future. In order to access your intuition, you have to be "in tune" with the now. It's impossible to know what is best for you in the moment if you are anxious about something in the future. For instance, Kate, a client of mine, was agonizing over whether or not she should pursue an entrepreneurial opportunity that had come her way. I asked her what she wanted to do, and she replied, "I don't know because I think I want to have kids in a few years." Huh? I asked her to elaborate. Kate explained that she wasn't sure how self-employment fit into her plans of having kids . . . which she didn't even want for two years. Instead of thinking about the job offer in front of her, she was worrying about the future and was muting her own intuition. She needed to stop thinking about the future in order to make a decision about the best thing for her to do *right now*.

The best way I know to get our minds in the present is through meditation. There are all sorts of ways to meditate — you don't need to visit an ashram or sit humming on a mountaintop. Some people use a simple, repetitive activity to still their minds, such as knitting, cleaning, gardening, jogging, or doing yoga. Others set aside a particular time of day to close their eyes, sit quietly, and "think of nothing." If you'd like, try focusing on your breathing to help to train your mind to be freer from thought. Simply bring your awareness to your breath, inhaling to a count of five, holding the breath for five counts, and then exhaling for five counts. You could also repeat a mantra or affirmation statement. One of my favorites is "Ham Sa, So Hum," which is a very powerful mantra affirming, "I am that, I am." With a mantra or phrase, you mentally repeat it to harmonize with your breath. You may start off with "Ham" on the in breath, "Sa" on the out breath, "So" on the in breath, and "Hum" on the out breath, and continue until it feels like a circle and you don't really know what is in or out.

> "I am proud that I have been true to myself. I did what felt right. I had a lapse where I slipped into caring what people thought, but I think I had to slide off track so that I could know what it feels like to be faking it. That way, I can identify when I'm starting to go down that road again and move in another direction.
>
> Life coach, 25,
> domestic partnership, Australia

For meditation to be effective, the important things are to develop a regular practice and to intentionally keep your mind focused in the moment. Especially when we first begin meditating, our minds can fly off in all directions, and it can seem like a lot of work to constantly let go of these thoughts and return to the present. Don't put any expectations on your meditation practice; let it be what it is. Thoughts will arise. You may not be able to clear your mind, but at least you are making the time to sit quietly with yourself. Meditation or any time of quiet self-reflection may be frustrating at first, but with practice it gets easier, and as it does your intuition will grow louder.

I developed my own meditation process, which has helped calm my very type-A mind and put me in more direct communication with my own inner knowing. Every day for ten minutes (and I set a timer so I can let go of thinking, "Has it been ten minutes yet?"), I sit quietly and focus on my breath. Thoughts and to-dos wander in, but I try to let them go and bring my awareness back to my breath. When I first started to meditate, I kept a piece of paper and a pen next to me so that if I thought of something I really wanted to remember, I could write it down. That way, I could mentally let it go since I had captured it on paper. Eventually, I learned to trust myself to recall whatever I needed to and I no longer need the paper. Similarly, you can develop a meditation practice that suits you, whether it looks like old-school "meditation" or not. If it clears your mind for a few minutes and helps you recognize your intuition, that's all that matters.

7. HOW DO I GET WHAT I WANT?

As we continue to navigate through the Twenties Triangle, slowly figuring out who we are and what we want — we start to become more concerned with the third question: "How do I get it?" As with answering the first two questions, answering this one involves focusing on and listening to our own unique process. No matter how packed and polished our résumé is, it won't guide us on the path to becoming a fulfilled, successful adult, which is scary.

Wouldn't it be nice to have college courses in How to Pick a Career You Actually Like; Getting a Job 101; Dating without Drama; How to Make Money Doing What You Love; How to Get Married Whenever You Want; Successful Finances for Those

"I have achieved two degrees and I'm working on a third. In this time, I have gone from being an immature child, seeking everyone else's help to tell me what to do with my life, to being able to make my own decisions. I have taken my work and life experiences and have incorporated them into a meaningful job and healthy way of living."

Children and family therapist, 26, serious relationship, Delaware

Who Are Broke; and Everything You Need to Know about Car, Health, Life, Renters, and Home Insurance? Can you imagine how packed those classes would be? Probably the reason they are not offered is because academia knows that nothing really prepares us for real life other than real life. Once we are on our own and faced with the decisions adulthood brings, it feels like school is *always* in session — and it is perhaps the toughest grad school there is.

FINDING YOUR STRIDE

Knowing who we are and what we want only gets us so far. As we begin to take action to make it happen, we enter the phase of the twenty-something experience I call "finding your stride." We continue developing our sense of self by listening, learning, and assimilating, but we also start making decisions and moving forward into that future we keep imagining. Making good decisions, and maintaining our stride without stumbling, means learning to develop our internal GPS system, tuning out the "shoulds," appreciating our "Life IQ," and maintaining our balance.

Developing Your Own GPS

You've begun figuring out where you are and where you want to go, but how do you get there? This can be the most frustrating point in the process of answering the questions of the Twenties Triangle because we feel stopped cold by everything we don't know, just as we develop some internal momentum. For instance, here is how Aaron describes this experience:

"I was driving home today and got really depressed. I was in such a funk that my stomach hurt the entire twenty minutes. I tried to chalk it up to being burned out and not getting enough sleep the night before, but then I asked myself what was really wrong. The answer is that I have only a vague idea of what I really want. I want to direct films, but *how* do I want to do it? *How* do I want to make my mark? *How* am I different from the eight million others who want to do the same thing? *How* do I send my 'vibes' out for a vague idea? Sometimes I feel so overwhelmed I don't do anything except sit around and think too much. I just feel unoriginal and unmotivated because I don't know *exactly*, detail for detail, what I want. I just know the general direction."

First, a general direction is a great start. It's a Google map at the lowest resolution, but it's still a map. With practice and experience, we slowly increase the resolution from interstates to highways to one-lane country roads that show every twist and turn we need to take. There is no easy answer to Aaron's questions, but I can offer some reassurance. By simply making choices and moving forward, we narrow our options and figure out all the "hows" that define our path. That is, we develop our own internal GPS navigation system by walking the roads; we don't download one ready made.

Today's workplace holds so many career possibilities and so many career paths it's easy to get caught in Cheesecake Factory paralysis. Even simple-sounding professions like "doctor" or "lawyer," with well-established paths and criteria, involve a host of decisions. What kind of medicine? What kind of law? What sort of practice? The truth is, you can't figure out all the "hows" and "whats" ahead of time; you figure out most of them as you go, throwing noodles and trusting that the blank spaces on the map do contain roads. You just can't see them yet!

My advice to those in Aaron's situation is to do something small every day to clarify your specific destination and the road to get there. Read books and magazines, watch films, take classes, practice at home, journal, contact people who do what you'd like to do, and so on. In chapter 11, we'll dive more into specific action plans, but for now, stop freaking out and keep moving forward!

> "The thing that made it harder for me to get what I wanted was caring way too much what everyone else thought about my decisions. Allowing myself to operate by 'shoulds' was not the best guidance."
>
> Professor, 30, married, California

Tune Out "Shoulds"

A critical step in going after what you want is to tune out the "shoulds" in your life. Even as you develop your intuition, these "shoulds" and "supposed tos" will still crop up and make you question yourself. One key to maintaining your stride and arriving at the destinations that feel a lot more like where you want to be is to take driving instructions only from your internal GPS.

"LISTENING TO MYSELF" by Jess, 28

DECLARATION: *The answers become clear when you commit to taking a first step.*

I had just finished design school and was exhausted. I didn't know the next step and I didn't have any answers. I went back home to my old job to pay off my student debt. I had to constantly reassure myself that this was okay: "Jess, you're not the only smart, talented person that is working a dead-end job."

I decided to sit down and fill out the answer to "Who am I and what do I want?" I asked myself, "Out of this whole progression of life events I have chosen, what was the end result I needed to achieve?" The answer: I had always wanted my own clothing line, an online clothing store.

But not everyone in my life thought this was a good idea, and many doubted my ability to make it happen. I started to tire of people telling me what they thought I should do or what they thought I should become. It all started a quiet fire in my mind, "Why are people shoulding all over me?" People kept telling me that I was "all over the map." They were right about this part; I knew what I wanted, but I didn't know how to get it. I froze. But then I realized that my life was at a standstill only because I was choosing to keep it there. This will only be a quarter-life crisis if I turn it into one.

I started to say to myself, "What are you doing just standing there? Time is a-wasting. You can do what you truly want. The catch is . . . you have to go and do it!"

When I felt a little doubt creep in, I reminded myself of things I have done, "You wanted to be with your boyfriend. You found a way to have him in your life. You wanted to meet new people. Lo and behold, they surround you. You hated your dead-end job. You quit . . . and the list goes on!"

My first step was to commit to baby steps. I've learned that being overwhelmed with something that I love just isn't going to feed the creative juices. I started by working on business plans, and now I am applying for grants and loans so that I can financially achieve studio space and equipment. I am also networking with people from school. It takes time, it takes planning, and it really takes a positive daily mind-set.

And I continue to be "shoulded" with questions: "Why don't you just get a job? Why don't you volunteer? Why aren't you living in bigger city and working in your industry? Why don't you contact my friend?" Once I realized "shoulds" are irrelevant, I simply answered, "I don't know," and smiled; they would back off. I've decided not to let questions from all the "should"-sayers take away from my positive bubble.

What surprised me the most in this discovery is how easy decision making becomes when I actually move forward with it. I heard a saying from Dr. Martin Luther King Jr. that I carry with me: "Take the first step in faith. You don't have to see the whole staircase. Just take the first step." I truly do visualize a spiral staircase moving upward for me. I can't see the top, but I know it's there.

Your Life IQ

Another reason we often trip as we're finding our stride is that we despair over our lack of experience. We're still young and seem to have few of the skills and little of the training we need to succeed. This is particularly true when we decide that what we really want has nothing to do with what we studied in college.

However, just because we change our focus doesn't mean that all of our experiences and education are useless. The skills we learn in one context remain and can be applied to any situation. Smarts are often equated with our IQs, but we should instead consider ourselves to have a "Life IQ" that is the sum of all we've done and learned. Our intelligence includes the entire collection of our experiences. Increasing our Life IQs is a cumulative and ongoing process that lasts our entire lives.

> "Everyone else seems to have a strong opinion on how I should be living my life, what job I should have, how I should act in my relationships, and when I should do this and that. It's overwhelming and exhausting trying to keep up, but the alternative, doing what I want, is even more overwhelming and confusing. Who can hear what they actually want when all we hear is what others want?"
>
> *Account coordinator, 22,*
> *serious relationship, Wisconsin*

Remember this whenever you feel there is only one way you can use or explore the skills you enjoy. You will always find new opportunities to apply what you've learned, just perhaps not in the exact way you expected. Indeed, there's no way to anticipate all the ways that your past experience will influence and help you, so never discount it. For example, I studied television and film in college and worked as a literary agent in Hollywood. Now I am doing something completely different, which I like a lot better, but what I learned in school and at previous jobs contributes to my work now. College writing prepared me for becoming an author; finding clients and reading scripts as an agent helped me learn how to solicit and edit stories for my books; having built a professional network in LA allows me to help clients find jobs and mentors; and having spent five years in the entertainment business helps me support and understand my TV-executive husband in his work.

> "I'm struggling with finding that balance of figuring out how to get what I want while maintaining the billion other things — friends, relationships, and responsibilities — that are thrown at me."
>
> *Events coordinator, 25, dating, Pennsylvania*

You see? It all adds up. Stop "compartmentalizing" your life and see yourself as whole, complete, and on the right path; have faith that you already have all the skills you need to do anything you want. Just keep tackling the "how" questions and increase your Life IQ. Passing life's test isn't about having the right answers; it's about continuing to ask the right questions.

Balancing Act

Some twenty somethings do not have a problem with committing to going after what they want; their problem is with *over*committing. They cannot say no and they do too much, often believing that if you want something done right, you have to do it yourself. They are trying to be Self-Sufficient Superheroes. However, not only is there no cool costume or movie sequels — all that activity can actually keep them from finding their stride.

One twenty-seven-year-old says, "Sometimes I feel like a

clown in the circus juggling so many balls — wowing the crowd with how many balls I'm able to keep up in the air at once. I know what I want, but there are so many other things that I have to do that they keep me from being able to dedicate myself to it 100 percent. Between social engagements, dating, networking events, volunteering, serving on committees, getting to the gym and yoga classes, and going to work, there isn't enough time in the day! I know I probably need to say no to more things, but it's hard to — I feel like if I do, I may either miss out on something or disappoint someone. But if I keep operating like this, I will never have the time to fulfill my dream of having my own graphic design business."

> "My type-A personality and expectation that I should do everything on my own makes me irritable to people who are only trying to help me. By doing this, I push good people out of my life and create a wall between myself and the outside."
>
> Student, 21,
> serious relationship, Louisiana

Whenever you feel that you're overextending yourself and overdoing it, I encourage you to start underextending and undoing. You need to maintain a balance. While you don't want to sacrifice everything to pursue one goal — such as, say, having no social life while starting a business — you also can't pursue all your personal, relationship, and professional goals equally at the same time. Having balance means focusing your attention and efforts, and letting some things go, at least temporarily. This can mean different things depending on your situation. If you've just begun an exciting new job, then you may need to step back from your social life a bit; let friends know that you need to take rain checks on their invitations. If you've just moved to a new city, you may want to give yourself more time to get settled and develop new friends, before plunging full tilt into career efforts.

Finding and maintaining your stride means avoiding burnout; slow and steady wins the race, right? Look at everything you have going on in your life and determine where you need to negate, delegate, or investigate ways to put things on hold. Home in on what you truly want and direct most of your energy in that direction. Checklisters: make two lists — one of the balls you will juggle now, and one of those you'll juggle later (and of which balls you'll put down when you do so). In other words, to have balance and keep moving in the direction we want, we have to be willing to admit that we can't do it all!

Not Independence: Interdependence

When twenty somethings describe the causes of their Expectation Hangovers, one of the most common ones is "independence." That is, twenty somethings feel they should be doing everything "on their own" or else they are not living up to what they and society expect of them. This misconception about independence significantly fuels quarter-life feelings of stress and anxiety.

I urge all the Hungover twenty somethings I counsel to replace their expectations of "independence" with efforts to create "interdependence." It's completely ridiculous to believe we can do everything by ourselves. This always leaves us either burned out or constantly disappointed in ourselves (usually both!). We won't get anywhere, but particularly to the grand destinations of our dreams, without the help and support of others. Don't be a

> "I took a big risk by packing up everything I own and driving across the country to a city where I knew no one, started a new job, and learned how to really survive independently. It has taught me that I can count on myself, even when things are really difficult. I don't know whether I would have been able to develop that kind of strength and self-sufficiency had I stayed so close to my parents."
>
> *Lectures division coordinator, 24, dating, Colorado*

Self-Sufficient Superhero. As you develop your plans and goals, create and gather your support system (and we'll get into how to do that in more detail in part four). Offer your help freely to others, and then don't be afraid to ask for and receive help in return.

"THE SELF-SUFFICIENCY STANDARD" by Lucy, 26

DECLARATION: *Strike an independent balance in life and you may discover more time, more opportunity, more freedom, more support, and more joy.*

Is this steady progression toward adulthood meant to prepare us for self-sufficiency in our twenties? It certainly seems so. When our college years come to an end and the ominous "real world" looms ahead, we get the increasing desire and responsibility to provide for ourselves — to be materially and emotionally self-sufficient. After all, our notion of maturity is linked closely to how well we are able to handle the challenges in our lives — getting a good job, a stylish apartment, moving into and out of relationships, and maintaining close bonds with friends and family. As twenty somethings, we want not only to appear self-sufficient but to feel as if we are taking our lives down their true and correct courses to meet the self-sufficiency standard.

> "I think the most valuable thing I have done for myself in my twenties is seek counseling, seek friends who are truly caring, and seek relationships all around that are nurturing and empowering."
>
> *Transportation consultant, 27, serious relationship, New York*

We think that self-sufficiency means we don't rely on others for help — that we are fiscally independent, emotionally unwavering, and professionally exemplar. Any deficiencies in these areas are interpreted as examples of our own shortcomings. We are overwhelmed and stressed with the seemingly never-ending list of to-dos. I have more projects, demands, and social engagements than I have time.

I know I am not alone in feeling this way; it seems to be part and parcel of living life. In the midst of our mini-crises is another emotion

— disappointment. We feel a nagging frustration that we aren't able to do it all and that in some way we failed at being self-sufficient. Add to that the feeling of not making enough money either, as we watch debt become the four-letter word of our generation.

Let's put this notion of the self-sufficiency standard on the examination block. True self-sufficiency would completely remove us from society. We would not pay rent, we would not buy food, and we would certainly not ask for a shoulder to cry on. We do not want to be so independent that we lose touch with our communities, our families, or our humanity. Neither do we want to be so dependent that we have no aspirations to leave our parents' home, borrow from our friends indefinitely, and forgo all adult responsibilities.

"Maturity" lies between the solitude of self-sufficiency and the burden of total dependency. For me, it's negotiating the territory of helping myself, providing help for others, and being provided for. I am becoming financially independent, but I am not afraid to ask for advice on how to do it. I have found balance by learning how to act responsibly in my own life, while knowing when and where to reach out for support. And this is the real goal, I think.

EXPECTATION HANGOVER RELAPSES

You've just had an epiphany about what to do with your life, you put it into motion, and everything is falling into place, when BOOM! All of a sudden something doesn't turn out like you thought it would and you're nursing another Expectation Hangover. You'd vowed to avoid it, but here you are again: not knowing what you want, or how to get what you want, or if you should even want what you want. And you were so excited over discovering your passion! But don't despair, and don't be surprised. Expectation Hangovers are like the common cold; they keep coming back until you boost up your immune system. In the meantime, you just have to keep trying to reduce the severity of the symptoms.

"STUCK IN QUICKSAND" by R.J., 25

DECLARATION: *I see the light at the end of this Expectation Hangover, but I keep getting lost as I try to find my way.*

At twenty-two, I had a corporate job with medical benefits, a brand-new BMW (which I bought myself), a fabulous apartment in a wonderful gated community, and excess spending cash. The "real world" was shaping up to be more than I imagined. However, at the end of the day, something was missing. I couldn't figure it out. Why was it that even though this is exactly what I wanted, I hated it? At the end of the day, I was left feeling drained.

A few months later, I was driving home from work when I heard Christine on the radio talking about Expectation Hangovers. Holy s#*t — that's me! I was empty, unhappy, and had been experiencing an Expectation Hangover for nearly two years. I continued to go through the motions because I thought this is what was expected of me.

I began to focus on what I wanted the rest of my life to be like.... Was I truly passionate about anything?

Yes! Dogs! The answer was dogs. I researched an idea and eventually launched my own business. I was challenged, motivated, and feeling among the land of the living again. My Expectation Hangover was cured! I quit my job.

But in just a few short months, I relapsed back into another Expectation Hangover when my passion didn't turn into an immediate success. I still didn't believe in myself and needed security, so I landed another corporate gig. Now I'm stuck again.

I recognize my passion and have a great business. I should be able to devote more time to my business, but I am still working full time, going through the motions. I need to move forward, but I am hesitant to take the risk, plus I have too many responsibilities that do not afford me the luxury of quitting my steady job.

I keep trying to get out, but get sucked back in. How do I get "unstuck" in order to continue to move forward with my passion and leave the corporate life behind? How can my childhood dreams become a reality?

When you're faced with a relapse, the first thing to do is identify any common threads connecting your Expectation Hangovers. Was the same expectation woven into your experience? Is there a lesson your experience is trying to teach you that you didn't learn the first time? As with R.J., self-doubt and the desire for financial security often lead to Hangovers. We all have bills to pay, and we often let our financial concerns keep us from pursuing our seemingly less-lucrative passions. But worries over money can also mask underlying fears and beliefs that have nothing to do with how much cash we need to live. We may equate emotional "security" with income and a certain lifestyle. Or perhaps we believe true grown-ups hold corporate jobs, so pursuing anything else is silly, foolish, and immature. Whatever the reason for the Expectation Hangover relapse, we should take it as a signal to investigate and examine our beliefs even more closely. I would encourage R.J. to look at why she doesn't believe in herself. Then reconcile those beliefs with more self-supportive actions, to avoid or minimize further relapses in the future.

> "I've learned that the less attached I am to this world, the more I'm able to love and embrace everything. The less expectation I hold, the more I can allow my life to evolve as it's supposed to."
>
> Graduate student, 24,
> serious relationship, Missouri

I can relate. After my first book came out, I got caught up in grandiose expectations of what my life would become. But Oprah never called, and I had an Expectation Hangover relapse of major proportions. For well over a year, I struggled and tried to talk myself out of it, but I couldn't stop feeling depressed, irritable, full of self-doubt and regret, and just "blah." Knowing I should know better made it worse. I was the one who came up with the whole notion of Expectation Hangovers in the first place — what a fraud to be relapsing!

So I put myself on a relapse treatment plan: I practiced gratitude, I reinvested in my own physical health, and I became proactive rather than reactive. In other words, I followed all the advice I give out in part 1. I learned from and cherished the people in my life. I gave thanks for the money I was able to earn and save. I saw my counselor more regularly, took an advanced yoga series, and cut back on my alcohol, sugar, and caffeine intake. I worked to transform my negative thoughts into something either neutral or positive. And I stopped complaining so much and started to consider my dissatisfactions as sources of inspiration.

It took a few months, but I recovered, and you can too. If you are relapsing — you find yourself in a situation you don't like and there's something else you'd rather be doing — then take steps every day to move toward it. At the same time, examine what beliefs you have that may be tripping you up along the way.

LEAVING THE TWENTIES TRIANGLE

There are usually two ways we leave the Twenties Triangle. One is the inevitability of turning thirty. For some, entering the next decade without feeling like we have successfully navigated out of the Twenties Triangle is disheartening. One man writes, "I am twenty-nine and single and feel that I'm running out of time. I feel like I've wasted my twenties in a cubicle when I could have been off trying to pursue my passion. I put myself in a position where I had a stable income and a roof over my head, but I wasn't happy. I wanted a job where I could travel and have great experiences, but I ended up in an office. Now, as I head into my thirties, it's hard to think about the opportunities I may have missed out on because I wanted security and was afraid to take risks and put myself out there when it comes to relationships."

If you are approaching the end of your twenties and do not feel like you are who or where you want to be, you did not fail at being a twenty something. Don't become discouraged or think you did something wrong. If you feel like you have wasted time, you are going to waste even more time beating yourself up for it. The questions of the Twenties Triangle are lifelong questions. There is a Thirties Triangle! (And I'm pretty sure a Forties Triangle, and one in our fifties, and...) In other words, it is *never* too late, and we are *always* challenged to be who we are and go after what we want.

> "I'm most proud of being able to derive life satisfaction from the inside instead of trying to control every aspect of my external world."
>
> Author and marketing communications executive, 30, married, Illinois

The other way we leave the Twenties Triangle is by reaching a point where we feel we have successfully answered all three of its essential questions. We feel we know who we are, we know what we want, and we have figured out how to make that happen. Congratulations — you made it!

What? Despite all you've accomplished, you still feel the grumblings of more questions? It's not surprising, for it seems the minute many twenty somethings start to feel contentment, they slip back into a "more, better, different" mind-set. They are just so used to a life full of uncertainty, pressure, and striving that they don't know what to do when they actually succeed at what they planned.

A twenty-seven-year-old advertising executive writes, "I accomplished everything I set my heart out to accomplish, getting my MBA, traveling, owning property, in a healthy relationship, having fun... I wanted and expected all these things for my life and have them, but somehow I am not sure I dreamed big enough. I often ask myself, Is it too late to dream bigger? If I were to leave this planet tomorrow, would my accomplishments be remembered? Have I short-changed myself? Do people see in me something greater than what I dreamed of for myself?"

STOP! At some point, it's important to stop questioning everything and truly relish the results of all of your navigation to this point. Stop thinking you need to go somewhere else. Stop looking back and wondering if you should have done something differently. Enjoy and appreciate yourself, your life, and the people in it. Admire the view from where you are.

PART 4

THE TWENTY-SOMETHING PUZZLE

Twenty-something life is like putting together a puzzle — and sometimes it can feel like it has five thousand pieces. The picture on the box — the one you come up with by navigating the Twenties Triangle — stares at you, taunting you as you struggle to get your life to resemble it. While it takes years to assemble this particular puzzle, it gets easier as we identify and find our "corner pieces." We can build from these, slowly filling in all those difficult middle sections. Most likely, as we painstakingly build our puzzle, we realize that some critical pieces are missing, while we have others that don't fit or belong anymore. And yet, unlike a real puzzle, we have the ability to create or reshape pieces, or even change the picture, until we've got exactly what we want.

Bringing your focus to identifying, or creating, those corner pieces in your life will help you put your puzzle together. I've learned, from talking to twenty somethings and in reviewing feedback from the online Manifesto Survey, that twenty somethings are most concerned with the following areas: relationships, career, dealing with emotions, how to make changes, and money management. In this part, we'll tackle all but the last, money management, which I'll address in part 5. First, we look at our support network of friends and family, then at romance and our "significant others," and finally at our careers.

> "If five years ago someone told me, 'You'll be in a job that you don't like, that doesn't challenge you, and that doesn't pay well at all; you'll still be in debt; you'll still be single with no prospects on the horizon; and you'll still be living at home because you can't afford to survive on your own,' I would have laughed in their face! I honestly thought that by now my twenty-something life would be put together."
>
> Membership services coordinator, 26, single and hate it, Canada

These are our corner pieces. When they are in place, the rest of the puzzle is often easier to assemble. Without them, we may never complete the puzzle, no matter how long or how many ways we try shoving pieces together. By the end of your twenties, your puzzle may or may not be complete, or you may be working on a different one altogether — and that's okay! You are off to a good start by being willing to crack open the box.

"I am proud of that fact that I have always done things my way and taken responsibility for my life, regardless of the consequences."

Account executive, 24, serious relationship, Rhode Island

8. FRIENDS AND FAMILY: YOUR NETWORK

No matter what life has in store for us, our friends and family are the ones who help see us through. But how supportive is our "support" network right now? And are we doing all we can to nurture and expand it? Most likely, there are some people in our lives who love us no matter what and provide trustworthy help and guidance, while there are others whose sole purpose seems to be to rev us up: by challenging us, discouraging us, or treating us poorly. Sometimes one person can do both.

As we assemble our puzzle, we need to identify who's helping us and who is getting in the way, and then determine if there are any relationships we need to cultivate. We have to decide: what do we do about the tense relationships — change them or leave them? And what, if anything, do we need to change about ourselves? How do we protect ourselves better, avoid toxic people, and ask more clearly for what we want? As a twenty something, you are in charge of your life now, and you get to decide who becomes part of your vital corner pieces and who should play a smaller part or perhaps be removed entirely from your puzzle.

INTOXICATING, OR JUST TOXIC?

At this point in the *Manifesto*, you are becoming an expert at identifying and treating Expectation Hangovers. But what do you do when your Hangover involves another person, and without some change in your relationship with him or her, you see no relief in sight? Are there people in your life that perpetuate Expectation Hangover–like symptoms, such as anxiety, frustration, confusion, lack of motivation, fear, and insecurity? Do you get these feelings at some point in every relationship, or only in certain kinds of relationships?

> "There are so many people pressuring me to go out and do things when I'm enjoying spending time alone or in quiet activities. But I don't want draining relationships anymore, so I'm very picky about how I spend my time. I spend it with people who build me up and encourage me."
>
> *Human resources manager, 28, serious relationship, Minnesota*

Remember, relationships change. People who may have been perfect at one point in our lives, who may have been fun and helped teach us valuable lessons, may not be supporting us now. Perhaps we've come to see that a particular friendship is imbalanced in an unhealthy way. And just sharing DNA or a long history with someone does not necessarily mean they should be part of our inner circle either.

Unfortunately, there's no donation center for negative friends, controlling family members, and condescending bosses. Instead, we need to clarify for ourselves what we want, and don't want, from other people, then set clear boundaries with them and — lovingly — stick up for ourselves. "Detoxing" unhealthy relationships makes room for supportive ones. It's like cleaning out your closet before you go shopping.

> "I spent many years beating myself up because I was not fulfilling my parents' expectations of me. But now I'm okay with my choices. Had I not done the things I've done, I would not be me."
>
> *Production assistant, 28, single and love it, Texas*

Ultimately, detoxing our relationships with friends tends to be easier than with family. If we need to, we can walk away from friendships, but shutting a relative out of our lives may not be an option. Although we can't change our families, we can change how we relate to them; we can change how we react to and interact with our families, or with certain family members. Obviously, the hardest relationships to change are the ones we have with our parents.

Do you have a parent, or two, with whom you don't see eye to eye? One twenty-four-year-old says, "It's trying to get my parents — particularly my mother — to treat me as a person in my own right instead of a reactionary force. I can't express an opinion different from hers without her thinking that my sole purpose for disagreeing with her is either ignorance or rebellion. It's hard to get her to accept that while I may not have her life experience, I am an adult, with my own thoughts and opinions, and that they have as much validity as hers."

This young woman has the right perspective: whatever anyone else thinks, it's her life! Others will have their opinions, but we are not obligated to agree with them or even to defend ourselves. It's easy for others to tell us how to live our lives, but we are the ones who have to live them! Of course, we want the people in our support network to challenge us as well as comfort us. We want their opinions and "constructive criticism," but we need to be aware when "constructive criticism" becomes just "criticism." At the end of the day, our own opinions are what matter most, even when we're wrong, and oftentimes that is when we learn the most. Consider everything that people do and say as a "buffet." You make healthy or unhealthy choices about what you choose to ingest. Each of us is on our own journey, and we cannot fault people for being who they are, and we can't expect them to change. Sometimes we have to accept that certain people may not be the right fit for us in terms of a close relationship.

> "Walking out on a verbally hostile, sexually and emotionally abusive boss was a triumph for me."
>
> *Real estate agent, 26, single and love it, California*

IDENTIFYING TOXIC RELATIONSHIPS

We all want to be surrounded by healthy relationships and supportive people. Part of achieving that is becoming aware of the people and relationship patterns that may not be supportive or healthy. Is there anyone in your life about whom you would say any of the following?

- I always feel crummy after talking to this person, or I feel guilty if I *don't* talk to this person.
- This person is really hard on me and judges me harshly.
- I feel like I have to walk on eggshells around this person.
- I feel bad about myself around this person; all my insecurities flare up.
- This person encourages my bad habits or addictions.
- This person is very negative, depressed, and does not take care of him- or herself.
- Our relationship is all about this person — there's not much room for me in the relationship.

- I am incredibly bored, uninspired, stressed out, or un-happy when I'm with this person.

If someone in your life fits any of the descriptions above, then that person, or something about your relationship with that person, is cluttering your life with toxicity! In a journal, make a closer inspection of this relationship: Are there particular circumstances or topics that are toxic, while others are fine? Does what's toxic seem mostly the result of the person's mood or actions, or of your reactions? Does the person seem aware of or oblivious to what you feel? If this relationship were gone from your life, how would you feel and why?

Depending on your answers, you can develop a plan for changing or shifting your relationship with this person — by having a conversation with him or her (to explain your feelings and perhaps set new boundaries), by stopping your interaction in certain situations, or by ending the relationship. Don't let fears of confrontation keep you from doing it. Often it's our fear of conflict that keeps us in toxic relationships far longer than we should.

For help dealing with a difficult person or situation, ask for support from the people in your life who make you feel safe. If directly confronting the person would cause more trouble than it would resolve, amend the time you spend around the person. In general, your goal is to reduce the mental energy you invest in thinking about and dealing with toxic people. Replace concerns and worry with thoughts of loving individuals and the love you have within yourself. Then draw from this emotional bank whenever you are in the presence of a person who challenges you.

FRIENDS

Friends are the family we choose, and they tend to make up the largest portion of our support network; in the online Manifesto Survey, 72 percent reported that friends are their biggest support system. We trust friends with our deepest secrets and rely on them for a good laugh or a shoulder to cry on. But friendships can be challenging. Not every friendship is alike, and all friendships change over time — some for the better, some for the worse; some fade, some persist. Sometimes people who were our friends can become our foes. A friend's betrayal, abandonment, or disinterest can leave us wondering what kind of judge of character we are. Nevertheless, our friends, and our friendships, teach us valuable lessons.

> "Choose your battles in life wisely, and know when to stand up for yourself, when to draw the line, and most important, when to accept that something just isn't worth the fight."
>
> *Accountant, 25, single and love it, Washington*

"RUINED BY A ROOMMATE" by Amanda, 26

DECLARATION: *I've learned the value of keeping a "friendly distance" from negative influences.*

For me, trusting people is a difficult thing, which makes a betrayal by a close friend even more painful.

I met Jen when I was twenty-three. We couldn't have been more different in personality, but I chalked it up to differences in our backgrounds and focused on the common interests we shared. When I decided to move across the country to pursue my passion, she was interested in moving with me. I was hesitant because Jen had been quite flaky in the past. But I thought it would be nice to know someone there, and Jen seemed so excited. So we agreed we would rent an apartment together for that first year.

The troubles started almost immediately. She did not reimburse me for shared costs, she used my things without asking, and she'd get mad at me for silly reasons. After only four months of living together, I got an email from her telling me she was moving in with her boyfriend the next month… leaving me strapped with double rent.

I lost it. After over three years of friendship, she was *emailing* me about this? I replied that I wasn't discussing this any further until we could do so face to face.

She didn't come home all weekend.

When she finally showed up on Sunday night, I had to separate my personal feelings from the reality of the situation. It wasn't worth it to talk about my hurt feelings. I needed to lay out the facts: she had agreed to live together for a year.

I told her that if she wanted to leave, she wasn't doing it without giving sixty days notice, like our contract said, and she had to pay back the money she owed me. She hemmed and hawed but ultimately agreed.

She spent the next sixty days telling me all about her wonderful new apartment and all the money she was saving as I was struggling to find a safe place that I could afford. She never once apologized. Instead, she managed to tell all of our mutual friends back home that I was so upset because she was dating someone and I was jealous.

The worst part was that I felt like an idiot. I knew that her mentality was "me first" through and through. I knew all of this, and yet I still didn't see this coming. Did I just allow myself to believe that because I would never treat someone that way that I could expect the same in return? When had I become so naive?

To this day Jen bears no responsibility for what happened. Although I've forgiven her (because what's the point of being mad?), I'm more cautious in my relationships. I've learned not to put myself in a vulnerable situation, but that doesn't mean I shouldn't be willing to take a chance on people. I just have to think before I act. Jen wanted to stay close friends, but to me she is a "friendly acquaintance." Ultimately, who I am friends with is my choice and my life, and it doesn't matter if other people don't understand my choices. What matters is that I am happy and healthy. And I am.

Amanda's story about resolving a toxic relationship has several elements that are common to many difficult friendships. The main one is the need to see people as they are, not as we expect or would like them to be. In general, people demonstrate who they are from the beginning and remain consistent. Amanda's instincts told her Jen might not be a good person to share an apartment with, but she went ahead anyway. Why?

Perhaps Amanda trusted or expected Jen to act with the same integrity she herself had and that Jen would become less "flaky" and "me first" as a roommate if she was kind to her. In other words, she hoped Jen would change. That expectation puts you at a big risk for a Hangover. People generally don't change or act like we want them to just because we think it's "right." This is a tough lesson to learn, especially when you care about someone. And "killing people with kindness" will not necessarily make them kind to you. I am not saying don't be kind; just don't be naive. As soon as someone shows you who they are, accept them for the way they are until they consistently show you something different.

> "I am proud of taking control of my life, filtering out and realizing that I don't have to be friends with everyone, and understanding what a real friend is."
>
> Job hunting, 23, dating casually, Pennsylvania

It could be that Amanda still needed to learn to trust and stand up for herself more: in this case, she overrode her own instincts about Jen to avoid feeling lonely in a new place, and it hurt their relationship. As with most relationships, both people bear responsibility for what happens, and it's to Amanda's credit that she sees and acknowledges her part, has resolved not to repeat her mistakes, and has moved into forgiveness.

Ultimately, your peace of mind is up to you. You choose who to surround yourself with. If you have a friend who is bringing more drama than peace into your life, politely step away from or otherwise limit that friendship. We can even be grateful for difficult friends, since it is usually through them that we discover what really matters to us in friendship.

What Kind of Friend Are You?

Often it's not our friends who are toxic; it's our own behavior as a friend! Whenever a friendship turns sour, we need to look at what we've done to create the painful situation. Our needs and expectations may be misplaced or out of whack. Perhaps we're expecting more from others than we are willing to give of ourselves. Or perhaps the Cheesecake Factory Theory applies here as we try to be "everything on the menu" to everyone. If we're trying too hard to please others, what kind of friend are we to ourselves?

"SUPERFRIEND" by Kelly, 26

DECLARATION: *I have come to realize that I can still be there for my friends without sacrificing myself.*

My friends are very important to me — I relied on them for support, guidance, advice, and love, and in return, my friends received the same from me. My friendships were 50-50, or so I thought. Looking back, I see that it was more 75-25. I was a "Superfriend" 75 percent.

I made my friends a part of me; therefore, they became a critical part of my life. I gave them cards telling them how much they meant to me. I'd keep a list of things they had expressed an interest in for when their birthday or Christmas came. I planned surprise parties, I'd call more than normal if they were going through something, and I'd wish them luck before a test. Anytime, anywhere, for every reason, Superfriend was there. When the expected reciprocation didn't come, I wondered if I had done something wrong. I had frequent "Are you mad at me?" conversations, and then I would feel bad for initiating the conversation. What was happening to my Superfriend powers?

To compensate for all my perceived shortcomings, I began to be what I call "too-overly" with my friends. I was too-overly nice, too-overly reserved, too-overly indecisive, as I didn't want to express an opinion different from theirs. My Superfriend lifestyle went on for about two to three years until I realized that I didn't want to be a Superfriend anymore — nor did I have to. It took me a long time and several rounds of tears to figure out that my friends cared about me just as much as I cared about them. The difference was they gave me what they could without depleting themselves like I was.

> "After spending time with friends who seemingly have everything, I get really down because all I can do is compare my life to theirs."
>
> Marketing and membership services coordinator, 26, single and hate it, Canada

I decided that I owed it to myself to transfer most of the energy I was giving them to myself. I'm much happier and realize that I can still be there for my friends without sacrificing myself. A phone call or text message is just as good as a card or gift, and a lot nicer on my wallet. It feels good to tell my friends how I am really feeling and even better to realize our friendship is strong enough to handle any disputes. I've learned that the characteristics I admire in my friends are those that I need to develop more in myself, and I can't rely on others to give me all the friendship in my life. I've learned that I have to be a "Superfriend" to one person only: myself.

The opposite "problem" of trying to be everything for our friends is falling into the toxic habit of comparing who we are and where we are in life to our friends. Throughout our lives we are measured up against our peers. From grading on a curve to competing against one another for coveted spots in college or grad school to applying for jobs, our peers have been the "competition." As twenty somethings create their lives, they keep measuring and comparing, and many feel bad that they are not where their friends are when it comes to jobs, salary, or relationships. If you are looking at your friends as the "standard" or the "competition," you are putting your friendship at risk because you are essentially demoting yourself.

> "I am working on not comparing my life to my other friends because we all have different goals. The older I get, the more I am able to understand this and to be happy with my accomplishments."
>
> Children and family therapist, 26, serious relationship, Delaware

A twenty-four-year-old says, "My friends seem to deal with life's obstacles more gracefully than I do. I feel uncomfortable telling them my fears and doubts. There is a lot of pressure to stand out and keep up, but I feel myself fading to the background, trying to avoid falling apart before their very eyes."

If you can't be honest with your friends, who can you be yourself with? Friendship is about accepting your friends for who they are and where they are; it's not about keeping up. So remember to be a friend to yourself and accept who and where you are. Also, keep in mind, that you may not know everything about how your friends are really dealing or feeling about things. We are all on our own unique path and judging yourself against a "friend standard" impedes your happiness and evolution through the Self-Awareness Continuum. You are who you are — be you. Stop competing with the people you would invite to your wedding unless you're playing a game of intramural softball or charades. Remember, there's enough abundance to go around. Celebrate yourself and your life with your friends, because that's what friends are for.

Where's My Coffee Shop?

Many of the typical twenty-something transitions can be hard on friendships, and twenty somethings confess this can be a very sad experience. One twenty-five-year-old reports, "I moved away from my college town for a job and focused on my career, not allowing time for much of a social life. But now that I have some time, I am lonely. I still have friends, but they aren't always available like they were before — friends get married, move, have boyfriends and girlfriends, and their own life." If you are experiencing a transition in your friendships, instead of focusing on loss, redirect your attention to where you can create new friendships.

According to *Friends*, and all the other twenty-something television shows, all you have to do is frequent a local caffeine haven, and your cool friends will be hanging out there having a fabulous time. They'll share your interests and take an interest in your life — and by season two you may even hook up with a few of them. That's Hollywood. The truth is that making friends isn't as easy as it was in college or high school. Your coffee shop is probably filled with busy people in their own worlds, talking on cell phones, working on laptops, or hustling off to work. Instead of enjoying lattes over laughter with your fellow twenty somethings, you may find yourself alone, friendless, and wondering how many more Friday nights you can spend with a Netflix envelope.

"FRIEND ME" by Justin, 23

DECLARATION: *My social life is composed mainly of "people I know" instead of friends, and I don't know how to change it.*

I don't think I have much to offer as a friend. I am insecure in conversations and have never had much of a social life. I don't have a new "clique" to belong to. My social life is composed mainly of "people I know" instead of friends. Because of my shyness, I seldom make an effort to reach out to anyone, all the while grasping the expectation that someone will reach out to me.

Social networking sites help but don't replace the authenticity of true friendship. So I recently forced myself to go to a party with a group of people I went to college with.

It was brutal. As I struggled to find someone to talk to, the awkwardness and nagging shyness took over. I have no idea what to say to start a conversation and feel like I have nothing to bring to the table. As a guy, it's just not cool to talk about this difficulty making friends. I mean, if I go to the self-help section of the bookstore, I am bound to meet a girl, but who is going to want to go out with a guy cruising the therapy section?

So what now? Well I guess I just wait . . . hope I grow out of this, hope that someday I can shake the person who I still see myself as, hope that someday I'll be able to walk into a room full of people and not immediately want to turn around and run out of there.

If you feel like your MySpace page is the closest thing you have to a "clique," it's time to put some effort into your three-dimensional social life. The first step for anyone who, like Justin, is feeling shy and self-conscious is to work on being a better friend to yourself. Don't rag on yourself at a party! You are not going to be putting out "Hey, talk to me" vibes if you are internally reciting your perceived inadequacies. Be nicer to yourself inside your own head. Then get out into the world and cultivate friendships.

One good way to meet people is to immerse yourself in situations that lend themselves to meeting people, such as enrolling in a class, joining a group, or participating in activities that you like to do. As you know, a class setting is a great way to meet people — be it a community-college course, a class at your gym, or an art class. As long as the class interests you, you are bound to meet like-minded people in it.

Next, say yes to any social invitation or opportunity that comes your way, and be open to surprising encounters. Remember, this *isn't* college, and you may need to get out of your comfort zone. My perfect example is my friend Meeghan, whom I met in a bar four years ago. I actually hate bars but forced myself to go to one for a birthday party. Feeling awkward as the people I was with started doing shots (I know, I'm a nerd), I made my way outside and stood under a heat lamp. Three minutes later, a woman my age walked up, and we started talking about how cold we were. An hour later, we were still gabbing away and exchanged numbers — brought together by our desire to stay warm in a cold outdoor bar! Three years later, she is one of my dearest friends, one I would never have met if I had not stepped outside my comfort zone.

> "Although I may not have a best friend or a huge network of friends, I feel good that I have many good friends to whom I have been a fabulous friend. I am always there for them when I am needed, and I get the same in return!"
>
> Insurance agent,
> 27, dating, New Jersey

PARENTS AND FAMILY

Without question, at least one of the "corner pieces" in our twenty-something puzzle will be occupied by our parents, or by other significant family members. However we feel about how we were raised, we would not be who we are without our parents. In fact, the impact our parents have on us becomes more and more apparent once we are on our own, entering into relationships and dealing with authority figures (a boss, perhaps?). We may see reminders of our parents in others, and in ourselves, everywhere. In chapter 6, I discuss exploring feelings about how we were raised, and here I talk about dealing with this directly as an adult.

"THOUSAND-PIECE JIGSAW PUZZLE" by Jessica, 24

DECLARATION: *With every ounce of understanding I gain, my twenty-something puzzle comes together, one piece at a time.*

I am twenty-four years old and scared to death of my father. I can't really remember a time when I wasn't. He was angry and abrupt, and I never knew one moment to the next how I would be received. Most of the time the typical response was a disinterested grunt without a glance, making it clear to me where I fell on the priority list. Often our conversations developed into full-blown, heated arguments. I had to shut off the side of me that felt rejected and even disliked by my own father — although as an adult I am becoming more aware of the hurt his lack of interest continues to cause me.

I recently took a new job with a small company. I love what I am doing, so I was caught off guard when I began to develop great anxiety and trepidation in dealing with my supervisor. I felt like I was walking on eggshells, constantly guarded, afraid that she would see through my confident exterior and shatter my fragile ambition and delicate dreams. If I had to ask her a question, I approached her office with great hesitance, speaking only from the safety of the doorway. Merely the angry tone of her voice was enough to bring tears to my eyes. I tried not to take her abrupt responses personally, as she responded to everyone in the office in a similarly unpredictable fashion, but her impatience and anger intimidated me beyond my own control.

I felt bullied and frightened because I never knew how I would be received (sound familiar?). I felt vulnerable because my slowly growing self-confidence at this point was based on how I had been received by authority figures in the past. Most of all, though, I felt angry about how she talked to people, mainly me. I couldn't disagree or tell her she was being an asshole; it just wasn't an option. I felt trapped.

One day, after a long discussion with a friend about how my supervisor was affecting my work environment, it became so clear to me: She was so much like my father! She had the same ability to make me feel tiny, worthless, and incompetent. She glared at me with similar disdain, and she flew off the handle with no forewarning as much as he always had. She was mad at the world, which is just like the environment I grew up in.

Given that I am still unresolved in my relationship (or lack thereof) with my father, this revelation didn't provide me with an instantaneous enlightenment on how to deflect her blows to my ego, but it did help me understand why I wanted to crawl under my desk when she raised her voice, while other people in the office were able to roll their eyes and let it go. I also realized why I would ask her questions from the doorway of her office in case I felt the need to escape — that's what I had done my whole life. It all seemed so silly — after all, the chances of my boss backhanding me were slim — but my responses of fear and intimidation also felt beyond my control, like involuntary reactions. They were learned behaviors, I guess.

I am still dealing with the situation day to day, and some days are easier than others. My interactions with her tend to parallel my current interactions with my father, and realizing this has allowed me to cut myself a little slack. I'm also able to look at her with a little more empathy than before. I can now look at her, much as I often do my father, feeling sadness for her misery and her inability to enjoy the people around her. I understand that my heightened response is merely a result of the trauma I experienced as a child and teenager.

Perhaps the most difficult lesson for me has been that it's okay for me not to agree with my father, and that the way he responded to me as a child — as *his* child — was not okay. Also, it's okay for me to be hurt and feel some sadness as a result.

Beginning to understand myself and what makes me tick is both terrifying and liberating. I look at my twenty-something years like a big, thousand-piece puzzle — with every ounce of understanding I gain, the puzzle comes together one piece at a time. What began as a tremendously overwhelming task grows into one colorful, ornate picture. I'm looking forward to seeing how it turns out!

With her growing realizations about the ways her father has influenced her, Jessica is clarifying a corner piece of her puzzle. As we all do, she developed learned behavior. When Jessica was exposed to anger from an authority figure, all her sadness and fear memories from her childhood were triggered. As she had done her whole upbringing, Jessica took any expression of anger personally. As Jessica said, she had "involuntary reactions" to her boss. Her response of withdrawing in trepidation was a learned reflex from childhood. And yet, as Jessica brings more awareness to her relationship with her dad, who was essentially her "boss" growing up, she can better understand why she is having difficulty dealing with her boss at her job — and this helps her learn to act, and react, differently.

> "I ask my dad questions to gain a better understanding of what his life has been like and why he made some of the choices that he did. I've come to learn that my dad is his own person. Understanding him has helped me better communicate and reason with him — and not take everything he says personally or want him to be different."
>
> *Editor, 25, single, New Mexico*

I want to highlight Jessica's liberating realization that it's okay to give herself permission to feel her feelings, which she never allowed herself to feel as a kid. Acknowledging buried feelings is an important part of the healing process. Repressing feelings only increases their toxicity and leads to continued Expectation Hangovers in our relationships.

If you are able to understand your family and deal with your emotions about them, you will be able to detox negative patterns from your adult life. As this twenty-five-year-old woman writes, "My father was an angry lunatic, and my mother appeased him. One would think I would be likely to enter some shady unions, yet I haven't because I've dealt with my feelings about my dad and haven't tried to look to a man like him to fill a void. I celebrate my ability to be choosy, to *not* go for angry lunatics just because they are familiar. And I have been in several healthy relationships, although I saw none of that as a young girl. I celebrate the fact that I stay in them, work with them, and do all I can to tell the men in my life that, yes, I am scared, but I will work very, very hard to overcome my fears because I want a healthy life, family, and existence with a healthy man."

IDENTIFYING TRIGGERS AND CORNER PIECES

What people or situations in your life get you revved up — much more, perhaps, than they deserve, as if you can't "let them go"? Does a boss make you crazy? An ex, a friend, a co-worker, a sibling, a parent? Why do they have such an impact on you? It could be that they are reminding you of someone or some relationship in your past, and they are triggering a learned reaction. Rather than complain, agonize, or wallow in victimhood, take all that negative emotional energy they've stirred up and put it to work for you. Learn from your involuntary reflexes. Very likely, they stem from your past and understanding it could be a significant breakthrough in putting the pieces of you together. Bringing understanding to something is how you transform it.

I encourage people who feel "triggered" by others to journal about it. This is an excellent way to help see and identify your learned behaviors from childhood, as well as to help you reexperience any repressed feelings. Another good technique for releasing emotions is to write a letter (one that you never intend to mail) to your parent (or to anyone you're having difficulty with) that says all the things you'd like to say and vents all the anger and frustration that may not be appropriate to say face to face. Also, as Jessica says she's learning to do with herself, I suggest cutting yourself some slack in your day-to-day interactions with any people who push your buttons. In time, as you understand the corner pieces of your support system, you'll develop new and healthier ways to be.

Becoming the Adult Child of Your Parents

Becoming the adult child of your parents, or of whoever raised you, means separating from the relationship you had with them as a dependent child and creating a new relationship as an independent adult. It means seeing them for who they are, letting go of your expectations of them, and not letting their expectations of you rule your life. It means understanding you will never change them, and realizing that you shouldn't change for them or in spite of them. It means no longer using them as an excuse for your problems or as a crutch when times are tough.

"I recently moved two thousand miles away from my parents, after never living more than twenty minutes away. It was a scary time, but it forced me to learn how to be independent with financing, love, and survival. I learned how to build my own support system in a new place."

*Teacher, 23,
serious relationship, Florida*

It is okay to set loving boundaries with your parents. Just know as you do, it may be difficult for Mom and Dad to see you "all grown up" and off living your own life — so just be sure to nurture your connection to them. A natural part of maturity is that our parents evolve from being our primary support system to being one part of our support system, which expands to include friends, advisers, other family members, and romantic partners.

Becoming the adult child of our parents does not mean we have to demote them within our support network. Parents and family members can be wonderful sources of support and encouragement. No matter what, they will always have more life experience than you and can often offer a perspective that a peer could not. If you have reasonable, noncontrolling parents who do not fall into the "toxic" category, their insight may surprise you as they begin to relate to you as an adult. They may even be more open, more honest, and better at advising you than when you were their responsibility.

Of course, parents may say a few things that inspire an eye roll, but read between the outdated vocabularies and capture the meaning of what they are saying. Often, they have been in your shoes. One thing to keep in mind: your parents are there to give you an opinion and support, not to tell you what to do. Allow them to love you, support you, and encourage you, but you are responsible for your decisions.

"SOMETIMES IT JUST DOESN'T MAKE ANY SENSE"
by Anne, 29

DECLARATION: *Letting go of my parents and their dreams for me meant I could come into my own.*

On my honeymoon, while sitting at breakfast, I read about the crash of Enron, my husband's new employer. A month later, Nat was without a job and I became the sole provider for our family. For the next seven months, I ran my business while Nat searched fruitlessly for a job and finally applied to business school. I was teaching dance twelve hours a day and under tremendous stress, which took the form of an intestinal disorder. I was twenty-four.

One afternoon I got the news by phone that my father died of a heart attack while vacationing on Fire Island. My dad was the owner of a prominent jewelry store, and as his only child when he died, I suddenly found myself in charge of two businesses, two houses, two dogs, and a marriage. I was barely keeping my head above water and nobody was throwing me a life vest. I was twenty-five.

As it turned out, the biggest surprise of my twenties didn't come in the form of my father's death, running my own business, or the difficulties of marriage. Instead, it came from what I thought would always be the one constant source of love and support in my life — my mother.

I have been described at various moments as stubborn, a fighter, decisive, morally courageous, and physically tough. My six-foot-three, two-hundred-pound husband often mentioned his perception of me as being bigger than him. I guess my mom thought the same, because when I hit rock bottom, she didn't see it.

I needed help with the financial responsibilities, the mental distress, and the tremendous pressure of the events of my early twenties. My mom did give me money during this time to see a therapist, which helped me more than I realized at the time. But I needed more than that, and I thought that she could (and should) give it. Maybe she thought it was Nat's responsibility to help me financially — but he wanted to go to grad school.

The final straw was when I turned to my mom and said, "You have got to help me. I can't do this alone, and Nat's not doing anything." She responded: "You promised Nat you would help him through business school. A promise is a promise." Ouch. In March 2004, after two and a half years of marriage, I filed for divorce. I was twenty-six.

The next two years marked a very strange and lonely journey through adulthood. I embarked on a new career, fell in love, moved to New York, and cut off all ties to my mom. The reason involves my mother's decision to invite Nat into her home immediately following my decision to get divorced. While I struggled to pay the bills, hire a lawyer, stay in my home, start a new career, and plan my move to New York, Nat slept comfortably in my mother's guest bedroom and ate dinner at her table every night. It just didn't make sense.

My mom and I didn't speak for two and a half years, but in many respects, it was the best time of my life. I was pursuing acting and was able to put much of my anger and sadness about the death of my father into my art. It felt good. It was healing. Letting go of my parents and their dreams for me so that I could come into my own was freeing. After a while, I was ready to return to Texas to start rebuilding my relationship with my mom — this time on my terms.

What I love most about Anne's story is her commitment to keep going and to heal. Despite all of her relationship challenges, she kept the spark inside her alive. She did not perceive every speed bump as failure or life-ending; she took things as they came and was proactive in dealing with them. She did not sit and stew. Sometimes, we may be quite surprised by the way our parents or our families treat us as adults; this is why it's invaluable to cultivate experiences in our twenty-something years that are solely for us, where we can heal and explore. Be it acting, art, journaling, music, therapy, or spiritual work — find something that gives you a safe place to exert and explore your emotions. Things that you enjoy doing or being a part of are a key component to your support system.

> "It was difficult to go against my parents' wishes and take a very menial temp job as an assistant. But it got me out of the slump I was in, I met new people, and it helped me get the job I have now. And it was a *great* experience to have lived."
>
> Coordinator of international operations, 28, engaged, California

Cutting Ties to Build Healthier Bonds

Sometimes a relationship needs to experience a break so that a healthier bond can be created. Anne's story about her relationship with her mom tore at my heart strings, since it mirrors a situation I went through with my mother. A mother-daughter relationship is complex, emotional, and unlike any other bond — put two related woman together for life, and there is bound to be some drama. But this can be true of any parent and child: sometimes even a good relationship needs to be shaken up so that both can come to terms with the adult the child has become.

My mom was my best friend my entire life. She stuck by me, kept all my secrets, and was the person I enjoyed being with the most. My mom stayed home and raised us, and she truly enjoyed being there. And as I grew up and out of my socially awkward years, my mom and I stayed close.

That was until I was twenty-six years old and made the fateful decision to move in with my boyfriend. I dreaded telling her, knowing she wouldn't like it or approve, but I didn't expect her to be as angry as she was. I remember her saying, "How could you do this? This is not what I wanted for your life." I cried and felt like the worst daughter ever, and at the same time I was angry too. I had always been a good kid. Why this reaction?

My mom and I didn't speak for a while. It was one of the most confusing things I have ever gone through — and now I am so grateful for it. Why? Because it brought about a restructuring of our relationship. I relied on her too much, for nearly everything: approval, validation, love, support, and friendship. Though it hurt, emotionally separating from her provided an opportunity for healing on both our ends. I cannot speak for my mom, but I suspect she had to come to terms with letting go of her oldest child. And I had to reconcile the fact that though my mom only wanted the best for me, her ideas were different from the ones I had for myself.

When my mom and I began to talk again, because it was important to both of us to work things out, I was able to really see

> "It's been hard for me to get my parents (my mother in particular) to see me as my own person who makes her own life choices. Their expectations hang over me like a black cloud, and they want me to live a certain way. The expectation to be perfect for them is overwhelming. It's a constant battle that I am tired of fighting."
>
> *Optometrist assistant, 26, serious relationship, Georgia*

her for who she is — my mother who loved me so much that she wanted to protect me from feeling any pain. She feared what ultimately happened — my boyfriend left me. She was right that we weren't going to last. But I had to learn that lesson on my own. Then we were able to forgive each other and begin a new phase of our relationship built on mutual understanding.

Our parents' role as our protectors and caretakers changes during our twenties — and often that change is messy, as in Anne's and my own experience. As painful as it is for parents to watch from the sidelines and see their kids suffer life's knocks, they now have to stay on the sidelines. And as painful as it is to request they go to the sidelines, however angry they get about it, it's necessary to change the dynamic between you. That doesn't mean you should cut off all communication; it just means your communication may need to change. Like pruning a rose bush, cutting old ties leads to healthier new growth, as long as you are willing to do three very important things: own your end of it, let go of being right and work through your emotions, and forgive — them and yourself.

9. LOVE

Love. The romantic kind. The knots in your stomach, lose sleep over, spritz aftershave or spray perfume in strategic places kind of love. Falling in love, being in love — it's like a drug, and we all want some. Romance is everywhere we look: musicians sing about it, movies become blockbusters over it, television keeps us coming back week after week for more of it. Boy, does love get a lot of attention! It's one of those corner pieces most twenty somethings consider essential to complete their puzzle.

By the time we are twenty something, we have likely experienced love, been burned by love, and spent time longing for our "soul mate." I should come clean now: I don't believe in the idea of one soul mate, but I do believe in "soul matches." I believe we all have a variety of soul mates out there. In fact, every person we interact with is a soul mate in one way or another. When it comes to finding a partner for life, look for someone who matches your soul (not who completes it): someone who flows through life like you do; someone who shares your interests, values, outlook, routine, and so on. Does that not sound romantic enough?

Our perception of love and romance is warped. I blame it on the movies. Guys especially have gotten the short end of the stick. Passionate love scenes that sell tickets have put expectations on them that are impossible to fulfill — unless they have a personal screen writer or romance novelist putting words in their mouth. As one twenty-five-year-old woman confesses, "My current boyfriend and past boyfriends have suffered from my huge expectations because they never seem to give me enough of what I think I should be getting. It doesn't feel like the movies or a fairy tale, so I assume they are not the right guys."

> "I expect my relationships to be just like the movies, written in the stars, and free of doubt. Yes, I'm still waiting for my Prince Charming to ride in on his white horse and sweep me off my feet. He's supposed to know exactly how to please me."
>
> Student and cocktail server, 25, serious relationship, Hawaii

If you are waiting for "big screen" love, you'd better take up knitting. Of course, romance happens, and it's something all good relationships experience, but not 100 percent of the time. There is a difference between romance and a long-term relationship. I like to compare a long-term relationship to a pair of shoes (I know, I should be writing romance novels). Each person is separate and unique, but together their differences fit in exactly the right way to make a great match. And the process of finding a soul match can be like shopping for shoes: you might have to try on a wide variety before finding a good fit, and even then you may get a few blisters before they are broken in and completely comfortable.

THE SINGLE LIFE

Being single is a blessing, and I encourage you to enjoy this stage of your twenty-something journey. Many twenty somethings spend a great deal of time longing to love. They despair over being single; every Valentine's Day is brutal, and watching other happy, frolicking couples is torture. But remember, you have the *rest of your life* to share a bathroom with someone. Only now do you have the chance to swing in your singlehood and to squeeze your toothpaste tube any way you like. If you focus on how much being single sucks, the more it will suck. Build friendships instead — you can never have too many of those!

More important, when you're single, you have complete freedom to explore and get to know yourself. And this is very important for attracting and finding your soul match. If you don't enjoy singlehood, you may get into a relationship only to look back with a sense of longing and the realization you missed an opportunity. As one twenty-five-year-old says, "When I was single, all I wanted was to be married, but now that I am happily married, I am jealous of my single friends and the fact that they get to date, flirt, and do whatever they want — I wish I would have appreciated that time when I had it!"

Sow your oats and explore life until you are comfortable in your own skin. Ironically, the moment we're standing firmly on our own two feet is usually when we swing into couplehood.

You Complete You

The film *Jerry Maguire* contains one of my least favorite movie moments of all time: the "You complete me" scene. No one else completes you. Period. People come in and out of our lives to share them with us, contribute, support us, and teach us, but they never complete us. This kind of thinking is very misleading; it's more likely to lead to an unsuccessful relationship than a successful one.

Seeking someone to fulfill us is tremendous pressure to put on another human being. It is an unfair burden to ask someone else to carry our self-esteem, and one they usually drop (leading to hurt, disappointment, anger, and breakups). I do not want to be responsible for completing my husband, nor do I want him to complete me. Sure, I depend on him, but I am not dependent upon him. I am dependent upon me.

> "I thought I might be married by now or in a serious relationship. I try not to dwell on that too much because I have so much else going on and I am 'working on me.' How can someone else love me if I don't love myself?"
>
> Salesperson, 28, recovering from a breakup, Virginia

Furthermore, if we are single and not completely happy with ourselves or our lives, we fall into the trap of hoping someone else will come along and fix, help, cure our self-doubt, or "complete" us. It's tempting to look for a lover to make you feel yummy about yourself, but no one can do this for you in a lasting way. Treat singlehood as the time when you get to fall in love with yourself. If you look with loving eyes, you will find that your most loyal companion lies within you.

"FALLING IN LOVE WITH ME" by Eileen, 24

DECLARATION: *The only person guaranteed to love me unconditionally, accept me always, and be my companion until the grave is me.*

I have never been *in* love. There. I said it. That was freeing. I love my family and friends. I have a deep, loving relationship with a male friend, who is gay. I've been infatuated. I've had countless crushes. I've slept with men out of lust. But I've never dated anyone formally — by "formally," I mean that I've never dated anyone for more than a week, and if I have seen someone for more than a week, we usually didn't see the outside of a bedroom.

My twenty-something goals really boiled down to dating and eventually marrying the perfect man while embarking on a career that was both intellectually challenging and financially lucrative, and being thin and gorgeous all the while.

I'm overweight, single, and in debt. There are plenty of days when I feel like crap: tired, cranky, frustrated, and fearful. However, beneath the emotions of the day, however unpleasant, is a base of optimism. Where did this optimism come from? It was born the moment I realized I was in control of my life: I decide if I will surround myself with negative people, I decide if I will stay in a job that I despise, I decide if I am going to lose weight, and only I can decide to let go of wants that result in feelings of bitterness and unhappiness. I have come to realize that as an adult, I must take responsibility for my life.

As a child, the adults around me wrote the script for my life. My parents separated when I was ten years old, and all at once my family was dismantled and reconstructed. At first I was overcome with inexplicable pain. In time my depression was replaced with anger, frustration, and eventually numbness.

It wasn't until my sophomore year in college that I realized I had constructed an impenetrable emotional wall. For years I'd quipped, "My parents are divorced and I'm fine." By "fine" I meant that I wasn't engaged in high-risk behavior and I was a model student. I was far from "fine." I had failed to recognize that emotional trauma manifests itself differently in each person. The emotional defenses I'd implemented as a child had created a woman unwilling to share herself emotionally with anyone. I felt I was unworthy of love, and I was afraid of being abandoned. In friendships I was possessive and jealous. In romantic relationships — well, those were unheard of because I had never let anyone get that close.

And yet I yearned for a relationship, but didn't have one. Why?

Maybe it was because I was too fat, too tall, intellectually intimidating, too pretty, too opinionated, biracial, too quiet, or just too inexperienced. Maybe it was because I was in the wrong city, or because I didn't go out enough, or because I went out to the wrong places or with the wrong people or on the wrong nights.

Each conversation with my grandmother inevitably turned to whether or not I was dating anyone. My best friend's mother queried why I wasn't seeing anyone — "I was so pretty." Friends' boyfriends wondered why I was still single. The message was constant and clear: you should be dating someone, why aren't you? *Don't worry*, they all assured me, *it'll happen for you.*

But what if it never did? What then?

In order to answer this question, I had to dissect the concept of "boyfriend." What exactly did this term mean to me? Did it boil down to love and sex? If so, I already had a strong network of friends, family, co-workers, and classmates who loved me and provided me with emotional support, healthy social interaction, and encouragement. I also had a functioning vibrator. What would I gain from a romantic relationship that I currently lacked? Once I quieted the constant questioning in my mind, I could hear the answer:

I wanted a man to "fix" me. I wanted transformative love, unending true love. Perfect love. I wanted a man to heal the pain I felt inside with his love. I wanted a man to accept my stubbornness. I wanted a man to appreciate my fat thighs. I wanted a man I could trust enough to open up to.

In my mind a boyfriend would provide unconditional love, acceptance, and companionship. What if he never came? Would I live my life without these things? The answer was and is no, because I have myself.

If I want someone to appreciate my fat thighs, I first have to appreciate them myself. If I want someone to accept my stubbornness, I first have to accept it myself. No one except me can heal the pain I feel inside. How can I ask a man to love me when I don't love myself?

Finding strength within myself does not mean that I have to stand alone. By acknowledging my emotional barriers, I have the power to deconstruct them. As I become more comfortable with my emotions, I am more willing to share them. As a result, I am a better communicator and a more confident woman. Through it all there has only been one constant, and she will be with me until my last hour. When I wrap my arms around myself and embrace the woman within, I realize that I have found a love that lives right now and will last forever.

Curing Emotional Numbness

Successful singlehood doesn't end in coupledom, it ends as Eileen's story does: by understanding and embracing who you are. If you look at your life with an investigative lens, you can detox negative thought patterns and behaviors that hamper your ability to create a satisfying relationship. You can allow repressed emotions that have been submerged for years to rise to the surface of your consciousness, to be acknowledged, understood, and released. Eileen discovered optimism and possibility the day she realized she writes the script for her life.

I read Eileen's story on a flight to Nashville on my way to speak to a group of college women. Twenty minutes into the flight, I went to the bathroom and returned to find a huge commotion around my seat. Apparently, the healthy-looking thirty-something man sitting next to me had begun to feel numbness in his legs and throughout the right side of his body. He immediately rang the call button. Fortunately, a nurse and doctor were on board, and thirty minutes later, the gentleman was getting some feeling back. He could move his legs and the right side of his face perked up. The doctor warned him that he should go to the hospital immediately upon landing, since numbness often signals a serious health concern.

I share this story because it's analogous to Eileen's experience of dealing with her childhood wounds. To deal with the intense pain of divorce and a broken family, she went numb as a child. Feeling emotional numbness is dangerous because it means that something is wrong — we have suppressed something and it has not healed. Since emotional numbness doesn't keep us from functioning in the world, it is a common defense mechanism. However, numbness affects how we experience our lives and how we relate. If we don't experience any great joy or great sadness — we just float along, often alone — then like Eileen, we may have formed an "impenetrable emotional wall." Nobody is getting in.

> "I feel like I am at a point where I have been hurt enough times that I could just close off and not let anyone in anymore. I sometimes feel like I have a lot of baggage, and as a result have tried to close myself off to new relationships because I assume they can't give me anything. But I am starting to see that not being willing to risk getting hurt again will only result in loneliness."
>
> Student, 24, single, Wisconsin

When our bodies go numb, we don't hesitate. We know something is wrong — like the man on the plane did. Yet we almost never react that way to emotional numbness. But if you are feeling numb, and wondering why you remain a wallflower at the romantic twenty-something dance of love — I urge you to start ringing your call button!

As Eileen discovered, singleness is sometimes the direct result of protecting ourselves from experiencing pain and loss. Her numbness may have kept her alone, but it also kept her safe — safe from risking falling in love with someone and then having them leave, and safe from having to reexperience the same loss and heartbreak she had as a child when her parents divorced. Yet as an adult, this numbness was keeping her from getting the one thing she wanted most — a relationship.

If lasting relationships continually elude you, ask yourself — "Where am I numb?" This place is likely to hold the keys to love and feeling that you have been searching for.

FINDING YOUR KEYS

To restore feeling when you've been numb, you need to get to the root of the numbness — why is it there and when did it start? It's like trying to find lost keys. You have to jog your memory and mentally retrace all your steps until you can identify the moment you set them down. Often, we lose keys when we go outside our normal routine and put them down in a place we don't expect. Similarly, the reasons we go numb are typically not "normal," routine moments. They may have become routine if a particular pattern or event repeated itself in your life, but the moment of "loss" was uniquely significant. It will stand out once we start looking for it. Finally, to keep from losing your keys in the future, you could set aside a certain dish just for them from now on.

Of course, searching for emotional keys in our memories is a more intense process than searching for house or car keys. To do this, choose a safe and private place where you won't be interrupted, and without any limit on your time. Relax or meditate, and take a trip through your past, creating visual pictures of your life as you go. Try to identify any painful moments that might be the source of your current numbness. What happened? How old were you? Who was there? What did the environment look like at the time? What conclusions did you draw from the situation? Write about any likely incidents, and answer these questions as fully as possible. Keep remembering, allowing as many pictures of the events to unfold as possible.

Things may be hard to remember at first, but I encourage you to keep trying. Just like when you lose your keys, it may take a while to reconstruct the past. Then, most important, allow the repressed feelings to come up, in whatever way feels appropriate and "cleansing": write, cry, scream, hit a punching bag, cuddle with a stuffed animal, and so on. Let yourself feel the stuff you've been holding inside, knowing that you are completely safe in the present moment. Trust yourself and your intuition, and you will know when you are done. Usually, relief is the clearest sign.

Finally, create a plan (similar to designating a dish where you put your house keys) for processing your feelings whenever they come up — to continue healing any numbness and keep it from returning. You could write in your journal, talk to a trusted friend or adviser, make an appointment with a counselor, or just repeat the above process.

Dealing with emotions is not a quick-fix process. It takes time, patience, and the willingness to see and embrace your past. Once you do, you may discover that many of the situations and things you fear are not based in your present-day reality.

"LET'S NOT JUST BE FRIENDS" by Eddie, 22

DECLARATION: *In order to be the boyfriend and not just the friend, I have to work on building self-respect and confidence in who I am.*

I'm a twenty-two-year-old male, and I've never had a girlfriend. It's not that I don't want one, but I lack confidence in situations with women I like because I don't see myself as much of a catch. I'm told I am attractive, but I don't really see it. I'm told I am smart, but I'm not super successful like a lot of my friends.

In college, I developed a crush on Erin. She followed her dreams seemingly without fear and won student journalism awards. By the time I was a senior, she was vice president of the journalism club, and growing more interested in fields that I was passionate about. What a turn on! I envied her and had this strange impression that if I became close to her, she would liberate me as well. She didn't know me too well, but we talked occasionally and she always said nice things. But once again, I didn't respect myself enough to think I had a chance with her.

When I couldn't afford to hold things back anymore, I instant-messaged her and told her I had a crush on her. Her response? The typical "I just want to be friends; I have feelings for you, but not *those* feelings." I was devastated.

Over the next few months, we stayed "friends." I was trying to be okay with that and told myself I'd just take what I could get. She continued to confide in me when something was wrong, but then I wouldn't hear from her for weeks and I felt placed on the back burner.

I got advice from a friend who told me women can sense that I am insecure. I concluded women don't like weakness when they detect it. I was so nice to Erin, hoping that she would like me, almost to the point where I would be willing to be walked over. Feeling as if I was not attractive, not masculine, and not what most women want, I began to see what a desperate loser I was acting like! Finally, I took a stand and told Erin that I couldn't be her friend because of my feelings for her. She never talked to me again. I don't know if she was hurt, but I sure was.

My conclusion is that I have to work on building self-respect and confidence in who I am before I can be comfortable with others, especially when it comes to dating. I have to love myself before anyone can love me, because if not, I come across as that guy girls just "want to be friends with." No thanks...I've got enough friends.

GRADUATING FROM SINGLEHOOD

If you would like to graduate from singlehood with honors, here are some suggested courses toward a degree in *self*-substance. Graduating does not mean moving into couplehood, but mastering singlehood. It's also not about "if/then" conditional thinking — as in, "If I lose five pounds (or if I get a great job), then I'll find my soul match." Superficial changes only get you superficial people!

My clients have reported great success and have actually enjoyed this curriculum — give these courses a try:

1. Relish your singlehood. Enjoy it, savor it, and be confident as a Party of One. Final Exam: Go to dinner at a restaurant and sit by yourself. Do this as many times as it takes to feel comfortable and to actually enjoy your meal.

2. Go out with a lovey-dovey couple. Be able to be around and celebrate other people's love. Final Exam: Last the entire evening without talking about your love life or feeling depressed when you get home.

3. Buy yourself an affordable gift that is meaningful to you — flowers count too. Final Exam: Attach a sappy card to yourself and write yourself a love or appreciation note. And yes, guys, this applies to you as well — you need the practice!

4. Plan a vacation for yourself. It does not have to be extravagant or pricey. Just take yourself to a new destination, and explore. Final Exam: Ask a stranger to take a picture of you, by yourself, then frame it and display it.

5. Go to a party or social function alone without drinking (alcohol is liquid courage — that's cheating!). Final Exam: Introduce yourself to at least three people while you are there.

DATING WITHOUT DRAMA

The perfect date does not just fall from the sky holding a milkshake with two straws. Even after we have successfully graduated from the school of singlehood, we have to put forth effort and get out socially to create opportunities. Dating can be daunting, and it will involve some let-downs, but it does not have to become an epic soap opera! Think of dating as a process of elimination. I know, not the most romantic of notions, but trust

> "Dating is like being on a roller coaster. Sometimes you're up, sometimes you're down, so you might as well throw your arms in the air and enjoy the ride."
>
> *Interior designer, 27, dating, Louisiana*

me, it's the truth. Unrequited crushes, embarrassing and awkward moments, and a string of terrible bad dates are required before romance blesses us. After all, we need to smell a few wilted carnations before we can truly appreciate the smell of a dozen red roses.

"DIVE IN" by Jeff, 24

DECLARATION: *The dating world is a big game of sink or swim.*

Let me start off by saying that I have never been mistaken for Casanova. In college, I did all right with women, but I never had them lining up to be with me. College was great because it was its own little world where finding dates was almost as easy as leaving the dorm. Places to meet people were everywhere.

As my college career was winding down, I was conditioned to prepare for the real world by budgeting and career planning, yet I was oblivious to the preparation required for dating. Once I moved away from my college town, I realized that the social ponds that I had fished in before had suddenly dried up.

Right away, I told myself it was all going to be fine; there were still bars. I soon realized that the bar scene was more like a casual-sex website. Not quite my style.

So I tried to initiate casual (more often awkward) conversations at random places like grocery stores. It seemed that every woman everywhere was on a mission and didn't have time to socialize. I live with two women (no Jack Tripper jokes, please), so I am frequently privy to complaints about what guys are doing wrong. I got educated in dating 101 "dos and don'ts": Don't text date requests. Don't call too early. Don't call too late (without a damn good excuse). Don't be a jerk. Don't be a nice guy. Don't be too forward. Be available, but not desperate. Have things in common, but not too many. Be able to talk a lot. Be able to listen more.

> "My two best friends got engaged within a week of each other, and my only single girlfriend moved. I was in this horrible rut, until I realized I have so much to live for and I don't need a diamond on my left hand to do it."
>
> Marketing assistant, 23, dating casually and waiting for the fireworks, Pennsylvania

All these rules made it seem like there could only be a very small possibility of success; scary, but I still wanted to try. I decided to get off the bench and into the game. After some hits and lots of misses, I started to get the hang of good icebreakers and became a little more confident in my approach. Then it was time for a real test.

One day, I see this very good-looking lady struggling with a ticket machine that *always* gives people trouble. Being the expert with random crap that I am, I thought that this could lead to a good conversation, maybe even a date. To make a long, embarrassing story short, I ended up looking like a hero by helping her with the machine, but quickly transformed into an idiot after asking this *married* woman out. Yes, I missed the ginormous rock on her finger.

The dating world is a big game of sink or swim. I have started to take off the floaties I had on during college and try swimming on my own. More times than not, I end up drowning, but I am optimistic that as long as I keep jumping in, eventually a good-looking lifeguard is going to throw me a rope.

Mars and Venus Dating Behaviors

It's often a stereotype, but it's my opinion that men and women really do have different approaches to dating (and relating). Men are less dramatic — they are the hunters, and they approach dating that way. They look for what they want, they see it, and they go after it. Men don't get enough credit for the courage it takes to be the hunter. I realize that the traditional rule of "boy asks girl out" is fading; however, men still do the majority of the pursuing. This takes confidence, creativity, and let's not forget — money!

Estrogen tends to account for a more emotional approach to dating than does testosterone. A bad date may leave women depressed for days and a lack of dates conjures up a slew of worries. When it comes to the opposite sex, women tend to be more anxious and overanalytical. We approach dating like shopping for an important purchase — there is lots of contemplation, trying things on, asking for the store clerk's opinion, and finally, when we do make a purchase, a lot of analyzing how we look in our new outfit. So guys, you best tell us we look great — whatever we are wearing.

Given these differences, getting Mars and Venus out on a date can come to seem like a miracle of celestial navigation. Ladies: If you are thinking, "There are no guys out there who ask me out," what has been your standard thus far? Are you expecting Dr. McDreamy to call up out of the blue? Or maybe your standards are too low. Do you consider text messaging an appropriate way to be asked out on a date? Do you "hook up" rather than wait to be asked to share a conversation over a meal? If you want a man to ask you out, you have to be acting like a lady — or start doing the asking. Men: Take a lesson from Jeff, and get off the bench. The worst thing that can happen is a woman can say no. Trust me, women are always flattered to be asked. But after you ask us, treat us like ladies. Call when you say you are going to, open our doors

> "I refused to think that I needed to resort to online dating to help me find my Prince Charming, but after a breakup I decided to check it out. I went in with an open mind and a positive attitude. The first person who contacted me via the site was the only date I went on. We moved in together nine months later and have a great relationship."
>
> *Hospitality manager, 28, serious relationship, Ohio*

(or at least try) — a little chivalry and respect go a long way.

Dating is a dance that does not come naturally to everyone, so just have fun with it and keep your expectations to a minimum. Stop sizing up every date to see if they fit your glass slipper and just try on a bunch of shoes. The same is true of same-sex relationships, where getting out there may be even more challenging; however, you have to be yourself and break up with any beliefs or judgments that are holding you back. We all have to open our minds, let go of our egos, and get playing the dating game in order to find a soul match.

Dating as Research

Right before I met my husband, I went on over fifty dates in four months. Before that, my fiancé had broken up with me, and I had spent four months alone and terrified of getting my heart broken again. After four years of being in a relationship, I was intimidated to date. I thought, "Good men are hard to find. I'll never find one like him." And, "Now that I am dumpable, I am not datable — who is going to want returned goods?" I was alone, depressed, and complaining.

So how did I become a dating diva? I shifted the way I was thinking about my status as a single. First, I worked to clear away my feelings of hurt and anger; then I changed my perception of dating. To bust through my toxic beliefs, I put notes on my mirror saying things like, "I am capable of love and deserve it," and "Men are trustworthy and dating is fun!" However difficult it was, I knew I had to have absolute faith that I would fall in love again if I ever wanted it to happen. To make that faith real, I had to open my mind, risk getting hurt again, and say yes to dating: in fact, I promised I would say yes to anyone who asked me out who wasn't married, an addict, scary looking, creepy acting, or more than fifteen years older than me.

Saying yes to dating keeps the energy of it alive. My openness attracted requests, but most important, I let go of expectations — I considered dating to be research. I knew with each bad date — and there were many — that I was a date closer to a good one. As I've said, dating is often a process of elimination, not a blockbuster romantic comedy. Eventually, you arrive at the "right" one.

And do you know what I learned? You can find something in common with *anyone* if you are willing to see them as a person rather than as a potential horizontal partner. In my dating bonanza, I learned about everything from quantum physics to medieval art traditions in France, because I was willing to get to know the people I was with. I discovered that a bad date didn't have to go badly if I was willing to find out something about the other person and ask him about what he loved. I figured out how to avoid the dreaded "interview" date ("So, where did you grow up? Where did you go to school? What do you do?") and those moments of "Mayday, mayday, uncomfortable silence!" when I stopped trying to say the "right thing" and just was myself. As long as I didn't care what he was thinking about me and I wasn't being overly judgmental of him, I was able to be more spontaneous, natural, and real, and this made for a more relaxed and fun time for both of us.

So say yes or have the guts to ask, and give people a chance. If you cannot find it in your heart to spend two hours with another human being, just how open is your heart? Be kind, be open, be honest, and be willing. Treat each date as an end in itself, not as a path to getting laid or getting a ring — but as an opportunity to get to know someone. Consider it research into other people, yourself, and the galactic laws of attraction.

Ready, Willing, but Waiting for "the One"?

I know, I know — you are sick of "researching." You are sick of dating to meet just anyone, or everyone. You want to meet "the one." Where the heck is Mr. or Ms. Right? Boy, if I could answer that for everyone, I'd be driving that convertible Mercedes I've always wanted. Wanting that relationship, the one that leads to marriage or a long-term commitment, and feeling like you're ready for it is frustrating if you don't have a good candidate.

When I was twenty-six, I went to ten weddings in one year. There seems to be a time in every twenty something's life when everyone around you is getting engaged or married. Before you know it, the clerk at Williams Sonoma knows your name. "Another wedding?" he asks, and then the dreaded follow-up: "So when are *you* getting married?" You either want to cry or punch him.

"ALWAYS THE BRIDESMAID" by Chrissy, 27

DECLARATION: *I'm tired of bridesmaid's dresses —*
I want a wedding gown and all that goes with it.

I've been a bridesmaid six times. I've never even had a serious boyfriend, and sometimes it feels like I never will. My mother always told me that when I went to college I would "be beating them off with a stick." I had the stick all ready to go — but never used it.

During college I was in a sorority and had a great social life. Bars, parties, and lots of friends. I've just never really felt all that comfortable around boys. Sometimes I think it's because I have two sisters. Or because I went to a small school. And then my high school graduating class was forty-seven kids. Other times I'm certain it's because I'm a bit over-weight. Whatever "it" is that's keeping me single, it's working.

When I graduated from college, I tried internet dating and went out on a few dates. I'm just not very good at dating. I have high ex-pectations and want to see "husband potential" right away. Or I get nervous and sabotage the date. I wish I could say that I'm living that wonderful swinging single life, but I'm not.

I work from home, so it's hard to put work aside — especially when there always seems to be so much to get accomplished, and I don't have a relationship to distract me. Plus, it doesn't give me many opportunities to meet men

There is an upside to my perpetual singlehood. I can take out the trash, paint a room, unclog a toilet, and put together Ikea furniture all by myself. I have to make all of the difficult phone calls myself and fig-ure out my taxes every year. I'm really great at being on my own — too great.

But I really want a husband and a family. I want a great guy to build a life with who loves me and makes me laugh. And I really want a family. I feel like I'm running out of time. At twenty-seven, my eggs are starting to wither up, and at this rate I'm not having babies anytime soon. Although my life isn't turning out the way I had imagined, I'm learning that I have to be okay with it — or I'll just be miserable. While I would really like to have a hus-

> "I was the girl who dated the bad boys, who were exciting . . . and who treated me like crap. I always believed I could change them. Over and over I expected the outcome to be different, but it never was. I finally stopped blaming myself and believed I would find a man to treat me with the respect I deserve!"
>
> *Social worker, 23, engaged, Hawaii*

band, I know that it doesn't control my happiness. I have to be happy with my life as it is and not spend my time waiting to be happy. I don't have to wait for things to be picture perfect.

Chrissy is right: we shouldn't wait for things to be picture perfect to be happy, but I would encourage her to have more faith in her picture. She wants to be married, and at twenty-seven there's plenty of time for that to happen — and for kids. (And just a side note to you twenty-something ladies: your eggs are not drying up, and if you are telling yourself that they are, please change that inner dialogue — your eggs are getting annoyed at your lack of faith in yourself to love and be loved.) As Chrissy acknowledges, our happiness is in our control; a ring and a date are not. But if we want marriage, we can do more than make the best of singlehood: we need to break up with any beliefs that are keeping us single.

Breaking Up with Beliefs

When it comes to love and marriage, we all have baggage, which is shorthand for our fears and insecurities. Our parents' marriage, our awkward teenage years, what peers have said to us, and our past interactions and romantic relationships all contribute to our expectations over whether we will partner up and with whom. Chrissy admits that her high expectations and fears lead her to sabotage dates, so in addition to being happier with herself (increasing her self-confidence and sense of self-worth), she needs to examine any beliefs that are undermining her romantic efforts. If we have negative beliefs about ourselves, our ability to attract or hold on to a significant other weakens. So, we have two choices: change our beliefs and the ways we interact, or accept ourselves the way we are. Remember, what we believe about ourselves is the vibe we give off to anyone we date — and self-doubt is not an aphrodisiac.

> "Once I finally allowed myself to fall in love and be vulnerable, I met my boyfriend. He loves me for who I am and supports my dreams. He has helped me break down my security barrier and realize I am worthy of being loved, even though I have made mistakes."
>
> *Makeup artist, 23,*
> *serious relationship, Georgia*

Self-doubt can be tricky. We may *think* we are a great catch, but we may not *believe* it, and our words and actions give us away.

A twenty-five-year-old writes, "My expectation was to be married right now. However, I am single. I bought a condo and hate having to change the light bulbs, unclog toilets, take out the trash, and shovel snow! When around friends that are married or engaged, I feel so inferior, like I am not good enough for anyone to want to marry me. I think that I would be a great catch for someone and hate that I let those feelings about not having anyone affect my self-esteem. It also makes me hate spending time with my coupled-up friends, because I envy them, and they have no idea what it is like to be me. Instead of embracing my life, I feel so ashamed."

> "I've felt that I must be doing something wrong to not be married at my age. I have to constantly remind myself that the reason that I haven't gotten married is not because of lack of interest in me by the opposite sex, but because I am particular. I am not the type of person who hastily jumps into things."
>
> Logistics analyst, 29, serious relationship, California

Though this young woman *says* she thinks she'd make a great catch, what she describes sounds more like she's suffering from a major Expectation Hangover full of envy, shame, and self-doubt. It seems that if she can unlock the reason why she feels inferior to her coupled friends, she might understand and be able to change the fears and beliefs that are holding her back. For anyone stuck in a similar dilemma, in which their actions, thoughts, and beliefs don't support their desires, I suggest the Finding Your Keys exercise (page 191). You *will* find your soul match... but only when you truly *believe* you are ready to be matched.

Attracting Your Soul Match

Where do I get off giving all this advice about believing in love and meeting the right person? Because I know firsthand. After my ex-fiancé broke up with me and I was back on the dating scene for a few months, I felt like I was forcing myself to believe that my soul match existed. Each time I'd get discouraged, I'd tell myself singlehood was fun, exciting, and what I needed to experience, but without losing faith that marriage was in my future. Then one night, I decided to make a manifestation list of everything I want and need in a mate. What I thought would be a few crucial things turned into a fifty-three-item list. I went from losing the person I thought I wanted to being able to be extremely specific and honest about what matters to me in a relationship and what I am capable of giving. After I finished the list, I lit a candle, said a prayer, sealed the list in an envelope, and tucked it under my bed.

Two months later, my friend Jodi called saying she'd met a guy she insisted I should meet. I agreed. However, though I was excited to meet this mystery man, by the time I arrived at the party where we were to meet, I was in a funk from a bad dinner date and painful shoes. We met, and I was "underwhelmed." But he asked Jodi for my number, and later he called me. We both gave bad phone, and I had a feeling that Jodi's intuition had misfired with this one. But he persisted, and we finally set up a dinner date.

I arrived at the restaurant about ten minutes late because my pants ripped on my way out the door (clearly, a bad sign). When I arrived, he was sitting at the bar, and as he turned to greet me, he smiled in such a genuine way — it got my attention. We sat down and within five minutes something in me shifted. I felt safe. It was easy. I could be myself with this man, and I was attracted to him — not in a running through a field of flowers in slow motion or fireworks blasting kind of way, but in an intimate and tender kind of way. After dinner, I asked him to get frozen yogurt. After yogurt, he asked me out for the following weekend. I was smitten — and so was he.

Three months into our courtship, I opened the envelope housing my manifestation list with nervous anticipation, anxious to see how many of the fifty-three items described Chris. My nervousness turned to bewilderment as each characteristic fit! Time stood still, and I sat in shock — part of me wanting to fall to my knees in gratitude, the other part wanting to pull out a pen and paper and create more lists! I eventually decided to share my list with Chris, and when I did, this unfamiliar smirk appeared on his face. "Did I spook him?" I thought. He got up, walked into his bedroom, and returned to the living room with his laptop. On the screen was a document entitled "My List: What I Want in a Wife." He had written it exactly one month to the day before I had written mine. His list was ten things, not fifty-three, but that is a man for you.

Exactly a year after our list exchange, Chris proposed to me in the most romantic and "me" setting. See why I believe in the law of attraction? What you believe in and the energy you live in creates your life.

MANIFEST YOUR SOUL MATCH

As I discovered, it helps to imagine your soul match before he or she appears. Make your own soul match list of attributes and qualities, and be specific. How does the person act, look, talk, and behave? What dreams, values, and hobbies does he or she have? How do you relate to each other? I encourage you to begin with the following statement: "I, [your name], do lovingly manifest my soul match [or, if you like, partner, husband, wife, love, and so on], who is the following, and I ask for this or something better for the good of all concerned. And so it is."

Follow this with your descriptions of how you see your soul match. Write in the present tense (you are writing about someone who is alive *now*, aren't you?), give it some serious thought, and *be specific*. For instance, if you say, "He is ambitious," in what way do you mean? Do you want a workaholic? Do you want someone who is driven yet does not hold down a job? Another example: if you write, "She is attractive," don't stop there. *Be specific.* Do you want someone who is constantly concerned with her looks? Who, perhaps, needs constant reinforcement of her beauty? And will you be okay with the attention she gets from other men? You get the drift — vagueness can dangerous.

When you complete your list, fold it up and put it away. You can look at it and reread it as much as you want. The only rules are that you have to be patient, review Expectation Hangover prevention tips, believe that this person does exist, and you will eventually match up.

BREAKUPS AND HEARTACHE

Before we move into relationships, we need to address a necessary evil that often comes with dating and relating: breakups. Let's face it, they can really suck. But heartbreak is often a necessary phase for any happy-ending story. If you are in the middle of a breakup, rest assured that there is another side that doesn't hurt so much, and you will get there. In fact, breakups are blessings — through them, we learn crucial lessons about love, loss, ourselves, and our hearts. True, sometimes these blessings reveal themselves much, much more slowly than we'd like, but we must learn to

"I have Expectation Hangovers with every breakup I go through! It sucks to be alone. It's a feeling of emptiness and insecurity. It's a hollow heart that beats for the anticipation of a phone call, email, or an instant message from HIM. It's waiting . . . and waiting some more."

Writer, 26, off-and-on single, Texas

keep our hearts open no matter how much they've been hurt or how often they've led us astray.

"CAUTIOUS COURAGE" by Jen, 28

DECLARATION: *I am able to recognize that the heartaches, disappointments, changes, and triumphs are all equally important to who I am and where I go.*

Four years ago, I was engaged to be married. I had a great job, a house, and my life looked great on paper. One day that all changed. I was visiting a friend in another city and had a difficult time reaching my fiancé by phone. My gut said something was "off." I immediately changed my flight and flew home a day early. I arrived to discover my fiancé and another woman in my home "playing house."

I struggled with moving forward, wondering what was next. Every day seemed like a blur. I had no desire or motivation to do anything or feel anything other than bitterness. I desperately wanted to wake up from what I prayed was a bad dream and have my life go back to the way it was.

After almost a year of tears, anxiety, and very little focus, I became frustrated over having no idea who I was. For such a long time, my ex was what was most important to me, and I lost my identity. His opinions were how I measured my likes, dislikes, thoughts, and even my own self-worth.

I needed a change, something drastic. With two suitcases of belongings and one full of cautious courage, I moved to a big city away from my friends and family. I had spent so much time being afraid of my life without my ex that I knew the best thing I could do for myself was to face the fear head-on. Plus, nothing could be worse than what I had been going through.

Everything was completely foreign to me. The city, the people, their lifestyles, me in this new city… everything. The first three months, I cried every day, missed my family terribly, and second-guessed my decision constantly. But then each day got a little easier. I was gaining self-confidence, and I began to feel comfortable in my own skin. By month four, I found a great job and pushed myself to step outside my comfort zone even further by meeting new people, experiencing the lifestyle the city offered, and discovering what things interested me.

During this time, I bought *Twenty Something, Twenty Everything* and learned so much about myself, my behaviors, and why I chose the paths I had taken in the past. Sure there were days when it was easier to revert to the old way of thinking. I would still ask the questions that had no answers. Why did he do this? What did I do wrong? How could I fix him? Instead of answers, I have turned to understanding and focused on what I can learn. I realized that for many years, I listened to someone else's ideas, thoughts, and opinions about who I was, what job I should have, where I should live, how I should act, and who my friends should be.

> "My ex-boyfriend and I broke up last year, and I've been having the time of my life since. It was unexpected for me, but so wonderful after I got through grieving. I love the life I'm living now!"
>
> Proposal coordinator, 25, long-distance relationship, North Carolina

In retrospect, there had been so many red flags over the course of my relationship that I chose to ignore in our everyday life. I heard my gut instinct screaming at me, but I let fear of being alone dictate many of my choices. I've learned that someone else's actions do not determine my value or self-worth, and the only person's happiness I am responsible for is mine!

I continue to put one foot in front of the other, and the more I learn about myself as an individual, the more I like who I am becoming and the more I enjoy the life I am building. It is as though a weight was lifted off of my shoulders, and I finally felt everything "click"! Without the heartbreak, I wonder how I would have learned to make the healthy choices I am currently making. My life today is well on its way to being everything I have ever imagined.

As I've said, one of the best things that has ever happened to me is my ex-fiancé breaking off our engagement. It forced me to learn how to build myself and my life on my own. If you are going through relationship rehab right now, consider that it is for the best. If it was meant to be, it would have been. Don't shut down emotionally if you have had your heart broken. Instead, take this opportunity to put yourself together even better than before, and move forward with your life! Your soul match could be right around the corner.

"PUTTING ME BACK TOGETHER" by Sarah, 25

DECLARATION: *Spending so much time picking over a broken heart means that we forget about the most important people in our lives — the people who still love us.*

I fell in love with James the first moment I saw him. After three months of dating, he told me he loved me, and there was no turning back. For the next four years we did everything together — everything seemed just perfect.

After attending wedding after wedding, we were both starting to wonder why after four years of dating we weren't heading down the aisle. The relationship started turning sour. I began to realize the person that I loved wasn't quite so eager to spend the rest of his life with me. As much as it hurt, we decided to end it. A big part of me wanted him to fight for us, but he never did.

The breakup threw my confidence. I lost the feeling of security that came with belonging to an exclusive team. I thought James was so impressive, and I missed him terribly.

How do two people who were best friends become so completely separate and unrelated? Isn't it funny (and brutal) how we can still think every day about someone we never see or speak to? He stopped loving me and wanting me in his life. I wondered, how long does it take to recover from that rejection? Will I ever be over it? It all happened so quickly, and I couldn't work out why it changed and ended, and how my life detoured so far from where I thought it would be.

Six months post-breakup, I realized now I was more in love with him than I was with myself. He was stable, secure, dependable, and said he loved me. It had seemed I had it all, but I've discovered there is a lot more to expect from life; what we had was good but nowhere near good enough.

Now, a year later, I know I have changed and time has been healing. The healing, however, is not complete — but I like it that way. The scars that remain remind me of the lessons I learned. At the moment I know I struggle with rejection probably because I know how it feels, the poetry I write still resounds with heartbreak, and I am fearful that I may never find love. Some of my friends feel that I am not giving love a chance, but I know what I want and I'm not going to make do with anything less. I think that when one dates, sparks should fly — anything less is a waste of time. So there is not even the hint of romance on the horizon, which is something I am reminded of when my father calls from Australia and says, "Come home, get married, and buy a house" — like I can grab all the necessities of life in a quick trip to the local mall.

I spend a lot of time talking with my single friends about their love lives. Have you ever noticed how many women the world over are suffering from heartsickness? Close girlfriends of mine are continually updating me on how they feel about the men in their lives, why it is not working, when he last called, and what he said. Every last detail is dissected and examined. It's not healthy! I did it. I spent so much of last year dissecting my broken relationship that I forgot about loving myself and the people who didn't leave me. Now I have a list of all the VIPs in my life stuck up on my wall. These are the people that love me unconditionally, the people I can't afford to neglect. Oh, and I'm one of them.

Of course your heart is going to ache when a relationship ends. But treat it like an Expectation Hangover; accept the pain, feel it, understand why it happened, and then behave proactively. It's easy to overanalyze or obsess about why a relationship has ended, but your heart cannot heal if you stay in the past. Thinking constantly about a breakup can become just a way to keep your ex in your life even though the relationship is over — and you need to stop using your heart energy on your ex. This means stop all communication as well for at least six months (and that means all forms of communication too — email, text messaging, IM'ing, phone calls, and so on). Your heart cannot heal if it's pulled in two directions. Healing from a breakup is a hundred times harder if you are still in communication with your ex. Don't try to be friends, at least not right away. Give yourselves space and time, then perhaps a friendship will be possible down the road.

> "I thought I'd be with my ex forever. It took me four years to get over him because I still wanted him back and kept my feelings for him alive. Finally, I went back and started undoing all of those emotions. It was like plunging into the ocean to a euphoric depth and aimlessly fighting to come up for air, and when I allowed myself just to float, I eventually reached the top, preserving enough air in my lungs to swim to shore and start over again on new terrain."
>
> Executive administrator,
> 26, serious relationship, California

And finally, don't let your heart atrophy. It's a muscle; you need to keep working it out. I love Sarah's suggestion of focusing on the love you do have in your life. Pour your love onto your VIPs — your friends and family — and not into a rebound relationship.

RELATING, SERIOUSLY

As dating becomes relating, a host of new issues comes up, such as: Is this the real thing or just a good time? Is my partner loving me or controlling me? Am I losing myself in the relationship? How do I communicate my heart's desires with this strange other person?

How do I, now "we," merge career goals with the needs of our relationship? And when should I ask or expect to be asked to get married? There are not always obvious answers to all the questions that come up in a relationship, which is frustrating, as we'd like to be "done" with dating in our twenties. Becoming a "we" in our twenties is yet another learning process; couplehood comes with its own set of challenges. As we gaze into our futures with or without our partners, often these challenges make us lose sight of ourselves. So as you relate in your relationship, keep how you are relating to yourself in clear view!

The Match That Fizzles

Ever had intense chemistry with someone? The kind of connection with another person that really lights your fire even though, deep down, you know they are not marriage or long-term commitment material? Sometimes, such a person might stick around long enough that you might start to wonder if the strong physical attraction might indicate a "soul match."

But are you confusing love with passion? We all know sparks can fizzle, so we want to be careful if sexuality is the major or main aspect of a relationship. Instead of sparks, pay attention to how easy it is to be with the person, how much anxiety you feel, how much you trust the person, whether or not you are completely yourself with them, how much you have in common (outside the bedroom), and how you work together as a team. To commit to a partner for life, we want someone who can stoke our fire without burning us, and whose commitment to the partnership includes all of life's messy chores.

> "I got married, and now I am headed for divorce. I knew I wasn't happy, but I played the part of the happy bride, not wanting to disappoint him or my family. I cried before I walked down the aisle. It's amazing what I overlooked hoping it would all go away."
>
> Information systems, 28, separated, Michigan

Great sex does not pay bills, wipe runny noses, hold your hand when you get bad news, or offer comfort when you lose a parent.

Passion can exist without love, and often it is easier to find than true love, which is partly why it is so tempting to believe that passion is love. Passion without love can be a dangerous form of infatuation. Getting too consumed by passion for someone can be toxic. Feelings of not being able to live without someone else, thinking obsessively about another person, allowing our emotional state to be dictated by the state of a relationship: all these things can literally put us in a spin cycle that disrupts our connection to ourselves. As we willingly ignore our other responsibilities, the rest of our lives are thrown off balance.

Passion is great, but it's not enough to base a relationship on, and it cannot substitute for love. Passion does not include room for growth, or change, or even contradiction — but love does and that is why love is what lasts.

Control Is Not Love

Okay, time for a relationship pop quiz:

- Have you ever had a relationship that looked good on paper but did not feel good in your gut?
- Have you ever felt extremely passionate toward someone but the only place you felt like you were on even ground or truly connected was in the bedroom?
- Have you ever felt like you were losing yourself in a relationship?
- Have you ever felt obligated to stay with someone just because they did nice things for you?
- Have you ever been scared to leave a relationship although you knew you should?
- Have you ever felt as though the other person dictated everything about the relationship?

If you answered yes to any of the above with regard to your current relationship, CAUTION! You may be in an unbalanced or controlling relationship — which is not the kind you want. If we cannot be ourselves in the relationship, or if we feel like we're losing ourselves in it, then something besides open-hearted love is probably present. We may be letting our fear of being alone, or someone else's desires for us, guide our decisions — not our love for the other person and for ourselves. In Tabatha's story, which applies to both women and men, do you recognize any behaviors or feelings present in your current relationship?

"WHATEVER HAPPENS, I'LL BE OKAY" by Tabatha, 23

DECLARATION: *I don't want to be an extension of somebody else anymore.*

I was raised in a strict Christian home. My dad read from the Bible at the breakfast table each morning — it was the foundation of our beliefs. My mother was born in China. She was taught to be obedient to her parents, and that men are always more important than women. I never rebelled against my parents. I had a sense my upbringing contributed to my submissive behavior and reserved demeanor, but it was my conversations with a counselor that helped me see the connection to my romantic relationships and own up to the feelings I had kept bottled up inside for so long.

In college, I dated someone older who became not only my boyfriend but also my friend, my mentor, my provider, and my co-worker. He did everything "right" — took me to all the nicest places, bought me all the nicest things. He was well-respected at my school and knew me better than anyone else because he made it his priority to know me. He was always there to "help" me. Always. Anytime, anywhere. 24/7. It was hard to recognize this was controlling behavior.

On the outside, it looked like we had a great relationship, but I never saw him as a boyfriend. When he kissed me, I felt nothing. When he held my hand, it felt wrong. I told him this, but he said he couldn't just be my friend. Scared to lose the security of Mike, I kept working at it, trying to *make* myself be in love with him.

I began to see a difference between someone doing nice things for me and being controlled by kindness. At the time, I wasn't aware that controlling behavior could come in the form of kindness. He helped me become dependent; he helped me feel that I could not do things on my own without anyone else's help. He used his "help" as a way to trap me, to make me feel obligated to be with him, and to meet his sexual desires in exchange for all that he did for me.

Therapy taught me I didn't have to feel guilty for not having the same feelings that Mike had for me. My psychologist said, "Attraction is not a faucet. You can't just turn it on or off." There was a time when Mike actually suggested the reason I didn't have this sexual attraction for him was because I might be a lesbian. That was the breaking point for me. I ended our relationship and started dating other guys.

But I fell into the same pattern. I let other guys control me, not to the same degree as Mike, but it was the same pattern. First, I dated a much older man who I fell for because he filled the communication and caretaker role that Mike had filled. He tried to convince me that "love is ageless." But I didn't want to be the Barbie doll with the old rich man. I wanted to be with someone closer to my own age.

So I started hanging out with girlfriends and stopped looking for a relationship, but then I met Danny. I think he is the first person I ever truly loved. For the first time, the relationship felt equal; our love for each other was mutual. I felt alive, a completely different feeling, a feeling from the heart. I found out I was capable of genuine romantic feelings toward someone, free of guilt and obligation.

I wanted to be with him, but I also wanted to be independent. I was torn. So I became submissive again, and I didn't speak my mind, and I ended up very unhappy. I ended the relationship. I told him I needed to grow on my own; I didn't want to be an extension of somebody else. I needed to find myself.

So it's been a learning and growing process. I've learned that I don't need someone else to complete me and that taking care of myself is more rewarding than having someone else take care of me. I've learned to feel confident in my decisions and not second-guess everything. I've learned that I don't need approval from my boyfriend or from my parents.

There is still work to be done and more to learn, perhaps there always will be. But now the future excites me. Now there is real hope in my heart.

Are you losing the "me" in "we"? If you think you may be in a controlling relationship, I encourage you to talk to someone about it — someone who knows you well and whom you trust to offer honest but kind feedback. I say that with three caveats. First, feedback is just that — someone else's opinion. Listen to what someone has to say without defending or justifying, and then let it marinate for a while. Really consider if any of it rings true. Take it home and digest it. Second, be careful who you choose, and don't overanalyze your romantic relationship with everyone. Resist making it the topic of all your lunch conversations, and keep the focus on *you*. Don't be tempted to gossip about, bash, or analyze your significant other with friends and family.

> "Leaving a relationship that was toxic for me, putting myself first and not feeling bad about it, has been the most empowering part of my twenties."
>
> Writer, 28,
> serious relationship, Oregon

And third, if you feel your relationship is abusive, find a trained counselor or support group that you can go to. Your physical and emotional health is more important than anything or anyone else. If taking a step to leave the relationship is scary, reach out to a friend or a volunteer — there is support out there; just find the courage to look.

Learn from Tabatha. She is willing to look at her past, but not become it. She is willing to see mistakes but not be ashamed of them. She is also willing to overcome the fear of being alone to discover who she can be on her own. These actions are supporting her in becoming a more healthier "me" so that she can find the "we" that really fits.

If you feel like you are losing yourself in a relationship, you probably are. It is time to readjust or get out. No one can control us unless we allow it. And sometimes things we don't like wear great disguises. As Tabatha says, controlling behavior can at first appear as "kindness," but kindness does not obligate us to stay or enter into relationships we don't want to. We have to be willing to look at how we are allowing ourselves to be treated and how we are treating others — does it embody love? Have we traded desire for security, or let someone else set the terms? In any romantic relationship, no one should be "one up" on the other. Both people in the pair remain their own "shoe."

> "I expected to be done with college now and already be a leader in the workplace, but I had so much planned and invested around the 'us' that I lost track of doing things for myself."
>
> Sales representative, 29, divorced and remarried, New York

He Said/She Said

As a general rule, guys are fixers, and girls are feelers. Of course, there are exceptions, but for the most part a frustrating thing about heterosexual relationships is that men's and women's brains are very different. This makes us behave, communicate, and love differently.

To demonstrate, how about a little "he said/she said"? Lucky for us, the following couple agreed to share their separate stories of how personal growing pains and issues almost came between them.

"HE SAID: WE DON'T HAVE TO FIGHT OR FLIGHT" by Tim, 25

DECLARATION: *The iron-fist approach and ultimatums*
are the best step to destroying a good relationship.

My girlfriend and I have just crossed the two-year mark in our relationship. Several months ago, we were discussing our future and some mental timelines for our career and life goals. Along came the crack in the flood wall that would eventually break open the dam. You see, I have a fantastic career that I like and that pays very well; whereas, Michelle is in the corporate world doing work she doesn't like. All of a sudden our relationship turned into a constant conversation about what she was going to do with her life and how I would fit into it. I think it was hard for her to see me go to a job that I love while she struggled to find her passion.

I am aware that relationships are all about compromise and sacrifice from both sides, so I was open to talking about what it would take for her to be happy. But the more we talked about her unhappiness and confusion about what she wanted, the worse it got. She thought she wanted to get into speech pathology, which meant she'd have to move away for school — and she wanted me to go with her. She was asking me to give up my dream for a career pursuit that she wasn't even 100 percent sure about.

She agreed to stay but wanted a timeline as to when I'd be ready to move "for her." I quoted her three to four years. But then some amazing things have been happening at my job, indicating that staying at this company could offer me a lucrative and enjoyable career — and fantastic opportunities for me to be able to provide a very good life for her and our future family.

When I pulled back from my initial timeline, there were tears and confusion. I panicked and couldn't stand to see her upset, so I reverted to my three- to four-year estimation. I have a difficult time seeing my sweetheart cry, and I went into "complete sacrifice mode" to get her back to happy. The resulting problem was that my own feelings of unhappiness were setting in. The more I thought about it, the more I realized that

Michelle wasn't looking for compromise, which just wasn't fair to me. The way I saw it was that I was going to be the base of financial support for us so that she could be free to pursue anything she wanted.

I always knew how to take care of her, but when the crisis-related panic attacks started, I had no idea what to do. Before I knew it, her quarter-life crisis kicked into high gear, and I found myself totally in love with a beautiful woman who felt I pushed her into making a decision between me and her career.

She wasn't forgetting about me and my career deliberately. I discovered she has an internal "deadline" when she felt she had to have all of her major goals accomplished (marriage, kids, career). Almost impossible by any standard — but how do I convince her of that?

I am constantly fighting off the urge to jump in, take over, and make her problems go away. I've learned to fight the urge to respond when she's talking because what she's actually doing is using me to "talk it out." There have been several times when she has been venting to me about how confused she is, and without me speaking a word she has a revelation about how she really feels about the situation simply by verbalizing it.

What I am starting to finally see is that it was never about me, it was about her. The pressures that females feel to "have it all" is nothing to take lightly or take for granted. Men need to be aware of just how influential this can be and how helpless our ladies are to harness the feelings it creates. The iron-fist approach and ultimatums are the best step to destroying a good relationship. We don't have to fight or flight. The best thing we can do is stand by their side, and just slightly behind them, letting them take the lead, but being there to help them up if they slip.

"SHE SAID: I WAS TAKING LOVE FOR GRANTED" by Michelle, 25

DECLARATION: *By becoming so focused on the few aspects of my life that weren't working, I was blinded from what was.*

I recently realized the internal deadlines I put on myself almost cost me the most important thing in my life: a relationship with a good man who loves me. At twenty-four I reached a point where I was completely lost and frustrated, and it bled into my relationship. You see, the problem was my boyfriend has a job he loves — and although I am happy for him, every day I was reminded of what I didn't have. It got to the point where I couldn't stand it anymore. I decided I wanted to go away to study speech pathology, but he did not want to leave his job. I felt completely trapped — not by him, but by the lack of direction I felt. It was as if I had to choose between the love of my life and the chance at having a successful future. I somehow felt that going away to school to pursue a career was the easier road, yet I knew in my heart that it was going to be the hardest journey of my life — and I wasn't even certain it was what I wanted.

It was on a Sunday morning that I left. I just felt like I needed to do something. As I closed the door behind me, sobbing, I feared I may have just lost my soul mate, and for what? To pursue yet another career path I wasn't sure about?

I started driving without a destination. I knew I needed to talk with someone, but I didn't know who to turn to. I didn't want to talk to my mom for fear that she'd tell me to follow the path of independence and self-success, and I'd actually have to really leave Tim. But I didn't know who would be better at a time like this; so I bit the bullet and drove to my parents' house. I had forgotten how great my mom can be in these situations.

My mom shared with me her experiences growing up and in her twenties. What she was able to teach me was that you can't always plan life. Life just happens. I had heard people say that so many times before, but it wasn't until that day that I really understood what it meant in the scope of my own life. I always saw myself being successful in a career that I was passionate about and meeting the love my life somewhere along the way. However, Tim came into my life sooner than expected. I realize now that I cannot plan *my* life anymore — I need to look forward to *our* life.

There were many realizations that she helped me see that day, many of which weren't necessarily a reflection of my mom's life experiences. Instead, she opened my eyes to the realities of life as a woman. She helped me see that making a hasty and panicked decision would be something I'd regret later. I began to realize that even though I am undecided on my career path, I am absolutely sure of the way I feel about my boyfriend…and I was pushing him away.

After our heart-to-heart, I quickly drove back to the apartment I shared with my boyfriend, hoping he didn't hate me for being such a drama queen. I walked in and told him I realized I had a mental separation between "me and him," rather than an outlook of "us" as a single unit. By setting myself on a deadline to fulfill so many expectations, I was giving myself no breathing room whatsoever. In his arms, I realized Tim has always given me breathing room — I am where I want to be.

Tim and Michelle are a great success story. And their two stories make clear the different ways men and women think and relate, as well as how couples can overcome these differences — with patience, love, and understanding. As you saw in Tim's story, guys are problem solvers by nature. They see a problem and they want to fix it. But as Tim learned, Michelle talked with him not in order to be fixed, but to vent, reflect, understand, and then when she was done, perhaps hear some loving words of reassurance. Women can get frustrated when men don't "get" this, and men can get frustrated when their helpful "fixing" only seems to make things worse. However, if we recognize the different expectations men and women often have, they can be shifted.

> "My boyfriend really tried to tell me that a lot of my expectations about life are unrealistic. I really tried to give up my expectations, but instead I just gave *him* up."
>
> Student and retail salesperson, 23, recovering from a breakup, Canada

As Tim and Michelle demonstrate so well, men can learn to sit still and listen for emotional "girlfriend" conversations, but women also have girlfriends and mothers they can turn to for this. We can't expect men to be our "girlfriends." Women can appreciate men for the ways they do express love (sometimes by patiently curbing their impulse to "fix"), and men can appreciate that women aren't jammed garbage disposals; you can't always fix us. It's incumbent on each person in a relationship to fix him- or herself.

Of course, this isn't just a gender issue. We all develop individual communication styles and have our own expectations (and baggage). Surviving as a couple means being clear about your expectations (for yourself and your mate), communicating them, and striving to understand and provide what the other person needs. Gay relationships, for instance, can have all the same dynamics and negotiations as heterosexual unions, but with the added temptation to assume that the other person "gets" you just because he or she is the same sex. In summary, when it comes to relationships, we all have to do our own work in learning how to understand ourselves and the people we love.

RELATIONSHIP 101

There are four crucial things a couple can practice to maintain a healthy intimate relationship. This is an exercise that you can do with your partner. I encourage you to let him or her read it and then have a "practice" conversation. Pick a topic or issue that is important to you or that you are frequently at odds with each other about. Then use this four-step process and notice if your communication and understanding of each other shifts.

1. Communicate: Honestly and calmly articulate thoughts, feelings, and expectations without blame, defensiveness, or manipulation. Each person should be allowed to fully

express themselves. Be explicit about how you desire the other to meet your needs.

2. Listen: Hear *exactly* what your partner is saying, not what you think your partner is saying. Resist the urge to fix or advise your partner or defend yourself.

3. Reflect: Repeat back to your partner what you think he or she is feeling or expressing. This confirms that you understand accurately.

4. Commit: After both people have expressed, listened, and been heard, brainstorm a next-step or action plan that resolves the issue or eases concern, then commit to it together. Sometimes the game plan is as simple as committing to this communication process each time you get into a disagreement or just feel "off."

Love or Career?

Michelle writes, "It was as if I had to choose between the love of my life and the chance at having a successful future." Another issue that comes up for twenty-something couples is balancing their desires for a lasting relationship or marriage with careers that are just starting to gain momentum. And quite often, they experience this dilemma exactly as Michelle expresses it: since it doesn't seem like we can have both, do we choose love or success?

> "I was always the girl who always said I would never get married... and then I met my husband. Funny how things work out."
>
> *Manager, 24, married, Ohio*

However, why is it that having the love of our life is not success? Attracting and maintaining a relationship with someone you are deeply connected with takes a lot of self-work, and it requires intimacy, vulnerability, courage, and selflessness. Equating "success" only with prestige in one's career is something I see among many twenty somethings. But this seems to me like a narrow, convoluted definition of success, and one that is very hard to live up to.

> "I've learned to seek wholeness, self-love, precious support, creativity, and fulfillment that bring true peace of mind; rather than status, money, approval, or other empty symbols of success I once chased."
>
> *Office manager, 26, single, Michigan*

As Michelle did, when we identify a successful area of our lives that we are not appreciating because we are focusing on something that isn't "successful" yet, we should shift our focus and expectations. Life does not unfold according to our deadlines.

If our career is booming but all we do is despair over our lack of a boyfriend or girlfriend, then aren't we undermining the happiness and contentment we might be enjoying from our work? By allowing negative feelings to overwhelm us, we risk losing out on relishing all the good things we've achieved. In Michelle's case, she saw that by despairing over her lack of a career she risked losing the person she loved. Michelle was wise enough to realize that "love or career" is a false choice.

How would you feel if you lost the thing you loved because you were worried about something you don't even have? Would it be worth it? I doubt it. So if you are lucky to have someone or something in your life that you love, nourish it. Don't take it for granted. And if you feel like you have nothing, I beg to differ. We all have things to be grateful for, things we cherish. And these things are the corner pieces from which we build our lives.

What can confuse us is when "success" appears in a different way or at a different time than we expect. "Having it all" is not the key to happiness; choosing to *be* happy about whatever you happen to have is. Focusing on what you *don't* have is not the way to get what you want. Instead, use one success to build more.

Appreciate what you have and keep your definition of "success" wide and inclusive of all that you deeply desire.

GETTING TO "I DO"

There are many paths down the aisle. I never thought mine would involve two engagements. Unless you have an arranged marriage, you never can truly plan the how, what, when, where, and why of getting married. Marriage does not happen on a schedule or time-line. It takes two people who want to get married for marriage to work — and if one of you is ready be-fore the other (yes, I mean you, ladies), no amount of pushing or putting pic-tures of rings on the refrigerator will help.

> "I thought it would be easier to find companionship with a woman without having to immediately start thinking about marriage. Can't we just get to know each other?"
>
> Analyst, 26,
> single and love it, Maryland

While I realize there are exceptions to this statement, in general women are more gung ho about getting engaged than men. The societally imposed "have it all" expectation combined with our biological urge to "find a mate" prime us for engagement. For twenty-something women who are building a career and also want to get married and possibly have children, feeling like there is a timeline to secure a ring and a date is very common. As women with biological clocks ticking loudly, we need to listen even more carefully to the voice of our intuition. We need to ask ourselves if we are truly ready or just think we should be. We need to look at the person we hope will get down on one knee for who he is today and not expect to change him. And we must be clear with ourselves about what we are willing to bring to a marriage. What kind of wife are we ready to commit to being? It's easy to get caught up in the fantasy of get-ting married and lose sight of the reality of what it's really like.

So before we say yes or do the asking, we need to have several very honest conversations with our potential brides or grooms. Issues like religion, whether or not to have children, commingling finances, savings and retirement plans, extended family and how to care for aging parents, merging families and where to spend the holidays, long-term goals, values, career and home life balance, time with friends, where to live, and even living behaviors are imperative to discuss before you even consider engagement. These topics are far more important than "chicken or fish?"

Getting to "I do" is just as much a logical decision as it is a romantic one. Guys are a little better at keeping this in perspective. So what motivates a guy to pop the question? I recently asked a group of engaged or married twenty-something men how they decided to get married. The men's answers lacked Hallmark sentimentality, but they made perfect sense. Men are romantic, but it's usually not the romantic part of them that decides to marry; it's the rational part. So guys, if you are feeling pressured to get married, rather than an actual desire, *listen* to that.

Twenty-eight-year-old Stewart shares: "Looking back on my decision to propose to Alex, I can't believe I fretted so much about the decision. In no particular order, these were the types of thoughts that ran through my head — 'Am I really ready to get married?' 'Alex is great, but what if there's someone who's greater out there?' 'Is it wrong that I feel like I'm settling?' Maybe that's what they mean by the expression 'settle down' — that is, settling on the fact that this person is not perfect, but you're realizing that this is the best that you've come across so far. And in my case, this was true by a long shot.

"Looking back on these thoughts, I see now how immature it was. While I still believe in the concept of settling down, I think a better word for it is 'acceptance.' That is, accepting that the person you're selecting isn't perfect in every way, but her pluses clearly outweigh the minuses. The pluses of the physical attraction, the conversational ease, the common interests, values, and ambitions, and her tolerance of my idiosyncrasies far outweigh the minuses. I'm also accepting that I don't know what the future will hold, but I'm betting on the fact that the two of us can grow together and can a) work through our differences and improve each other, and b) change together. It is worth the investment."

Stewart's thoughts don't ooze with red-hot romance, but they are honest, real, and *very* common. Marriage is a partnership, not a movie. And he is right, no one is perfect and there are no guarantees. A relationship takes work, dedication, honesty, and an acceptance of the person you are with.

Twenty-seven-year-old Brendan says: "When it came down to finally popping the question, it was about three things: the right girl, the right time, and a certain collection of external pressures. I now understand that asking a woman to marry you is not as simple as just finding the right girl; I believe that timing plays just as big of a role. I was done with college, was starting to think about having a family, had financial security, and most important, was in a career that I loved. I knew marriage was inevitable; it was time."

I know, I know. Brendan doesn't have a future as a greeting card writer, but he is being honest. Also, he's right that stepping into the commitment of marriage does involve the right timing as well as the right person. Taking vows together is meant to be *for life*. So if you are hesitant, maybe you are not ready to say yes or to ask. You'll know when you are, since having the confidence to make such a serious commitment requires a strong sense of self and of personal (and sometimes financial) security. There are few promises we'll ever make as big, and when it's right, we usually know.

"MY HAPPY ENDING" by Jonathan, 29

DECLARATION: *Marriage isn't something you can plan for. At some point, you just know. It's really that simple.*

In my early to mid-twenties, I knew I was not ready for a serious relationship. I was not sure that I ever wanted to get married down the road either. My parents' marriage was not exactly a great advertisement for heading to the altar. Plus, at twenty-five, spending the *rest* of my life with one woman scared me to death. And truly my main focus was working my way up the corporate ladder and making money. So when it came to dating, I just wanted to have fun.

But then at around twenty-seven, something happened. I was settled in my career, I was starting to get sick of the same old Saturday night routine of going out with the guys, and I was actually starting to want a relationship (of course, I did not admit that to the guys). I really wanted kids too. Not tomorrow, but someday.

One Friday night I was out with friends and noticed an attractive girl. She smiled at me — green light. I made my way over and began a conversation. Her name was Jen. "And that is not short for Jennifer, it's just Jen," she informed me with a sweet smile. We talked for a while and I started to feel a special connection.

Fast-forward two years — I knew I loved Jen, but some part of me was still scared of that next step: marriage. I wanted some kind of crystal ball that would show me 100 percent that this was the right thing to do — that thirty years later we would not be sleeping with our backs toward each other and fighting over petty things. But there was no crystal ball, only the concerned look that I would see in my girlfriend's face each time we left another friend's wedding.

I tricked myself into believing that I was stalling for more stability, that I should wait until I am able to buy a house before we get married, and, wow, if I save a little bit longer I could afford a better ring, and so on. I had many reasons — well, really false justifications — to deal with my fears.

Until one Sunday afternoon when I went to teach my mother how to use email (talk about a generation gap). After informing her that "spam" is not just meat that comes in a can, she confronted me, "So when are you going to ask that amazing girlfriend of yours to marry you before she gets impatient and leaves you?" I was floored. First, because the most intimate conversation that my mom and I have ever had about my love life was about who I was going to ask to the prom and even *that* was awkward. And second, because my mom hit on my other deepest fear: losing Jen.

I bumbled around for words a bit, and then I just lowered my head, defeated, and mumbled, "I don't know." My mom then asked me what I was scared of. Again, "I don't know." She took my hand, tipped my chin, and looked into my eyes. As I looked into hers, I saw tears. She quietly asked, "Is it because of your father and me? Has our relationship made you scared of marriage?" In the past, I could flawlessly lie to my mother about why I was out too late or who broke the neighbor's window, but in this moment, I had to tell the truth: "Well, maybe a little…yes."

She then said to me what years of therapy could probably not accomplish: "Son, please don't let our past be your future. Your father and I did not have the connection you and Jen have. We married because we had to, not because we wanted to, and we've been blaming each other ever since. It is not marriage that has made us this way; we were like this from the beginning. You have the power to make your relationship what *you* want — you are not destined to be like us. In fact, I believe in my heart you are destined to be different."

One week later I proposed to Jen. Our wedding is next month.

10. WORK AND CAREER

The puzzle pieces of twenty-something life that are often the hardest to put together revolve around the question, "What do I want to do with my life?" Career is hands down the number-one issue among twenty somethings. From not knowing your passion, to not making enough money, to not being respected, to wanting to make a difference, to not being able to find a job — there is more confusion and dissatisfaction with this generation of twenty somethings than ever before. Why? It all comes back to expectations. As a society we work more than ever before. "What do you do?" is often the first question you're asked when you meet someone. And if you don't like your answer to that question, you are probably experiencing an Expectation Hangover.

In this chapter, I discuss how to create job satisfaction, how to overcome the fear of quitting a bad job or pursuing a good one, and how to start a business. But first let's tackle the most popular career advice given out today, which is: "Follow your passion, and you will be happy and successful."

Yeah, right! Most twenty somethings do not even know what their passion is, and yet the concept that each of us is born with a fire burning in our bellies for a particular career has spread like a bad flu. Many twenty somethings obsess about finding their passion — believing that without it they have no purpose in life.

> "I spent my time and energy for the past four years going after a career that I now realize I chose for all the wrong reasons. Now I have no idea where to go or how to proceed. Since I'm working on myself now, I figure I'll just deal with it until I reach a better place and revisit my options, hopefully having a better idea of what my life's purpose is."
>
> Account coordinator, 22,
> serious relationship, Wisconsin

Or, as Tasha says, "I am a twenty-five-year-old dental hygienist. I have a great career with an excellent salary. I am engaged to the most wonderful man in the world. But I am striving to 'have it all' — including passion. I love what I do but I am not passionate about it. I do not want to be a clinical dental hygienist all my life, but I don't know what I want to do. I look at my fiancé who loves his volunteer rescue squad. He would have a fit and break out in a rash if he could not be an EMT on an ambulance. I look at my co-worker who loves yoga. She practices yoga three to four times per week and talks about yoga seven days a week. I look at my boss who lives and breathes dentistry. As for me... there is nothing that I do in life that I am passionate about. I don't have any activity or subject that excites me beyond a few weeks. Just because I have no passion, does that mean I have no purpose in life? How do I reach my inner passion?"

SEPARATE PURPOSE FROM PASSION

From my perspective, Tasha already "has it all" — she is just having trouble seeing that because she is focusing on the buzzword: passion. She has a job she likes, and she is in love. I would disagree that Tasha has nothing in life she is passionate about — and I hope her fiancé would too! And if a single activity only interests her for a week, perhaps she is passionate about exploring different things, and what's wrong with that? Passion is a matter of perspective and can be created in many different aspects of our lives. It's even possible to approach a "mundane" job with even more enthusiasm. One of Tasha's purposes now may be to have compassion for her patients. Anyone who has been to the dentist would agree, having a friendly dental hygienist makes what could be a rather miserable experience actually enjoyable. It's important that we don't underestimate the work we do, despite how "passionless" it can feel at times. Avoid confusing passion for a career with your purpose in life.

Life purpose is *not* determined simply by who signs our paychecks. It is about learning lessons about ourselves and our lives — to smell, taste, touch, see, feel, and experience. Purpose in life includes our entire lives, not just our working lives. If we look for life purpose solely in a career, then we are forgetting that life purpose is also expressed by falling in love, laughing, dancing, traveling, having families, connecting with friends, celebrating holidays and birthdays, and so on. If life purpose really was found only in our work, we would be robots.

> "Why can't just having a job be good enough?"
>
> *Administrative assistant, 28, serious relationship, Illinois*

But we are not robots. We are multidimensional human beings, and our work is just something we do; it is *not* who we *are*. Granted, having a job you like makes life more pleasurable. When I was working a job I hated, I used to get terrible Sunday night blues, and there were knots in my stomach when I got off the elevator Monday morning. Though it can take a lot of noodle throwing, we all can strive to find a career path we truly love — it just may take time.

> "Passion is an unwavering state of being in all circumstances: a passion to be free and impart that feeling to others, a passion to give and support others no matter how seemingly large or small the impact, a passion for compassion with oneself and others regardless of circumstance. Rich passion is embodied in a person, it is not something that can be described as merely a hobby — and it's not a job."
>
> Substitute teacher and bartender, 26, married, California

However, what we do does not constitute or define our purpose in life; rather, it is one of the many ways in which we fulfill it. Our jobs provide opportunities to actively realize our purpose in life by expressing our creativity, our compassion for others, and our desire to help society. For instance, I believe my purpose in life is a personal, individual journey in which I am consistently learning lessons and sharing with others. To fulfill my purpose, my life's work is to allow that to be reflected in everything I do, not just in what I am paid to do. If you are at a loss for your purpose, consider that your purpose now is discovery. Allow it to unfold, rather than constantly questioning it.

Passion Is a Journey

We spend a big chunk of our lives working, so it's natural to want to love what we do, or at the very least like it. But most of us assume passion arrives like a thunderbolt of inspiration, instantly spreading wonderfully warm feelings and clarity about our careers.

But do you know what the word "passion" truly means? *Webster's* defines "passion" as "powerful feeling" and "great enthusiasm."

Further definitions include "emotions as distinguished from reason," "suffering," and "anger and rage." Passion is not logical; it does not express itself in tidy, left-brain career steps. Nor is passion easy. The road to passion of "great enthusiasm" may require some "suffering." You may experience "anger and rage" and "emotions distinguished from reason" to reach the "powerful feeling" of discovering passionate work.

Living out all aspects of the definition of passion was absolutely true for me. I did not discover what I enjoy doing until my late twenties, and I was not able to make a full-time career out of it until almost thirty. Along the way, I encountered frustration, disappointment, jobs I hated, dead-end career paths, and having to do things I didn't really want to. The most valuable thing that I learned is that passion is a journey. I realized passion in a job takes preparation, experience, a great support system, and, yes, often a few emotions distinguished from reason.

But just being passionate about

> "I wanted to quit my first job after two weeks, I was so frustrated. But I have stuck with it for almost two years to get the learning experience and because I knew I had to give it a chance. Perhaps I haven't found my perfect place yet, but I'm finding out more about life and myself in the process."
>
> Salesperson, 25, dating, Wyoming

something is not a formula for fast success, and if you try to rise too fast, you might miss important lessons along the way. Having passion doesn't keep us from experiencing pit stops in our career: sacrifices, fear, doubt, confusion, lack of money, and jobs we don't like. Don't let being stuck in one of these pit stops make you think you lack passion! Remember, passion is more a way of being than a destination, and it does not create satisfaction or ideal employment all by itself.

A career path is not always a joy ride. And for some people, their passions never fit the nine-to-five world. That is okay. As long as our jobs afford us an acceptable quality of life — pay what we need, are reasonably interesting, aren't abusive, foster a pleasant work environment, don't require us to be workaholics — what is wrong with that? Why not be grateful for our jobs, rather than question them? In fact, there are plenty of ways to improve the quality of our work lives without looking for a new job or obsessing about career passion.

JOB SATISFACTION: IT'S NOT WHAT YOU DO, IT'S HOW YOU DO IT

Forget your career goals and expectations for a moment. What's your job like right now? Do you work passionately — not necessarily all the time, but enough to enjoy what you do? Whatever you want for the future, you have the power to make the present better right now. Your state of mind is a choice.

Have you ever met someone working an ordinary job — say, the guy who takes your dry cleaning — who does it with such genuine, smiling good cheer that you leave feeling better? Do you really think it's a passion for dry cleaning that inspires that person? Possibly, but more likely he makes a choice every day to bring joy into his job. Perhaps he takes pride in doing his job well, no matter what, or perhaps he likes people. Whatever the reason, he's decided to bring enthusiasm to his work, and you can too. Usually, no matter how much you say you hate your job, you can find things to enjoy about it, places where it's challenging or creative, new things to learn, innovative ideas you can generate, or people to interact with. At the very least, you can leave each day without knots in your stomach! If you can't find any redeeming aspects in your job, then you probably need to start looking for another job (see the exercise on page 239).

> "It's an awful feeling to walk into a building and want to turn around and walk right back out again."
>
> Investment banker, 26, dating casually, New York

"I HATED MY JOB" by Justin, 27

DECLARATION: *I always thought the answer
was finding a different job, until I realized
the real answer was just deciding to be different.*

I hated my job. As I drove to work each day, I could feel my zest for life deflating. I constantly questioned what was wrong with me. I picked an industry that I thought I liked, but now that I was working in it, I had my doubts. People talk about passion, but I didn't feel it. The only excitement I got from my job was leaving at the end of each day. I am normally an optimistic person, but each day I felt myself dying a little bit. It was hard to see all my buddies kicking butt in their careers and enjoying it — they actually feel like they matter to their company. For me, on the other hand, it was life in cubicle hell, wondering when I was going to have some big epiphany about what the heck I was doing with my life. My life was like an episode of *The Office* sans the funny commentary and cute receptionist.

> "I've learned to vocalize what I want and what I need help with, which is a very scary thing to do when you are first starting out. But I've found out that people listen, and your managers actually *want* you to be happy because they realize that you'll perform better when they let you do work that you would like to do."
>
> *Corporate banking analyst,
> 23, engaged, Pennsylvania*

One of the biggest issues I had was my boss. He is a miserable person and likes to make sure other people are miserable as well — I think he puts depressants in the break room water cooler. And in terms of what I do, I was not challenged anymore, and I don't respect the work the company does, anyway. So why haven't I looked for another job? Well, I have — but I can't seem to find anything.

Finally, I had an "aha" moment — only it was not in the form of a job offer or an awakening to what the meaning of my life is. I was at poker night with a bunch of my buddies, and everyone was talking about work. One of my friends, who has known me since college, asked how my job was going and I rambled off something negative and pathetic. He slammed down his beer bottle on the table — and he gave me some tough love. He told me that my attitude sucked, I wasn't the same fun guy to be around (he actually compared me to blockhead Charlie Brown), and I wasn't doing much to change anything. He reminded me that I was making good money with health benefits, and that my hours were reasonable. To really drive it home, he asked me if I thought life was supposed to be like it is on TV, where work is full of expensed fancy lunches, hot secretaries, and high-powered meetings at big conference tables. He ended his sermon by saying, "J, be a man — work is work. It is what you make of it. If you don't like your job, then be the one to do something to make it different. A job is so that you can live, so suck it up and start living, man!" Finally, and I think this was the beer talking because I don't know where this came from, he quoted Gandhi and said, "Be the change you want to see."

We all had a good laugh about this little intervention, but I couldn't help but see the truth in what he was saying.

So I made my new job to change my old one. I made a pact with myself that I had the power to make it more enjoyable. In school, I was the class clown, I made people laugh, and I have completely turned that part of me off. So I revved it back up — I started cracking jokes, making people smile, and most important, taking myself lighter. I've already seen how it is changing the office vibe. People are actually excited to see me. I'm even beginning to think that one of my purposes may be to bring some life back into this cubicle hell!

I am not trying to make a difference "out there" anymore; I am trying to make a difference in my own life. I get my work done and disengage from the office bs, I'm planning a kick-ass vacation, and instead of just surfing the Web, I am calling people and setting up networking lunches to see what else is out there. But now that I am actually enjoying my job more, I don't feel so desperate to leave. I guess Gandhi had a point.

Justin is an example of someone who kept waiting for the Passion and Purpose Police to come and haul him away to his dream job.

Once he realized, thanks to poker night, that he was the one responsible for why he hated his job, he began to see possibilities. Like Justin, sometimes we find ourselves in an uninspiring job, and then make the worst of a bad situation by not taking responsibility for our attitude. We wait for passion to arrive, and keep waiting, doing nothing to create it. One twenty-nine-year-old says, "I was passionate about my career when I first started, but the spark has fizzled as I've gotten older . . . and I wish I could get that spark back." Certainly, reevaluating your job or career path is necessary, but before you pack up your cubicle, reevaluate your current job: how can *you* reignite the spark inside yourself, rather than relying on a job to provide that spark? Is the problem not so much the job, but that every morning you leave your passion and sense of humor at the door when you clock in?

"I HATE MY JOB" SURVIVAL KIT

You hate your job. Nothing about it feels right. You have no passion. Okay — but you still need to pay your bills. Here are some quick tips and "to-dos" to help you thrive at a job you feel like you are barely surviving, as well as suggestions for taking steps toward more possibilities.

1. Up your quality-of-life (QOL) quotient at the office: Make aesthetic changes by adding pictures, bringing in flowers, getting a cool mouse pad, rearranging your desk, and so on. Then make attitude changes: Remember, your reality each day is created by your thoughts. Approach the day with a positive attitude, "play" more with your co-workers, think graciously about your job and the things it affords you (such as health care and internet access), and so on.

2. Reap the benefits: Take advantage of health benefits if you have them and get all your checkups; enroll in your company's 401(k) plan, if offered; and use your vacation days.

3. Rescue your résumé: If you really want to get out of your job, do more than post your résumé online and surf the Web. Hire a career coach, and at least get help writing your résumé, such as with a résumé service like www.JobBound.com.

4. Network: Research people to meet, not just job postings. Set up informational interviews, cold call, send emails, and join online networking groups.

5. Make an impact: Want to make a difference in the world? Start with the people in your office. They matter too!

Are the Dues You're Paying Too High?

Livebreatheeatsleepwork. Has your career swallowed your life? Are you paying your dues and then some? Donald Trump thinks you should. Many successful entrepreneurs and businesspeople wear their sleepless nights, overtime, missed holidays, and neglected personal lives like badges of honor. Some actually get a rush out of it; the long hours are just a sign of their total commitment to their goals. And if the symptoms we're suffering aren't any worse than being tired and perhaps a little out of shape, we assume there's no real problem.

> "To do something that positively impacts someone else's life is the only type of passion in life that has eternal satisfaction."
>
> Business owner,
> 29, single, Massachusetts

Some occupations, because of their importance or complexity, require a pretty hefty personal sacrifice — those in the military, investment bankers, doctors, lawyers, and more — and they frequently command our highest respect. We may think, if we aren't sacrificing as much, is what we are doing worthy of the same admiration?

To some extent, every occupation requires us to "pay our dues," or suffer through a period of working harder for less pay and reward, which isn't fun. By paying our dues we gain the real-world experience and expertise we need to earn the perks and respect of our

> "I left a job at a social service agency because of how I was treated. When I told the staff, they all told me they wished they had the guts to leave too. I realized that my mental health must come first and no job is worth that."
>
> *Social worker, 29, married, Florida*

chosen profession. But how high are the dues you are paying, what are you willing to pay, and what do you expect to get in return? Your answers to these questions will determine what you should do if you're unhappy.

However, most often, twenty somethings aren't sure what to think: they don't like paying dues, but then they think maybe that's just the price for what they want and they need to change their attitude. Or, maybe their unhappiness means their profession isn't right for them, and they should find another. Or maybe, the dues *are* too high, and even though in theory they'd like to be a doctor (or lawyer and so on), the professional sacrifices are too much; they'd be happier with a less-consuming job in the same field.

The first thing to do is to *try* and change your perspective and attitude by implementing the QOL suggestions (page 239). Change your perception and see what you learn. If you successfully change your attitude and are going to work in a good mood, and you still feel in your gut that this career is not the right fit, then it's time to explore other options. Give where you have landed a chance before you job jump.

Another common dissatisfaction is not feeling respected enough. As this twenty-four-year-old describes, "Being underestimated at work and not being given challenges that I know I can handle because the higher-ups feel I 'don't have enough experience' is incredibly frustrating." Rather than stay frustrated, see this as an opportunity: seek advice from others, learn from their mistakes, and find ways to demonstrate your competence. Remember, you don't have all the responsibilities of the "higher-ups" yet either, so you're freer to experiment, extend beyond your reach, and fail without serious consequences. Enjoy this.

There is no "normal" when it comes to anything — we are all unique, and we have different thresholds for what we are willing and able to endure. Pay attention to your mental and physical health, as it is a good indicator of whether or not you are pushing beyond your own "paying your dues" threshold. Is your well-being worth that paycheck? Is the end result and doing what you're "supposed" to do worth the dues? In your eagerness to succeed, are you trying to fulfill unreasonable expectations (yours or someone else's) and paying too much? It helps to look around at everyone you work with, particularly the thirty- and forty-year-olds who have already "made it." What kind of lives do they lead? Are they happy? Or do you suffer a sea of dirty looks when you leave the office "early" at 7 PM?

A twenty-six-year-old woman writes: "I had a boss who worked around the clock and is incredibly smart, successful, and respected. He was always pushing harder and harder. He has two young kids that he virtually never saw, and his wife is nearly a single parent. Everything he ever does is planned by his assistant and in his Outlook calendar, including his romantic anniversary getaway with his wife. I was somehow swallowed up by his energy and enthusiasm in the beginning and began

> "I expected to be happier in my career. The only thing I can think to do to change that is to find a new career. But then I am scared that I will also not like that career either, and then what do I do? So for now, I grin and bear it and try to make the best of things."
>
> *Engineer, 24, single and love it, Texas*

working the hours he worked with the determination he did. Three years later, I looked in the mirror and realized I had neglected my boyfriend, family, friends, and most of all myself for something I now hated. I love my job and many of the people I work with, but I have grown to resent it because it owned me. I had to stop. Over the past six months, I have made great strides in controlling the way I work — I set limits, I exercise in the morning before I start work, and I am working more remotely. For so long I felt like I was a victim to it, when really I just needed to take control back."

The All-Important Work-Life Balance

"Paying your dues" is supposed to be a limited experience. For short periods of time, we can survive out of balance. But a life with no life other than work and big personal sacrifices is not quality. Opt out. We must set boundaries for ourselves and maintain a personal life. Becoming a workaholic is a toxic habit. Come in at a set hour, take a lunch break every day, and leave at a reasonable time. No ifs, ands, or buts. No one will tell you to take a break because you are doing too much work — your boss and co-workers will probably just expect more. Make sure your job supports your life, not the other way around. Enjoy vacations and spend time with friends, significant others, and family — these are priorities as much as work. Your company will not fall apart without you! And if you are self-employed, it's imperative to separate your work and home life — or else they'll blur together and life will become one big to-do list!

> "Having a passion means wanting to do something to the exclusion of all else. However, sometimes being really great at one thing is not worth the sacrifice of relationships, other interests, or your health."
>
> Consultant, 28,
> serious relationship, Georgia

"PAYING MY DUES" by Jeannette, 27

DECLARATION: *From the outside I had it all; my life was picture perfect. The inside was a different story altogether.*

I graduated from college with a degree in accounting and immediately began working for the largest accounting firm in the world. It was the "perfect" job. However, I spent so many hours working that I did not have the time or the energy to do much of anything else in my life. I was all about work. The times that I left at a decent hour (6 or 7 PM), I felt guilty or uncomfortable because I knew that my seniors or managers were unhappy that I was leaving "early."

I was constantly exhausted, irritable, had trouble sleeping, wasn't eating properly, had a negative attitude, and suffered from terrible stomach pains and migraines. At one point I developed a rash on my chest and arms that neither my general doctor nor dermatologist could diagnose. Deep down I knew that my body was telling me something, but I stayed.

I felt that if I left my job, then I would be considered a failure at my own goals. I was so focused on making it work because in my mind working for this company was something I was striving for since I was sixteen years old. My family was so impressed with my accomplishments I felt that if I changed, then they would see me as a failure. So I convinced myself I was in my early twenties and was "paying my dues."

> "When I first got into the workforce, I wanted to impress my manager, so I started taking work home at night and on the weekends. Slowly, my work life started taking over my personal life. Now I live under the rules that work stays at work . . . and my manager is still happy with my performance."
>
> *Internal auditor, 25, single and hate it, Ohio*

Eventually, I reached a point where I had to make a change or I was going to lose it. The first and most drastic thing I did was quit my job with no backup plan. I knew that for things to get better in my life, I had to leave my job. After dissecting the negativity that had consumed me, I realized I could choose to look at it as a mistake or as a series of positive experiences that I could learn from. I chose the latter.

I enrolled in a six-month women's empowerment course and met women who were able to push through challenging situations and move on to the next thing in their lives. I was so moved and inspired by them that I was able to let go of my expectations and old beliefs, and live in my own joy.

One April morning I woke up feeling completely renewed. I actually was smiling for no reason and could not wait to start the day! It was then that I realized that I couldn't even remember the last time I suffered from any of my physical ailments.

> "The stress I am under over work makes me not enjoy the simple things anymore or laugh at the littlest things. I've missed out on many opportunities to meet new people because of my mood or lack of desire to go out or try something new."
>
> Consumer researcher, 28, dating, Illinois

Upon reflection, I think my fear of others seeing me as a failure stems from my parents constantly expressing to my siblings and me that "life is hard" and that "life isn't fair." I guess I was made to believe that life was a struggle, and if I didn't struggle, then I wasn't accomplishing anything. But this is a belief system I was ready to shed — and it feels great!

Currently, I am working as an accountant for a small real-estate investment firm. Since I now have a job with normal working hours, I have the time to enjoy my passions outside of work — and I'm finding there are many! I feel that now that I've let go of so many negatives in my life, it's time to create a foundation that supports me in living life on my terms.

DECIDING TO MAKE A CHANGE: THE FEAR TRIFECTA

If, after careful consideration, we decide the dues we're paying are too high, it's time to quit. So why do we so often stay in jobs much longer than we should? Because of what I call the

"Fear Trifecta." People who are in very demanding jobs that fit a
particular career path, especially if it's a career they studied for in
college or have dreamed about since
adolescence, suffer from this. Jeannette's description of the reasons why
she tolerated her misery as long as she
did are a perfect example of this trifecta in action.

> "There is no such thing as a dream job.
> Nothing is perfect, and you will only know
> if it makes you happy once you try it."
>
> Production assistant, 25,
> single, London, England

First, there is the perceived failure.
When our jobs fit our hoped-for career
goals, we don't want to quit because leaving would seem to negate
our success and doom our dreams and efforts to failure. That is
hogwash — which is why I call this feeling "perceived" failure.
Leaving a job that makes us miserable is not failure, nor does it
doom our careers or waste all our efforts. Looking at it that way
only keeps us in a job we hate. Furthermore, realizing the job we
always wanted isn't actually what we want does not make us terrible decision makers. On the contrary, we should be proud: we
took a chance, worked hard, and followed our dreams. Now, experience has shown us things we couldn't know until we tried, and
we're making a new, better decision.

Of course, it is not just our own perceptions of failure that we
have to deal with. Jeannette believed that her parents would also
see it as a failure if she left her job. When we start thinking along
these lines, we have to remind ourselves that other people can't define success for us. We can't let their perceptions guide our lives
or reality. As Jeannette realized, she had bought in to her parents'
perception of life as "hard," but she could opt out.

Second, there is justification. Jeanette told herself that paying
her dues, no matter the price, was a phase that she needed to endure. Since following our passions does involve sacrifice, justification is easy to slip into. Any time you find yourself justifying

something, consider: are you trying to convince yourself, or do you really believe what you're saying? Think about it, if we know something is right, do we need to defend it? Not usually, so take any justification as a sign that you may need to make a change.

Part three of the trifecta is fear of the future. Our jobs may be bad, but how do we know something else isn't worse? We don't, and Jeannette admitted she quit her job with no "plan B." I love that Jeannette handled this fear by joining a women's empowerment group. How awesome is that! Uncertainty about the future is not an excuse to not find ways to be inspired in the *present*. After all, if our jobs are bad, we at least know that, and moving on could be the best way to access inspiration. Plan B will reveal itself and you too will be "smiling for no reason." Note that Jeannette didn't abandon her career in accounting, either; she merely got a different job that allowed her to better balance her life so that it was filled with a wide variety of passions.

> "I wish someone would have told me that making decisions based on fear — whether that's fear about money, stability, relationships, etc. — would only make me unhappy. Decisions made in spite of fear tend to be the right ones."
>
> *Graphic artist, 25, recovering from a breakup, Virginia*

PURSUING YOUR PASSION

If you have a skill, dream, or desire that you are passionate about pursuing, perhaps the biggest obstacle you will face will be your own fear: fear of failure, fear of asking for help, fear of the unknown, fear of not being secure, and so on. Fear can keep us in bad situations, and also from pursuing our passions. Fear can often be a stronger motivator than the desire for success, stopping us in our tracks before we even find out what we want.

But here is the good news — you have youth on your side, which means you have time to overcome your fears. You can go for something you truly love even if it feels scary. When it comes to going for what we truly love, fear often hides in conditional thinking: the if/then and when/then thoughts that divert us and hold us back, waiting for the right moment. It takes courage to go beyond our fears and act on our desires. We just have to do it. Often taking that first step is the hardest; trust the steps that follow will be easier as long as you have a sense of the direction you are headed and commit to it fully. It takes boldness to risk embarrassing ourselves, to risk rejection. And sometimes, as this next story demonstrates, it takes tragic events to wake us up to the fact that life doesn't last forever, so we need to make the most of *right now*.

> "I'll never forget the day I decided to go with my gut and make the leap to leave my job. I wasn't completely sure how I was going to pay my bills, but to me it was worth it to not be miserable. I slept like a baby that night, and I'm now on a path that is much more 'me.'"
>
> *Recruiter, 28, serious relationship, Maryland*

"SOLID GROUND" by Jon, 29

DECLARATION: *Life is not about living up to other people's expectations. It's about creating your own reality every day.*

I was always an overachiever. I think it had a lot to do with the fact that I came from a dysfunctional family that always argued about money. I drowned myself in schoolwork and extracurricular activities. I believed that if I got into the best school, I would then get the high-paying job that would lead to me being rich, which would make me happy and erase all the bad memories.

I was always good with numbers and after seeing the film *Wall Street*, I figured the logical life choice would be a career in finance, which would get me the fast car, big house, and beautiful woman on my arm.

When I got to Wharton School at Penn, I encountered people the likes of which I previously had never known existed. Here I was, with my pierced ear and Doc Martens boots (remember those?), entering a world full of eighteen-year-old prep-school kids in blue blazers who had their whole lives planned out. They were the sons and daughters of the Wall Street elite, and they spoke in a foreign language, casually tossing words like "arbitrageur," "leverage," and "VC" into conversation. I always felt like a misfit, but I was intent on keeping the focus because of the end goal.

A curious thing happened along the way, however. I found I was spending much more time with my hobby of playing music than going to class or studying. I had taught myself how to play the piano while in high school; I had grown up obsessed with the music of Billy Joel and dreamed of being like him. After all, here was a misfit, a short kid from Long Island who married Christie Brinkley, the most beautiful woman in the world! Since I didn't have a piano in my dorm room, I took up guitar while at Penn, and I spent countless hours learning to play the entire Beatles songbook when I should've been doing spreadsheets.

After a summer internship at an investor magazine, I returned to Wharton sophomore year, excited about moving forward with my education in finance. Again, though, I eventually found myself skipping class so I could play guitar and sing. I even started writing songs of my own.

Then a life-changing moment happened. My idol, Billy Joel, came to Penn as part of his "Master Class" tour. The event was half concert, half Q&A. Through much footwork and good fortune, I obtained a front-row seat in the crowd of over two thousand students.

Two hours into the incredible event, my enthusiastically waving arm got Billy's attention. When he called on me, I asked if I could perform "I've Loved These Days" with him. It was my favorite song, and a lifelong dream. He said yes! The next five minutes were literally an out-of-body experience for me, the greatest high of my life.

I graduated Wharton and started my plum job as an equity trader. While I never forgot about my love for music, it certainly took a backseat to my life on the fast track in New York City. Whatever spare time I had was spent on the couch vegetating or working on my golf game, because of course I needed to play golf well to entertain clients and one day join a stuffy country club in Westchester.

I never really stopped to think about the fact that I wasn't gratified in my career. I was making tons of money and doing what I was "supposed" to be doing, so how could I complain? But there was something missing. It took two other life-changing events to bring things into focus.

The first event was 9/11. This obviously was a wake-up call for people all over the world and especially those of us living in New York City. I realized that I had been missing not only my music but also a part of myself. I started performing at a small venue in downtown Manhattan.

My attention was altered again, by the death of my stepbrother, David. He was thirty-one. David had been a dialysis patient from the time he was seventeen and had received several unsuccessful kidney transplants. He lived every day like it was his last and will always be a great source of inspiration to me. After he died, I took a long, hard look at my life and asked myself what would make me happy.

I walked into my boss's office one day and just said, "I'm done." He wanted to know what competitor had hired me away and what they could do to stop it. They didn't believe me when I told them I was simply walking away from Wall Street to pursue other things. I felt really strange as I walked out of Eleven Madison Avenue for the last time, but I knew I had done the right thing. I was twenty-seven years old, scared, curious, and exhilarated — and I was a musician. Finally, I had ignited the match that would take me on the most incredible journey of my life.

I'm now at the end of my twenty-something journey and entering my thirties with more passion than ever, and no regrets. I used to feel pangs of doubt when I went to visit my old friends in New York and recall how relatively easy it was to make a good living. Now I just wish them well and always feel incredibly grateful to have made the choices I did.

Life as a musician is certainly a struggle and I have my ups and downs. But I am proud of myself. What I have accomplished as a musician is both different *and* better than Wall Street because I am selling something I really believe in, that I've created. It took a lot of events, some very tragic, to light the fire, but I am holding the flame and passing it along to others.

Jon's when/then thinking — when I am a successful investment banker, then I will be rich, successful, and adored — kept him numb from the quality of his life in the moment. The danger of if/then and when/then thinking is that it lives in the future — that place we are under the illusion we have control over. And what lives in the future? ANXIETY! WORRY! STRESS! But also, this mode of thinking is one way we justify or distract ourselves from the bad situation we're in: I'm not happy now, but if and when I get to this particular place, I will be. If your thoughts are consistently of the if/then variety, stop and see if you're missing important cues from the present. Happiness is always available to us right now when we overcome our fears and take steps toward the pursuit of what we love.

> "I have felt truly immobilized by fear or anxiety at times. I wasted so much time worrying and not acting. At this point, I would have been so much further along in my field if I had given it a shot and not spent so much time analyzing."
>
> *Student, 27,*
> *serious relationship, Connecticut*

Don't wait for tragic events or a breakdown to motivate you. Don't allow your fears to force you into being someone you are not. One of Jon's songs is entitled "Wasting Time" — which is exactly what he isn't doing anymore.

HOBBY VERSUS CAREER

Jon did something that almost every twenty something thinks about: he turned something he loves doing, his musical hobby, into a career. But does every hobby make a good career, and how do you turn it into one and actually get it to pay? I am frequently asked these questions, and I always begin by asking the person the following question in response: "If you were doing your hobby all day and it turned into the thing that paid your bills, are you absolutely positive that you would still enjoy it as much as you do now?"

If you can't respond with an emphatic yes!, without any doubt in your mind, then more reflection may be necessary. Our hobbies are often our escapes. They are a break from work, a way to "zone out" from stress. How would your experience of your hobby change if it *became* your work? How would you feel about it if you *had* to do it to financially support yourself? Would what you love about it get lost?

I, too, once tried to do this. At twenty-six, my primary hobby was yoga and working out, and I thought, "Why don't I turn my hobby into my job?" I quit my "career" job that I was miserable in and became a personal trainer and yoga teacher, hoping doing something I loved would solve my quarter-life-crisis career concerns. Within three months, I realized I had made a big mistake. After training and teaching yoga to people all day, the *last* thing I wanted to do was stay an extra hour and work out or do yoga myself. What had been my place of solace and stress release became my "daily grind." I share this with you as a gentle warning, not to deter you. "Follow your passion, and money will follow" is a suggestion, not a rule. It's okay that not all of our passions fit into jobs or career tracks, and that's good — we all need playtime! I'm glad I pursued my hobby as a full-time job because it helped clarify my career goals, and it helped me realize

> "My love for music was becoming something I hated because I was trying to turn it into my career. Now I am able to keep my passion as my passion and my work as my work."
>
> Student, 21, single, Texas

the importance of my rejuvenating hobbies; it turned out to be a fork in the road that sent me on my current path.

If you are absolutely sure that what you love to do as a hobby is what you want to do for a living, then first, be grateful that you've identified your passion. Then ask yourself: Do I want a job where I get paid to do what I do as my hobby, *or* do I want to start my own business?

If you're looking for a job, then the simple answer is to start looking in the fields that correspond with your hobby — research, network, talk to people in the field (or that share your hobby), identify which jobs fit your interests most closely, and create a résumé tailored to getting that job. Don't be vague about what you are looking for. For instance, a twenty-five-year-old once wrote to me that she wanted "something that I am passionate about and that leaves me with a sense of fulfillment. A job where I can make my own hours, work for people I respect, have some level of intellectual thought, and work for people who appreciate me and the job I do." That's fine, but what specifically does she find fulfilling, what specifically stimulates her intellect? Take your hobby and research the best way to apply the skills it uses and the results it produces. Articulate why it's a fit for you professionally. What exactly makes you passionate about it? The process, what you produce, who you interact with? Remember, it may take some noodle throwing to match what you love to do with the perfect job.

> "When I was younger, I thought everything would happen so quickly, but now I know reality. Sometimes the steps you have to take to accomplish your goals take longer than you imagine. There is a big difference between imagining and actually doing."
>
> *Administrative assistant, 27, single, Connecticut*

On the other hand, if you want to start your own business, then you've really got your work cut out for you — welcome to the path of the entrepreneur.

BECOMING AN ENTREPRENEUR

If you are embarking on the entrepreneurial path, pack a backpack of patience and manage your expectations. Manifesting the business of your dreams is not about being an overnight sensation. It requires both personal and professional work, patience, a plan that remains open to possibility, and faith. Starting a business can be daunting, but it can be done. All you have to do is *take the first step*. I recommend making that step the creation of a business plan — or what I like to call a "Mission Vision." You don't need to go to business school to do this. It's a creative and logical process that begins with you outlining what it would look like and determining what it would take to turn your dream into a job or company. There are five steps to your Mission Vision.

Mission Vision Plan

Step One: Write Your Mission Statement

Your mission statement encompasses the primary purpose of your business. Think of it in terms of what you will be providing, not what you will be doing. For example, if you want to start a jewelry-making business, a good mission statement isn't "Making beautiful handmade jewelry." It would be more like "Enhancing the style and beauty of women with unique handmade jewelry." In other words, the mission statement should characterize the underlying purpose of what you hope to do, and the reason customers want what you produce. Research what other companies similar to your dream company use as their mission statements (often you will find a company's mission statement on the About Us page of its website). If you get stuck, start by just writing down words that come to mind. Think of feelings your hobby creates, what it looks like, what you hope it brings to others, and so on. I also recommend creating a "vision board" (page 321), where you collect and display pictures, words, drawings, and so on that represent what you would like your business or job to look like.

Step Two: Do Your Homework

Research and investigate businesses that are similar to what you would like to do or that pertain to your hobby. What services or products do they offer? Who is their target consumer? How do they market? How big is the company? Where are they based? Do they have storefronts, warehouses, online shopping? Read company bios, product and services descriptions, About Us pages, investor information, and terms of service. Become an expert in your market before you dive into it. Know your niche inside and out. Write down your research findings and bookmark company websites that you like.

Step Three: Build a Team of Advisers

Building a team of advisers is critical because you are stepping into new territory, which will generate a lot of questions — support and feedback is critical. Although being an entrepreneur may imply you do it on your own, the most successful entrepreneurs usually have a team of people who have advised them along the way.

> "You would really be surprised by how much help people are willing to offer you if you just ask. Give people a shot to surprise you with their gift of help."
>
> *Retail salesperson, 24, recovering from a breakup, Canada*

The primary member of your team of advisers is a mentor. Your mentor does not have to be someone who does the *exact* thing you do; he or she can be someone who does something similar. Make sure the mentor you seek has a business similar to what you envision for yourself in terms of number of employees, the goods and services offered, and target consumer.

The rest of your team of advisers consists of people who will act as your personal and professional support system. Building a business is an emotional investment as well; don't assume you can do it on your own. Former professors, counselors, and family friends are good people to consult. Also, identify people you know who are "experts" in areas you may need advice in, such as lawyers, Web designers, accountants, business advisers, sales gurus, and so on. Reach out to everyone and remember the "six degrees of separation." You know more people who know more people who know more people than you think! Don't be afraid to reach out to strangers for advice or a connection, either; the worst thing that can happen is that they say no (and most people are flattered to be asked).

Step Four: Brainstorm and Strategize

Steps one and two will give you ammunition to really start to see your business. Write down any ideas you have about marketing, product creation, sales, types of services, names of your business, potential partners, how many employees you will have, where you will work, your website, and so on. Capture all of your thoughts first; organize them next as you begin to strategize. Warning: This step can feel overwhelming — remember, you are not committing to anything; you are effortlessly getting your ideas on paper. Feel free to change and tweak them as you go.

Next, it's time to get to the "Nuts and Bolts" part of your plan as you begin to put together a strategy for your business. Ask yourself questions like: When will you start? How much money do you need to get it off the ground? Who is your customer? How will you market to them? Will you need

> "I wish someone would have told me that trying to find a job that is your passion is kind of bullshit. You should look for a job that intersects what you're interested in and what your skills are. I think a lot of people use the term "passion" because it sounds more romantic, but it doesn't really reflect how a job is. I think teaching young people that they should find fulfillment in a job can be misleading."
>
> Graduate student,
> 25, dating, New York

to hire a staff? What aspects of your business can you do on your own and what will you have to outsource? Will you have partners? What is your revenue model? These are just the beginning of the questions that will be presented to you as an entrepreneur, but all the answers won't be there in the beginning (remember I said to manage your expectations!). Just keep asking, continue to research, and reach out to your team of advisers.

This is also a good time to consider what kind of initial investment you will need to make and what type of financial support you will need. Investigate taking out a small business loan; some companies target specific types of businesses, like women- or minority-owned companies, or nonprofit organizations. A small business loan is something to consider when your ideas are firm but you need a boost to get your dream off the ground.

Step Five: Do It Part-Time

Don't quit your day job until you've tested your business. Pursue your business part-time initially. As a rule, wait to jump in full-time until your "side business" has been generating income for at least three months that is equal to *at least* half of what you are making at your current job. Going into debt is a surefire way to stress yourself out and zap your ambition and inspiration. Do a little something every day that takes you a step closer to transforming your hobby into your full-time job. This can range from simply adding a picture to your vision board to setting up a meeting with a bank to inquire about a business loan. Just keep the energy of your goal in constant motion, visualize your success, and remember to pay your bills along the way. Above all, remember that what you do is *not* who you are, so treat yourself kindly, set attainable goals, maintain hobbies that have nothing to do with work, and trust your intuition. And if in the end you decide your hobby should remain "just" a hobby — that is okay too.

> **MISSION VISION OVERVIEW**
>
> 1. Write Your Mission Statement
> 2. Do Your Homework
> 3. Build a Team of Advisers
> 4. Brainstorm and Strategize
> 5. Do It Part-Time

Becoming an Overnight Success Takes Years

All right, you've taken the plunge and started your own business. You are "working your passion." You created your Mission Vision and did everything you were "supposed" to do, but you can't seem to generate enough income to support yourself. You are doing what you love, and you love what you are doing, but love does not put food on the table or gas in the car. This is incredibly frustrating and a discouraging place to be in, but it is part of the growing pains that come with starting a business.

Stick with it. Remember, following your passion is a journey, not a magic wand; success is not immediate, but that doesn't mean it won't come.

"I LOVE WHAT I DO, BUT I CAN'T PAY MY BILLS"
by Christina, 28

DECLARATION: *Finding your passion is just the beginning. Making it profitable is the real challenge.*

My oldest sister got engaged my freshman year in college, and I helped her with all of the wedding plans. I scouted locations, talked flowers, and helped with the minute details. During one of our many conversations about the wedding, my sister stopped and said, "Hey — why don't you do this for a living?" I changed my major from education to hospitality and tourism the next day and knew it was right for me.

Five years, a college transfer, two years of summer school, a catering company internship, and a few beers later, I was ready to be a wedding planner. Mind you, I had no experience in weddings or business — but I believed I was ready. I sent out nearly a hundred résumés to wedding planners in the area where I wanted to live. I didn't hear back from most, and the rest said they weren't hiring. It turns out I had chosen a career that is dominated by small businesses. It's just not like that J.Lo movie *The Wedding Planner.* There are no long hallways filled with racks of gowns, beautiful flowers, planners, and brides bustling about. In reality, wedding planners work from home and meet clients in hotel lobbies or Starbucks.

> "The most fun job I had was as a lifeguard at a waterslide park. I thought that it wasn't good enough to make a job like that a serious consideration — my parents' expectations were riding on a 'better' career. After a stint in hospitality, consulting, child care, and bookkeeping, I'm going into substitute teaching and bartending because being around people makes me happy."
>
> *Teacher and bartender, 26, married, California*

Nearly four years after graduation, I have started my own company, and I love what I do. But it's not all roses and satin ribbon. It turns out that running my own company is really difficult. I've had to take on a part-time job and am actively looking for something full time.

I have learned that just because you're passionate about and good at what you do, it doesn't mean you'll be able to make the big bucks. At least not in the beginning. It takes a long time to establish yourself in any new industry when other people have been doing it longer. It also takes a lot of experience before you can command the fees that are required to make enough profit to live on.

I am constantly asking, How do I pursue my goal of being a full-time wedding consultant (a job that really does require weekday hours and a large time commitment) while supporting myself financially?

The Quarter System

I've noticed that once people identify their passion and start building their businesses, they dive in head first and expend large amounts of mental and physical energy. Any new venture requires a substantial initial investment of time, resources, and money, and each day is a new adventure, as an entrepreneur juggles many balls at once. Often, though, what results is a haphazard approach that leads to burnout and burning a hole in your wallet. Creating your Mission Vision supports you in planning your business, but as you start working your passion, you need a strategy to maintain your momentum. I came up with the "Quarter System" during my own career haphazardness as a way to streamline my efforts and focus while increasing productivity.

After a Mission Vision is created and a business begins to evolve, the Quarter System supports an entrepreneur in prioritizing across four main areas: further developing skills and knowledge, networking and creating relationships, building operations and revenue, and evaluating progress. I recommend the Quarter System to anyone who works for him- or herself or owns a business, especially someone like Christina, who has discovered what she wants to pursue but is struggling to make it work.

> "I expected to go to law school and become a lawyer, but it turns out that I have no passion for the subject. I now regret not having carefully thought things over before taking the plunge."
>
> Law student, 21,
> single and love it, California

Committing to the Quarter System consists of dividing your focus and work day into four types of work-related activities, which I call "quarters." Your time and energy may not be equally divided into fourths, but I encourage you to strive for equal balance in terms of your attention, awareness, and dedication to each of the four parts. It is challenging not to develop tunnel vision about certain aspects of your business, and consequently losing sight of long-term goals and being too frazzled to notice immediate opportunities or problems. For instance, a highly creative business owner tends to spend more time in the making of the product, since tasks like bookkeeping or financial forecasting do not come as naturally. Similarly, an overly ambitious entrepreneur may spend too much money on marketing materials or advertising without taking time to partake in free networking and relationship building opportunities.

> "As an entrepreneur, you will encounter disappointment and you may fail, but it does not mean you are wrong for your career. You will not be perfect at everything, and sometimes it takes time to learn!"
>
> Web designer, 29, engaged, Minnesota

Take an inventory on how you spend most of your time now. What quarter do you play the most in? In which quarter are you the MVP, and in which quarter do you play the third-string substitute? Perhaps you'll notice there is an aspect of your business that you are not investing enough of your resources in. For the next six months, commit to the Quarter System and balance your efforts to become MVP at every position. In order to win at the game of business, you have to play all four quarters. The Quarter System will organize your efforts so that as you give your business time to grow, you are investing your time and resources wisely.

First Quarter: Be the Expert

Just because you've done initial research while creating your Mission Vision does not mean your homework is over. Now it's even more important to become an expert in your field. We live in an age of information overload, so every day presents us with an opportunity to learn, research, or evaluate something. Be an information hound. Set Google alerts to receive links to articles on the Web that pertain to your business. Conduct competitive research to stay abreast of what your competitors are doing, and monitor their strategies. Subscribe to newsletters from companies or individuals in your field or that have to do with owning a business and being an entrepreneur. If you continue to do your homework, you may discover products and tools that could help your business and possible ways to generate income.

I suggest beginning each work day in "learning" mode rather than "working" mode. Before you check email and return phone calls, invest thirty minutes to an hour in continuing your education. If you come across a person or an opportunity that you believe may be helpful to your business or to you as the business owner, act on it! The more you learn, the more primed you are to being an expert in your field. Build up your expertise and status in your field by sending cold emails to other experts in your field and ask for an informational interview; volunteer to be an expert or to write for an article or trade publication; and post advice or articles on relevant blogs. Remember, continuing to do your homework and upping your expert status is paramount to your success at becoming a straight-A entrepreneur.

Second Quarter: Network

The team of advisers that supported you in your Mission Vision become even more important as your vision becomes a reality. I suggest setting a designated time once a month to have a ten-minute phone call with each of your advisers and mentors. Continue to add to your team. Every entrepreneur needs to align with people who do similar things, who can be colleagues, not competition. For example, I would advise Christina to reach out to another wedding planner in a different state and begin a rapport. Trade stories, secrets, business tips, and so on. Identify people who are a few years ahead of you on their entrepreneurial journeys and learn from them. It's extremely valuable to take on an "apprentice" mentality (and I don't mean Donald Trump's reality TV show). My most valuable training has been from my own coach and therapist — because the relationship comes with advice and support.

Seek out and take advantage of networking opportunities. Attend networking events, even if you have to go alone. Never leave your house without a business card, as any situation, from standing in line at a grocery store to going to the gym, can lend itself to meeting someone who can be valuable to your business. Join online networking groups and keep your profile up to date. I recommend trying to make at least one new introduction per week — either in person or online. Build your database of contacts.

Third Quarter: Execute

This is the "doing" part of the Quarter System and where entrepreneurs spend the majority of their time. Execution will be much less overwhelming and stressful if you are complementing it with the information database you, the expert, are building and the connections you are making from networking. It's best to be in execution mode during your most productive hours. If you are a morning person, play hard in this quarter then. This is the time you are actually doing the work that is your business. It's the time you spend with clients or customers, generating sales, fulfilling orders, completing projects, dealing with employees, making and returning phone calls and emails, and so on. Execution also involves the behind-the-scenes work you do to market and sustain your business, such as

> "It's easy to say, 'Follow your passion; the money will follow,' but I truly think this is not always the case for everyone, and it's a scary leap to make. Being successful is finding balance as well as making an effort to recognize all the positives in your life, and being grateful for them."
>
> *Corporate banking analyst, 23, engaged, Pennsylvania*

developing campaigns, designing and updating your website, creating and fine-tuning your product, building your mailing list, producing brochures, paying your bills, and meeting with your bookkeeper, accountant, graphic designer, and so on.

In this quarter, it's helpful to stick to a schedule. Make appointments and keep them. Put reminders in your calendar of days and times to complete tasks. As your own boss, you are responsible for your own accountability. In the early stages of your business, this is where you have to "hustle" and "burn the midnight oil" a bit. Christina has this part down — the only thing she is lacking is faith that all her efforts will pay off. This is a very common feeling among exhausted entrepreneurs. Before you forfeit the game, take a time out and remind yourself of your mission statement or take a look at your vision board. Self-doubt, even a twinge, inhibits your ability to execute, and it is toxic to your success.

Fourth Quarter: Evaluate

At the end of every day, dedicate time for evaluation. This is time you spend reviewing the day — what worked and what didn't? What follow-up items do you have? What should you be delegating? What needs can you identify? Who did you meet? How much money did you spend? How much money did you make?

> "Your degree is just a calling card to get in the door, not your ticket. My 3.92 GPA wasn't impressive. It didn't land me a job. Education does not equal dollars, work ethic and experience do!"
>
> University fund-raiser, 26, divorced and remarried, South Carolina

Quarterly, meaning four times a year, it's important to make an in-depth evaluation of your entire business, preferably with a professional. Budget and allocate resources that will enable you to consult with experts like business managers, accountants, and lawyers as you evaluate your business. You have to invest money to make money, so once your business is off the ground, you cannot rely on favors from friends. With an expert, conduct a comprehensive analysis of your business so you know exactly where you stand. It's not possible to grow and move forward without evaluating where you have been. In this phase your critical next steps may be identified, like forming a partnership, applying for a loan or increase in credit, hiring a staff, and so on.

Something that is hard to swallow for many entrepreneurs in this quarter is realizing you are not staying afloat financially. Building your own business takes time, and if it's not earning money, you may need to evaluate whether a supplemental source of income is necessary — that is, taking on a part-time "pay-the-bills" job. If you do get a second job, I encourage you not to think of this as a step backward or "taking away" from your own business or dreams, but more as an additional, yet temporary, investment. Outside work can fall into the first quarter, as you build your knowledge base and skill set. All of the seemingly random part-time jobs I have taken over the past five years while on my own Quarter System have improved my overall expertise. They've sustained me financially and taught me things that have absolutely helped me in my own business — although, admittedly, I did not always realize it at the time and would have rather been playing all four quarters of my own game. But success is a lot sweeter when it's experienced as steady growth as opposed to a growth spurt.

> "Working for yourself is not what you imagined it to be. Don't go in with expectations, go in with an open mind — be humble and willing to learn. It's going to be painful at first!"
>
> *Entrepreneur, 25, single and hate it, Kansas*

Also, balance your "work-life" support with personal support by setting aside time for sessions with a coach or therapist and for activities with family and friends.

QUARTER PLAN OVERVIEW

1. Be the Expert
2. Network
3. Execute
4. Evaluate

CAREER 101

The best advice about work comes from people who are out in the trenches working their way through obstacles and celebrating triumphs. Here are some words of wisdom from fellow twenty somethings putting their work-life puzzle together. Their tips are valuable to keep in mind regardless of your employment status.

Read each quote, and then in your journal write down your thoughts and reactions. Do you agree with their advice? Have you experienced similar "aha" moments? If so, how have you experienced them? What would you add to their comments? You have already learned more from your career (even if you just started) than you probably realize — using the advice from others as inspiration, summarize your own best advice, in your own words.

"You won't always enjoy what you're doing, but look to what you can learn from each job and take that with you as you move on. Working is actually a learning experience."

— Executive assistant, 28, serious relationship, Utah

"When it comes to how you are seen at work, you are what you do, not what you say you will do or claim to have done."

— Buyer, 27, love/hate relationship with being single, Arizona

"Work isn't utopia. It doesn't define your intelligence, your potential, or your aspirations. It can be rewarding, and it can be difficult, but it is the impact you make outside of the office that makes a true difference in your life and in the lives around you."

— *Research assistant, 29, dating, California*

"No one was *born* knowing how to do their job well. Mistakes are essential to the learning process. You must be patient with yourself and learn not to personalize criticisms. Take them in stride."

— *Student and administrative assistant, 24, single, Pennsylvania*

"Just because you love your job doesn't mean you will always like your job. Even the best job will have office drama or clashing personalities. You either work through it or find something else. But try not to let the 'like' get in the way of the 'love.'"

— *Student and nanny, 22, single and love it, Tennessee*

"Don't be a sellout. Work can consume you and more money, benefits, and security can lure you into staying in a job that you truly find miserable!"

— *Transportation consultant, 27, serious relationship, New York*

"Work is work, and your personal life is separate. Don't bring your personal problems to work, and maintain your professionalism."

— *Women's clothing salesperson, 22, serious relationship, Canada*

"One of the most valuable skills I learned was that it's critical to pay close attention to workplace politics. It's important to think about what motivates your boss, your clients, and your co-workers."

— *Web developer and life coach, 30, married, Colorado*

PART

SURVIVING AND THRIVING

As if the twenty-something years aren't hard enough, sometimes life deals us a hand that makes it even harder. In part 5, I have gathered a collection of topics that focus on helping twenty somethings survive and thrive in the face of difficult challenges that can affect us in any decade, at any time.

Interpersonal dramas, divorce, dislike, discrimination, disorders, and debt are not the sorts of things that make the list of "What do I want?" in our twenty-something years, but they happen, and when they do, we must survive them. Not every challenging issue is covered, and not everything I cover is necessarily a standard issue of a twenty-something journey, but they may be part of or similar to yours. Read them knowing you too will survive anything you are facing now or may be faced with in the future.

> "I think we are so trained to always strive for more, pushing ourselves into getting what we want and overcoming that which we don't, that we lose sight of the journey."
>
> *Nurse, 26, single, Missouri*

From my own experience and from talking to thousands of twenty somethings who have faced every disaster and heartache you can imagine, I have learned this: Not only is it possible to survive even the toughest stuff, we can learn how to thrive. Whatever happens during our twenty-something journeys, there is a light at the end of the of the tunnel. Trust it will illuminate your path toward tremendous insight, wisdom, healing, and lasting well-being.

11. TOUGH STUFF

When life throws us a curveball, what do we do? It can bring us to our knees, asking, "Why?" Our rage, grief, confusion, and despair may become so overwhelming that we lose ourselves in it completely. There is no way to anticipate or avoid all the ways that life can knock us off course; we just have to deal with it. But in doing so, we can transform these experiences into opportunities for healing and inspiration. Our challenges can become our most precious gifts. We can find a way to let go, forgive, and remain open in our hearts.

THE ACCEPTANCE PROCESS

The method I describe here for dealing with tough stuff covers all the situations discussed in this chapter and the next. To get through any difficult situation, it helps to deal with it in stages rather than trying to just "get over it." We all need time and patience with ourselves when it comes to healing and acceptance. This Acceptance Process is similar to the stages of the grief process (denial/shock, anger, bargaining, depression, and acceptance). Understand that this is a process for getting *through* something. When something terrible happens, we have to face it. The more we try to go around it, over it, ignore it, or change it, the more stuck in it we become. Understanding each stage will help you to move through the process so you can get beyond whatever has happened and continue living, growing, and thriving.

> "I have been able to keep my head above water through much heartbreak, changes in what I want to do with my life, deaths of friends and family, broken friendships, money issues, and more. It's better than sinking, and I think in your twenties all you really can do is try to get your head above water and just get through it, knowing that things will turn out in the end."
>
> *Law student, 25, single, California*

1. Stage One: Shock and denial — "I can't believe this is happening."
2. Stage Two: Big emotions — "I am so mad, sad, scared, ashamed, disappointed, heartbroken," and so on.
3. Stage Three: Seeking support — "I need help relating to this; I can't get through this alone."
4. Stage Four: Understanding — "I want to learn from this."
5. Stage Five: Acceptance — "I don't like what happened, but I can accept it."

I think the most powerful way to explain this process is with an example. In the following story, Giscelle is going through these stages. Consider applying the lessons and insights she shares to any "tough stuff" you may be dealing with.

"I DON'T GET IT!" by Giscelle, 26

DECLARATION: *Despite having heard that such things have happened to other people, you never really think it could happen to you. You're never ready for it.*

My boyfriend, and the man I considered my best friend, failed to call at the usual time. After I waited a few hours anxiously, my phone finally rang. I answered the phone in a bubbly voice, happy he was calling. Nothing but silence greeted me. "Marc?" I kept calling out his name, wondering what joke he was pulling by not replying. And then I heard him sobbing.

That was the beginning of my education in the real world. I was from a good and stable family and was lucky with my experiences. I believed that people innately wanted to be good to each other, and injustice existed in a parallel world, like mine but not mine. Like I said, I was lucky... and maybe naive.

Apparently, my boyfriend's mother had been looking through our pictures, and my Filipino features and the closeness of our relationship finally struck her. "Do you know what, Marc? If you marry a Filipina, it's like marrying your maid." Marc immediately told her she was wrong, and then the conversation escalated into a raw and heated argument about family loyalty, race, and responsibility.

When he finished relating all that had happened, all I could say was, "I don't get it." I knew what he was saying, but I could not understand the thoughts behind it. In my mind, I would make a good daughter-in-law for any family. Still, in her eyes, I was not good enough, just because I am not Chinese. This was the first time I wished to be somebody I was not so the person I loved could love me.

That evening we considered ending our relationship, but we didn't. The next few months were full of uncertainty, irregularity, and hiding, but we treasured stolen moments we could spend time together. Out of fear, perhaps, Marc would sometimes hang up on me the moment either of his parents entered the room. Unable to resolve the issue in myself, I could not help but bring up the subject whenever I could. Marc chose to ignore the problem most of the time. Talking about it frustrated and angered him, most of which was directed at himself. I neglected to be understanding and assumed that everything was always about me. Our relationship took a turn for the worse.

I knew we loved each other and I was not ready to give up. At first I felt like I was a victim of an unjust rejection, and I began to experience anger and hatred. But I didn't like being so judgmental, so I continually sought to understand it.

I entered internet forums to foster discussion between the Filipino-Chinese community and myself so I could understand the different views that might perhaps have contributed to his parents' way of seeing things. I began to learn his family's language. I tried to open my mind to understanding and loving them, because no matter what, they are still the parents of the man I want to spend the rest of my life with.

> "I constantly find myself trying to prove to others that I'm knowledgeable in my field. It's difficult and frustrating to face age discrimination as a twenty something."
>
> Event planner, 24,
> single and love it, Delaware

It has been a slow process, but I believe that I will eventually be able to love them despite all that they have said and done. Just the same, we continue to pray that they have a change of heart and accept us as a couple. Regardless, Marc and I have begun to enjoy each other's company again without letting the conflict interfere with our love, our expression of that love, and our appreciation of each other.

We no longer feel that the world is against us. Instead, we realize that we have been fortunate to find a love like ours in our lifetime to help us overcome all adversity, and to have parents like mine to offer their support for our love.

When an unexpected, emotional-charged incident occurs (such as Giscelle's first direct experience of racism), we initially react with shock and outrage. Our sense of the world has been shaken, and it's normal to ask, "Why did this happen? Why me?" I encourage you not to get stuck trying to answer the "why" questions. Those answers may reveal themselves in a later stage. Initially, it's more important to your own healing to fully experience your feelings, whether anger, sadness, panic, embarrassment, jealousy, fear, grief, and so on, instead of intellectualizing why something happened. Trying to figure it out keeps you stuck in the stage of shock and denial.

Giscelle describes feeling anger, hatred, and shame, and not only did she allow herself to feel these emotions, but she acknowledged and "owned" them. Expressing and recognizing all that we are feeling is a vital step, and I recommend journaling, talking to others, crying, screaming — anything that opens the flood gates in a safe, private way.

As we experience and express our emotions, we should take the initiative to seek support, which is the next stage. It is likely that our emotions will become overwhelming. We may feel we are losing control, or be afraid of the intensity of our emotions. To numb the pain, we may turn to drinking, drugs, overworking, overeating, or any other addictive or suppressive behavior. These things will not solve our problem, only prolong it. Giscelle reached for support by joining online groups that focused on her particular issue; through these, she connected and communicated with others who both empathized and understood what was happening with her. This is what a good counselor or support group provides — some context for our feelings (yes, you're reacting normally; no, you're not crazy) and a bridge to understanding.

Next, Giscelle moved from understanding the cultural differences at work (which helped answer her "why" questions) to lovingly accepting her boyfriend and even striving to accept his parents, even though they had yet to embrace her. She was able to enter acceptance by understanding that their racism wasn't about her personally and by experiencing gratitude for what she had.

"For a long time, I believed that emotions were out of my control, that you just 'had them.' Now I know I can choose my reactions to things and not let my emotions and feelings rule over all."

Licensed veterinary technician, 29, serious relationship, Michigan

Acceptance is often the hardest stage. We work through our emotions, we come to understanding, but we still hold on — refusing to accept or forgive. We may think, "There is no possible way I could ever forgive so and so or accept that such and such happened."

I emphatically say, yes you can! Buddha says, "Holding on to anger is like grasping a hot coal with the intent of throwing it at someone else; you are the one who gets burned." No matter what has been done to us, we burn ourselves and deepen the hurt by hanging on to the hot coal of our emotions. Once we let go and move into acceptance, we experience a huge relief — even better than the falling into bed at the end of a really long day when you are exhausted kind of relief. Acceptance creates space for gratitude, love, and change — just as Giscelle is able to see how blessed she truly is and to leave the door open for a change of heart in her boyfriend's parents.

THE ACCEPTANCE PROCESS

1. Shock and denial
2. Big Emotions
3. Seeking Support
4. Understanding
5. Acceptance

This exercise can be done as a mental reflection, but is most beneficial if you write it out. Take a "tough stuff" situation and see if you can accurately identify where you are in this Acceptance Process. Are you stuck in one of the stages? Have you tried to skip a stage and wonder why you do not feel any relief from your issue? If you do not have an issue that you are dealing with currently, consider something that has happened in the past. How did you move through this process? Is there any stage that you think you may have been able to take to a deeper level? Understanding how you have dealt or are dealing with challenges in your life will actually make you better at dealing with them.

THE INTERPERSONAL MINEFIELD

Like Giscelle, we may discover in our twenties that the world is a more complicated, difficult place than we experienced growing up. We are thrown into situations we didn't expect and don't know how to handle. Some people will upset us, some won't like us, and some will push buttons we didn't even know we had. From family relationships that explode to marriages that go sour to bosses who turn out toxic — sometimes it seems hell really has to do with other people.

And yet, all of these people are messengers with important lessons. They are our teachers. By challenging us, they help us develop into strong, independent, self-sufficient, and self-sustaining human beings. As we learn to navigate the minefield of relationships, we begin to emerge from even the most annoying, difficult, and scary encounters without serious harm. Don't believe me? The stories in this section may convince you.

Warning: Not Everyone Is Going to Like You

The twenty-something years are a time when self-confidence is often tenuous. When it's new or challenging to like yourself, it's natural to want everyone to like you. Not everyone will, and experiencing this becomes even more infuriating when you "have done no wrong."

When someone in your life actively dislikes you, it's unnerving, to say the least. The key, as Giscelle's story and the following story make clear, to regaining and maintaining your peace of mind is to work through your own emotions, understand the person's perspective as best you can, and let go of trying to change his or her mind. Don't waste your energies on a lost cause, but put your energies into living your life in the best way possible.

"MY SOAP-OPERA LIFE AS A SECOND WIFE" by Angela, 27

DECLARATION: *I now know that all this has happened for a reason. I once cared about what that reason is, but now I just live my life.*

I met my husband when I was twenty-two years old. He had been married before and had two young boys, a six- and an eight-year-old. I moved in with him before we were engaged, into the house he had lived in with his ex-wife. That was the first mistake.

At first his ex-wife was cordial with me. I remember the first day I met her. I was nervous, anxious, and I wondered how it would turn out. I was naive. She came to the house, her old house, and was friendly, almost *too* friendly. I chalked it up to being lucky.

Soon my luck started to wear out. It started the day she dropped their *good* shoes off for the *Big* Day. She had this look on her face. I would eventually come to know that look. For the first time in my life, I had to deal with someone really not liking me.

My life became a soap opera. First, I wasn't allowed to work with the boys on their homework anymore. Then I would get weird glances from the other mothers on the soccer teams, the teachers at school began to avoid eye contact with me, and our neighbors began to shun me. The worst was when his parents no longer called us, but began a relationship with her. I agonized over it: "What is it? Why is this happening?"

I tried desperately to get her to like me. The more I tried and didn't succeed, the more frustrated I got. So I continued to be a good wife and a good stepmother. I did everything to make everyone else happy. But the more I did and the better I did it, the worse my life became.

I did not know what to do. I was hurt, sad, depressed, and angry! Never in my life had people regarded me in such a terrible manner. I knew I had not done anything to deserve this. I was never a mistress — I just fell in love with a man with children. So I went inside to figure out why this soap opera was happening. My gut told me his first wife hated me, hated me for all that she wasn't. She hated me for all that I brought to her ex-husband that she walked out on. All of a sudden, I could see so clearly. I was living her life, but better. I created a bond with her children and had provided a happy, stable home for them — a family.

And five years later she has not changed a bit, but I have. I have grown, matured, and realized what is important in life. I am never going to get her to "like me." Every day is still a challenge, and I still obsess about why things cannot be better for all of us, especially for the children. But I owe it to myself to live my life every day to the fullest, to not look back with regrets, to be there for my husband and stepchildren, and to thank God every day for the wonderful people who have been brought into my life. We are a family.

We Can Only Change Ourselves

At first, Angela responds to being disliked by trying to change the ex-wife's opinion of her. Perhaps it's the wistfulness of the twenty-something years that makes us think we can change people, but we can't. Sometimes, as Angela found out, trying to do so can have the exact opposite effect; the person becomes even angrier, ruder, more unforgiving. Instead, we have to take the high road of acceptance. We have to focus on changing how we react, not on the other person.

I acknowledge Angela for realizing that her best was being wasted on a lost cause. Turning her best on herself and her immediate family liberated her from the drama. When she stepped out of the emotion, she stepped into understanding where the ex was coming from and she was able to "not care." Her cure for being naive was to add wisdom. Once we reach a place of understanding and forgiveness in our hearts, we immediately improve our lives, even if it doesn't resolve the situation. We are only the victims of other people's toxic behavior if we choose to be.

Up for a challenge? Like yourself so much that someone else not liking you cannot threaten you. Build your own healthy emotional foundation, and you will be better armed to deflect difficult people. Be patient; it takes time to develop the inner fortitude to survive a "hurricane." With practice and age, this gets a lot easier!

"MY LESSON, IN THE FORM OF A HURRICANE"
by Brianne, 26

DECLARATION: *Letting other people control our lives is useless and a waste of our energy.*

"Hurricane Lindsey" and I met in design school and ended up becoming partners. Two smart, creative workaholics seemed bound to make a perfect, successful team. The only catch? We hated each other and have blatantly opposite personalities. I call her "Hurricane Lindsey" because she is loud, obnoxious, controlling, pays no attention to her physical appearance, and has absolutely no filter between her thoughts and what bellows from her big mouth. On the upside, she is also very fast and efficient at work. I, on the other hand, am slow, deliberate, quiet, fit, and attractive. It's the perfect "sibling" rivalry, even though we actually aren't related.

We had a tumultuous relationship in school, fought a lot, but also liked working together because the outcome was incredible. As graduation approached and the job search began, I knew I had to get away from her. However, when she asked me to join her for her dream job in New York City, at the "hottest" firm in the business, I couldn't say no! But I wish I had.

> "Sometimes people will dislike you for reasons you will never know. And worrying about it is not worth your time."
>
> Communications director, 28, single and love it, Iowa

Once we hit the cutthroat corporate environment, the rivalry got worse, and I let it bring me down. Way down. It was my worst nightmare. I felt like I was becoming Lindsey's bitch. She publicly tried to humiliate me to remind people she was the "boss" of the team. Since fighting with her was like sticking my face into a blender, I let her have her way most of the time. I became more self-conscious and unsure of my creative abilities than ever and actually believed I had no power to change the situation. I was treating myself as badly as she was.

Eventually, I had to figure out what was going on. *Why* was I doing this to myself and letting one person bring out the worst in me? I didn't want to quit — I liked my job and the opportunities it provided. So I did some soul-searching and realized that Lindsey is like the terrible controlling beast that comes out in me when I am feeling insecure. The only way to defeat her was to defeat her inside of me and remind myself of how great I really am despite the way she treats me. If she can't live in me, she certainly can't affect me as much on a physical level. First, I started to pity her for being someone nobody likes being around. Then I began to connect with the sweetest and compassionate side of myself. This was the way I combated her.

I made an effort to do more things for myself outside of work and to appreciate my own creativity even if other people did not. Every time she was vicious, I reminded myself that she is just angry at herself and I represented everything she is not. I became more patient and understanding and stopped taking her so personally. I started standing up for myself a lot more because I was valuing my own self-worth.

Eventually, I stopped paying as much attention to her. I brushed her off when she acted like a psycho-bitch. A bad encounter would affect me for five minutes rather than five days. Now she hardly even bothers to push my buttons because she knows I won't pay attention if she does. Or I may even push one of hers to keep her on her feet (okay, so maybe there still is some sibling rivalry left!).

From this I learned a lot. But the best thing I learned is that letting other people control my life is a useless waste of energy. We have no control over anyone else. We can barely take command of our own little worlds, and it is in "our" worlds that we have the most hope for making personal changes. According to Tom Robbins, we're all "pimples on the ass end of creation." It's not worth getting so hung up on another zit.

Like the typical schoolyard bully, the people who push our buttons do it to get our reaction: they want us to argue, defend ourselves, complain, fight, or play the victim. As Brianne learned, if you opt out, if you don't take the bait, sometimes that's enough to ease or end the conflict. We may be perpetuating the conflict, even willingly adopting the role the other wants; sometimes seeing ourselves through the other's eyes makes this instantly clear. Once we own our end of the relationship, and depersonalize the conflict, it will be possible to accept and forgive the other and move on with our lives. As we get a glimpse behind a person's exterior, we depersonalize their actions toward us and can see ourselves as part of the person's larger worldview, one we had no part in creating.

WALKING IN A BULLY'S SHOES

If someone dislikes you or treats you badly for reasons you can't name, put your feelings and ego aside, and try to see the world, and yourself, the way they do. No one is born nasty. Nasty stuff happens to people, and instead of learning from it, they become defensive, angry, judgmental, and even aggressive.

So take a bully in your life and put yourself in his or her shoes. How does the other person see the world? What has happened to the bully? Have you unknowingly pushed this person's buttons? Has the bully cast you in a "villain" or "victim" role to justify his or her actions? Is the person projecting his or her fear and anger onto you? Is anyone bullying the bully?

Try to tell this person's story to yourself in order to reach a place of empathy. Look past the behaviors and into the real person, versus who he or she has become. At the heart of every bully is, indeed, a heart.

Divorce

Breakups are an expected part of the twenty-something experience, but not divorce. There is a taboo about getting divorced at such a young age, which makes the prospect of divorce even harder to face for twenty somethings. But what is the implication? It's better to stick out a bad marriage until your forties, when you have kids, a mortgage, pets? I think not. Divorce is hard enough as it is. It is challenging emotionally, socially, financially, and legally. If, for whatever reason, you feel your marriage is beyond saving, and your relationship with your spouse can't be reconciled, perhaps recognizing and ending a soul-mismatched marriage will be a blessing. Please do not feel ashamed if divorce becomes part of your twenty-something journey — haven't you been through enough?

"HONORING A VOW TO MYSELF" by Josie, 30

DECLARATION: *The hardest decision in my life was to walk away from my marriage to take care of me.*

I "had it all" before the age of thirty: a successful career, my MBA, a nice home, and a fairy-tale wedding, in which I married my college sweetheart. I had never really failed at anything, especially if I had worked hard for it. So how did I end up divorced before I turned thirty?

Shortly after being married I became seriously ill. The doctors I spent countless hours seeing told me I could have anything from MS to a brain tumor. All of the illnesses the doctors began testing me for would greatly change my future. At least I had my husband to stand there by my side, or did I?

This was the first time in my life I truly needed someone. I went from working out five times a week to not being able to walk to the bathroom by myself. My parents were there for me, but I was married, so this was the time my husband should step up and take care of me, right? Well, not really — he was physically present, but emotionally missing.

I guess this was when I noticed, or at least I admitted to myself, that my marriage might be less than perfect and that forever was going to be a very long time. Being sick magnified what I needed out of a partner and what was missing from our relationship. I had someone next to me, but I had never felt so alone in my entire life.

I tried so hard to make the relationship work. I gave up what I wanted and needed from someone just to stay married. I needed communication, affection, time, laughter, and an emotional connection. I stopped being me. I was sacrificing the most important thing, myself, to not fail at being a "Mrs."

With my urging, we went to counseling, separated, and we tried, but things got worse. The hardest decision in my life was to ask for a divorce. I was so worried what people would think of me; I was especially worried that people would think I was a failure. Looking back now, if I had stayed in the relationship as it was, I would have been more of a failure than I ever could be for ending the marriage.

I am not saying just because you are having problems in a marriage you should get a divorce. Rather, you should look at the foundation on which your marriage is built. Needs and wants change as you grow older, and unfortunately, our relationship did not grow in a way that supported each other. He was there for me in the way he could be there for me, but that way was very different from what I needed. He was who he was and I am who I am — and those two people were not good partners.

I am a strong believer that "everything happens for a reason." When I was going through the divorce, I had no idea what that reason was. I spent so many hours crying and wondering, "What had I done wrong? How could I fix it? What would people think of me if I got divorced?" I never thought I would stop crying, but I did. It took a long time for the tears to stop and the pain to subside, but that's okay. I was grieving. I had lost a relationship and a man that had been in my life for ten years. As time passed, I realized that I was not a failure; rather, I was finally taking care of me.

Today, at the end of my twenties, I am a much stronger and happier person than I ever was. At the time of the divorce, I could not look to the future and understand that I could survive and I would be okay, and do I dare say, be happier? Why yes, I do, and I am, because I hold true to who I am.

The Power of Forgiveness

Again, often the hardest stage in dealing with tough stuff is the last: acceptance and forgiveness. Many of my clients reach an emotional roadblock at this stage, as they think that feeling forgiveness would in some way excuse the person and the behavior. But forgiveness does not mean we condone someone's actions or agree with what he or she thinks or says. This stage is about accepting the situation as it is and letting go of our own desire to blame the other, remain angry over a perceived injustice, or try to justify ourselves or change the other's feelings. Forgiveness opens space inside of us by clearing out all the anger, resentment, and hurt we are holding. When we reach understanding of the other, all of a sudden we have access to a place of relief and freedom inside ourselves.

Furthermore, forgiveness does not have to happen face-to-face. Forgiveness is something that occurs inside of us, and its main purpose is to help us move on. I have found it helpful to write forgiveness letters (that do not have to be mailed) to others and to myself. Be patient and loving with yourself as you move into self-forgiveness and forgiving others, as this isn't a one-two-three, easy-as-pie process.

The following story demonstrates the beauty and power of forgiveness and how it is always possible, no matter how much loss and sadness we experience.

"DEPORTATION TO RESTORATION" by Jacqueline, 24

DECLARATION: *Confronting my fears and resentments allowed me to reach a state of peace, forgiveness, and love.*

Understanding the relationship I had with my mom is the most complicated task I have ever had. My first memory of my mother acted as the impetus for the terror I developed toward her. While watching the scene from *The Color Purple* where the character Sofia is hit in the head, I remembered my mother hitting my older sister when I was three years old. I don't recall what my sister had done to set off my mother's "bad temper," a characteristic of hers I would be exposed to on multiple occasions. Frightened by what I'd seen, I pushed the memory deep into my subconscious, and it traumatized me enough to prevent me from loving her.

Perhaps the incident explains why I never called her "mother" and referred to her as "Ya Marie" to distance myself from her [Ya is "aunt" in Kiswahili]. As a child, I did not comprehend that this woman was in fact my mother because she did not show me love.

When I was fourteen, my mother returned from one of her routine doctor's appointments. Her image in the doorway was that of a drained, gaunt woman. As usual she spoke with authority, repressing all emotion: "The doctor says I have lymphoma cancer." I entered a state of shock as I anticipated what would happen next; she was going to die. "See," she said as she watched my eyes well with tears, "this is why I did not want to tell you because I knew that you would cry."

The week before my mother died, when I was fifteen, I found out that she had full-blown AIDS and never told me. I also found out that when she brought me to the United States legally from Africa when I was four years old, she failed to apply for my citizenship. When she died, I had been left not only without a parent, but without a country.

I resented her for abandoning me. I hated her for not telling me the truth that she had AIDS. I despised the fact that she never once told me that she loved me; was I that hard to love? I decided never to forgive her for not securing my safety here; if she cared about my well-being, she would have applied for my citizenship.

I saw myself as a victim of my mother's faults and blamed her for not petitioning for my citizenship. It was because she had failed to nurture me and to be honest with me that I developed emotional handicaps. As long as I maintained such a mentality, I could continue to avoid addressing the problems within our relationship and the gravity of my situation.

Eventually, I had to fight for my immigration status; blaming my mother was not going to get me a green card. After countless attempts to petition for my permanent residency, an immigration statute addressing battered children was my final hope in pleading my case. I was forced to testify against my dead mother, disclosing details of the abuse to a courtroom of strangers who would decide if my life experiences were sufficient to qualify for consideration under the statute.

The experience was excruciating. As the words fell from my mouth, my heart began to bleed. An urge to defend my mother surfaced within me, an urge to make sense of how she acted toward me, and somehow paint a fuller picture of who she was.

From that moment and thereafter, I committed myself to reviving my mother's memory in order to commemorate her life. I had to do so not only for her but for me. To do this, I had to excavate and accept my past on my own terms.

In order to truly walk in this woman's shoes and to humanize her, I could not view her from the perspective of my mother's daughter. This woman had survived several miscarriages, three marriages in which her husbands abused and cheated on her, and six of her children being essentially kidnapped from her when she could not provide for them. She survived her last husband from whom she might have contracted AIDS. She spent the last years of her life painfully keeping a secret from her youngest child, which not only killed the relationship, but also killed her. I started to make sense of her long suffering. Suddenly, this monster of a woman became a delicate and wounded soul. My mother became a fallible woman just as I am today.

She showed me love the best way she knew how, which was limited because she experienced more pain than love in her lifetime. This time, I accepted her love. My resentment and fear started to slowly dissipate, and in the midst of all the agony, as I started to love my mother…I started to fall in love with myself.

Triggered Memories and Buried Feelings

Jacqueline shares how a scene from a movie triggered her memory. This is a very common experience in the twenty-something years, when the "survival" and/or "dependency" instincts of childhood

wear off and our minds become more open to information that may
have been suppressed. Often difficult memories will stay buried
until we have the emotional maturity to deal with them. It's a
self-protecting mechanism that is just one of the many fascina-
ting parts of the human subconscious.
Stream-of-consciousness journaling
and the "Finding Your Keys" process
(page 191) are great ways to access the
subconscious and open the floodgates of
your memories.

Jacqueline also says she recognized
that blaming her mother was a way to
keep herself from feeling her deeper
sense of anger and sadness regarding her mother. During our
twenty-something years, we are learning to manage many new aspects of life, and often we maintain our "status quo" by keeping
the lid on certain difficult or old feelings. In other words, we fear
that if we open these up and fall apart emotionally, our entire lives
will fall apart. Like Jacqueline, we may be afraid to move forward
until something forces us to. On the surface, we may say or think
we're fine, but pay attention to persistent anger, depression, stress,
or addictive behaviors. These may indicate deeper, repressed feelings we are avoiding and, consequently, we're going numb. Don't
wait for a "breakdown" to bring these forward and start the
process of healing.

Follow the stages as if the event just occurred: feel your emotions, seek support (a counselor may be especially helpful), and
move into understanding and acceptance. Though it may seem
overwhelming, allow repressed feelings or memories to be recalled,
no matter how much you want to resist them. As Jacqueline is discovering, sometimes our most painful experiences can lead to
love and a reawakening in ourselves.

> "I am proud that I had the courage to seek help for myself due to the extreme amount of stress I had been feeling. It is such a relief to know there are ways to overcome what seem like such large emotional hurdles."
>
> Supervisor, 24, single, North Carolina

12. BODY, MIND, AND MONEY

The combination of the common quarter-life stresses and the additional "tough stuff" life brings, coupled with the unresolved issues from our pasts, can lead to larger issues in our twenties — such as eating disorders, drug addiction, dangerous sex, and spiraling debt — that become obstacles to navigating successfully through the Twenties Triangle. Also, increasingly, many twenty somethings have grown up wearing labels about who they are that have nothing to do with the clothes they wear or their social status: such as a mental or behavioral disorder. Beyond the diagnosis itself, the stigma of being labeled and seeing oneself as that label presents its own challenge to figuring out who we are and what we want. Rest assured, though, as with the other "tough stuff" described in part 5, we can learn to cope with these threats to our mental, physical, emotional, and fiscal well-being, and continue along our twenty-something journeys.

DEALING WITH PHYSICAL ISSUES

Your body is your temple. You know that, right? Twenty somethings often act like they are invincible, focusing more on paychecks and relationships than wellness. In the online Twenty Something Manifesto Survey, only 7 percent rated themselves as having a healthy diet and good nutritional habits. However, not only are twenty somethings rarely thoughtful about how they take care of themselves, in the name of "having the time of their lives," they frequently put their physical health at risk. Engaging in unprotected sex, binge drinking, and developing a recreational drug habit, can have serious consequences. Plus, sometimes twenty somethings do these things not because they are "fun," but because they are ways to cover up unhappiness, fear, anxiety, and repressed emotions. So they take their emotions out on their bodies until their bodies give out, and then they have no choice but to face what they've been avoiding.

> "I am realizing that instead of avoiding my life, I need to take ownership of it. I am learning not to overcompensate for my mistakes by eating and swiping credit cards."
>
> Fundraiser, 26, divorced and remarried, South Carolina

I don't want to be a complete buzz kill. Please, have fun and enjoy your twenties! But don't wait for a wake-up call from your body to make your health a priority. Pay attention if your "good times" coincide with feeling bad. Get regular checkups with your physician, and during these years when your body is still young and malleable, establish an exercise plan and routine that makes you feel good inside and out. Take care of your vehicle — your body is your transportation to doing what you love, to falling in love, and to being loved. Finally, regard healthy eating and exercise as investments in yourself, as ways to make yourself feel good, and not as a form of torture to fit an unrealistic societal expectation of physical "perfection."

How Do I Look?

Equally as important as how we care for our bodies is what we think of them. Twenty somethings tend to obsess about how they look, and for the most part, they are very critical of what they see. The online Manifesto Survey asked twenty somethings to rate how much they like their bodies on a scale of 1 to 6 (with 6 being the highest rating). Most responses were between 2 and 3. That's a low average, it seems to me, for a generation in its physical prime. Our elders may have encouraged us that we could be anything we wanted to be, but they forgot to teach us how to accept ourselves the way we are, probably because they never learned themselves. There is a generation-wide and society-wide lack of acceptance of our bodies, no matter what they look like. But if we don't learn to appreciate and accept our bodies now, when youth is on our side, how hard is it going to be in five, ten, twenty years?

> "When I found out that I have an STD, it made me reevaluate the way I approach sexuality, and also how little I have valued my own health in the past. I will never sleep with someone to please them again."
>
> *Student, 23, single, Indiana*

We may be able to sprint five miles uphill, wear a size four, bench press two hundred pounds, and jump into a handstand — but none of that guarantees we will have a healthy body image. During the twenty-something years, our bodies change — metabolism slows down, we become more sedentary, and suddenly, nights of being able to have a few drinks and stay up past midnight transform from the norm to something that leaves us hung over for an entire day. Eventually, what has to change with our bodies is our states of mind about our bodies and our approach to taking care of them.

> "The trouble is that, as anyone knows, it is easy to see inner beauty in others, but much more difficult to discern it within yourself. But not facing your demons can easily rob you of your life and all of your creative potential."
>
> *Administrative assistant, 24, dating, Pennsylvania*

We can begin to transform the way we consider our bodies by focusing on all the wonderful things our bodies allow us to do: move, taste, smell, touch, laugh, sweat, see, and so on. Legs that are "too short" can still run and swim. The sensuality of our skin is not affected by our pants size. Like a car, the body's most important function is to move us, to get us where we need to go, and this depends on maintaining the engine, the wheels, keeping the tank full, and so on. Sure, we wash and polish our cars, and we admire their curves, but those things won't matter a bit when the engine breaks down. We should eat better and exercise because it improves our energy, abilities, and well-being, not as a way to get six-pack abs or impress others.

A twenty-eight-year-old says, "I finally get it. I actually feel better when I go to the gym in the morning — I feel accomplished, energized, and cherish the alone time I have. It's funny I no longer care about how many calories I burn or how much weight I am losing. Now that I have taken the pressure of the outer physical result off of myself, I am so much more motivated to work out!"

Think of your body in terms of how you feel rather than how you look — by doing so, you too may find more motivation to take care of yourself.

"MY BODY IMAGE CRISIS" by Ashley, 28

DECLARATION: *I have allies like intention and action
in my corner, which when combined with patience
and compassion, make a pretty formidable team.*

The cruise control that propelled my body screeched to a halt at age twenty-three. Seemingly at once, I found myself ten pounds heavier and realizing that this was the beginning of something new. Coupled with the other stresses and responsibilities of my twenties — career, independence, and relationships — it seemed too much. I lacked the energy to properly address these concerns. This was the start of my twenty-something health and body-image crisis.

At twenty-eight, I am now twenty pounds over my "cruise control" weight. Depression, driven in part by a deep dislike for my present sedentary employment, as well as a love of food, led to my status as a physically unhappy person.

Like many women, I was taught that physical appearance attracts attention. It will make us more popular and perhaps even more successful. Daily, we see images of beautiful, digitally enhanced women with words such as "sexy" and "hot" printed nearby. For me, these images produce the inevitable result of internalizing that my physical form is intrinsically tied to my sense of self. I perceive the women being portrayed as "having it all" and feel if I look a certain way, I can "have it all" too.

The question that I must ask myself is "How can I prepare myself to meet the challenges that my body presents to me?" I have learned that when I have a plan, and commit to my decisions, I feel a hundred times more confident and resolute in the face of a challenge. My plan of action consists of starting an exercise routine of just thirty minutes a day. I am also attempting to shift my focus from the desire to "lose weight" or to "be thin" to the desire for health, happiness, and an increased energy level. I try to steer clear of wanting my body to look like it did when I was twenty. I am also making an effort to positively restructure my feelings about myself.

When I wonder, "Will I ever be fit again? Will I ever feel truly sexy again?" sometimes I feel downright ludicrous for being so concerned about my body, especially since there are so many women (and men) in much more physically challenging situations. But still, the thoughts, the questions, the doubts, the anxiety persist. When those doubts grab hold of me, I try to help improve my body image and restore my confidence in myself through many different avenues. I have practiced yoga, I've done a bit of Pilates and some cardio, and I've tried to take more walks on my work breaks.

Although each of these excellent physical activities has had an immediate endorphin-driven impact on my psyche, I need more. I credit a part-time job that I took at a wellness center as the key to restoring my capacity to face my body-image crisis. Through the amazing friends that I made at that job, my confidence levels increased, consequently creating a spiral of positive energy surrounding me and my new plan of action.

> "My need for perfection led me to try cocaine and fall into addiction. Today, I am clean, but I will always be an addict — that is something I never expected. But accepting responsibility for my addiction has put me down the road to recovery."
>
> *Programmer, 27, single, Washington*

Don't get me wrong; friends and networks are not *the* solution by themselves. The choice still lies within me, to either open my heart and my mind to encouragement and support or to face my challenges alone.

I've also learned that I can't force myself to become something that I am not ready to become. I taped a quote to my wall that reads, "Accept the anxiety of feeling yourself, in suspense, and incomplete." I believe the author was saying that we need to be patient with ourselves. Without patience, I would perpetuate the feelings of doubt and insecurity that ravaged my spirit, and subsequently my body.

Looking at me, I am not a testament to health and fitness. I am a young woman, faced with weight gain, anxiety, depression, and a laundry list of minor but discouraging health concerns. I had no reason in the recent past to be patient with myself; after all I was the one who allowed myself to consume way too many potato chips and chocolate. I had no reason to be compassionate toward myself, because after all, I was the one who lacked discipline and resolve toward physical activity. I had no place in a "wellness center" because I was not "well" enough to be there, nor was I "well" enough to be friends with healthy and positive people. But I *did* do all of those things, and now I have begun to realize the reason behind the action. I did not want to remain a prisoner to my negative body image and negative sense of self. I wanted to change...and I am.

Eating Disorders and Addiction

The reasons some people develop eating disorders and addictions are complex and beyond the scope of this book to address in detail. However, a good place to start is by looking at how not dealing with our negative body image, our low self-esteem, and/or our repressed emotions may lead to or perpetuate these issues. Not everyone who parties hard or despairs over how they look develops these problems, but these problems are certainly the ultimate way that emotional issues are expressed physically.

Perhaps the unifying thread that weaves through all the "tough stuff" stories submitted by twenty somethings is depression and a sense of hopelessness. Whether you consider your own relationship with drinking, drugs, eating, and exercise as "normal" or not, if you consistently struggle with dark moods and bouts of self-hatred, I encourage you to reach out for support. You do not have to struggle alone.

Ignoring these issues because we fear facing them or we think "they are not that big of a deal" only makes them feel bigger, more out of control. Yet sometimes we have to suffer serious consequences, we have to "bottom out," before we find the motivation to finally walk down that very difficult road to deal with our deepest fears. I encourage you to do so, sooner rather than later, for these difficult issues can become gifts, providing tremendous opportunities to heal and learn — and be an inspiration to others.

"NUMBING THE PAIN" by Kurt, 25

DECLARATION: *Addiction helped me to learn that I control my life; my drug of choice does not.*

On December 31, 2005, while attempting to gather laundry in the basement, I slipped and fell down the stairs. I was not severely hurt, but I had trouble sitting and walking and had to lie on my side whenever I wanted to sit down.

I went to see the doctor about the tremendous pain that continued after the fall. Since there was little he could do to heal the problem, we decided to manage the pain with narcotic painkillers. That was fine with me. I had taken them before at fifteen when I broke a leg. However, at twenty-four, I was in charge of my medicine and found it easy to be generous with what the doctor had ordered. Not only did the painkillers help with the physical pain I was feeling, they numbed my mind to the emotional and mental pain of depression that had taken over my twenty-something life.

I steadily worked my way up to taking five or six pills at a time to reach the high and numbness that I was seeking. My addiction got so bad that I started to ignore my responsibilities to my job, my family, and school. I lived day to day for the next time I could get high. I saw two or three doctors for different physical issues so that I could get more prescriptions.

I used the painkillers to numb myself from the heartache of a breakup and the frustration of trying to finish my master's degree. I considered myself a responsible user. I only took them at home, never drove under the influence, and didn't think I was hurting others. Looking back, I recognize that I still managed to hurt those who love me simply because I did not care enough about myself to stop using.

Intellectually, I understood that what I was doing was unhealthy. I started to experience blackouts and memory loss. When I could not get a prescription filled right away, I would hide severe withdrawal symptoms, like upset stomachs and migraine headaches. I started to hit bottom when I was up to twelve pills at once, just to escape the depression I was feeling. At my worst, I managed to swallow ninety pills in four and a half days. Most people do not take that many painkillers in one year. The day after that, I confessed to my mother and a friend, and they insisted that I go to the emergency room and then get extensive help for my addiction.

In the ER, doctors explained that the amount of medication that I took is often lethal. They had no real explanation for why I was healthy and how I had not damaged my liver.

Once I left the hospital, I checked into a treatment program. Never had I been more scared. For two and a half days, I fought the overwhelming desire to check myself out and get back to my life. I wanted to leave so bad it hurt. But somewhere deep inside, instinct told me that if I wanted to get control of my life and my future, I needed to get healthy. Staying would be the only way to ensure this. When I checked out of the treatment center, I left knowing that I had a support system and a plan for ongoing treatment. I was ready to get on with my life and knew that I did not need drugs to do that.

I have been clean and sober since August 6, 2006. Certainly, there are days when I am tempted to relapse. Cravings for an addiction never just disappear. To this day, I fight them successfully, since I have developed positive coping skills. This experience was one of the most challenging in my life, but it opened the door for me to learn so much more about myself and discover my strength. Now, by volunteering and attending support groups, I try to help others who are in the same position I was in. It's a gift to be able to understand what others are going through because I've been there.

LABELS

Many twenty somethings grew up with or live today with a behavioral label or a mental diagnosis of some kind, and depending on the medical issue, these may be accompanied by ongoing treatments and prescriptions. Whatever the particulars, all such labels come with assumptions and beliefs; they set people aside as "different" because of their mental functioning. Twenty somethings may have been diagnosed with ADD, ADHD, a learning disability, an addiction, bipolar disorder, depression, and/or an anxiety disorder. In the Manifesto Survey, 32 percent said they are currently taking antidepressants or anti-anxiety drugs, and 70 percent reported "anxiety" as the feeling they experience the most.

I am not qualified to speak about medical disorders. However, I would like to talk about labels and how they can impact one's life and self-perception. This is such a prevalent issue that if it doesn't affect you, it probably affects someone you know.

> "A DUI charge felt like a permanent label, and I was humiliated and ashamed. But it humbled me. I began to see it as an opportunity to reevaluate the careless way I was approaching my life, rather than as a black mark on my moral record."
>
> Salesperson, 27, recovering from a breakup, Arkansas

Let me begin by introducing my friend Steve. If I say, "Steve is manic-depressive," what comes to mind? Though I have only given you a diagnosis, most likely you've already made a series of assumptions about his behavior and personality. You may think something like: "Steve must be really sad, unpredictable, probably cries a lot, maybe even gets a little crazy at times."

Now, what if instead I introduce Steve by saying, "Steve is a famous and celebrated artist"? What springs to mind? You're likely to assume he has some envious combination of talent, ambition, creativity, and intelligence.

Steve is a real person, and he's both. He has a depressive disorder and he is a talented artist. But how does the label "manic-depressive" change your view of Steve the artist? Is he now a tormented creator? Do you assume his artistic impulses are driven by his behavioral issues? Or do you think he creates in between bouts of illness? More to the point, what is Steve's perception of himself? Does he see himself as an artist who deals with depression or does he view himself as a depressed person who paints?

The way we perceive a diagnosis or label — whatever it may be — determines whether we believe we *have* a disorder or whether we *are* our disorder. What I have noticed is that twenty somethings often see themselves as victims, and they use their diagnosis or overwhelming feelings that they clump together as one label, like "anxious" or "depressed," as the reason or excuse for why their lives are not where they want them to be. The label morphs into their main identity. I can relate. At twelve I was diagnosed with depression and prescribed Prozac, and until my late twenties, I saw myself as a depressed person.

However, in my personal experience and my experience with clients, I've learned that it is possible to gently peel off the label we once thought was permanently affixed. We need to learn to separate ourselves from our labels and to see the diagnosis as a dynamic lesson rather than a static trait. As we've already learned, when we change our perception of ourselves, we open to new possibilities and ways of being.

"FROM EUPHORIA TO THE PSYCH WARD" by Carla, 27

DECLARATION: *I have had to become less driven, and permit myself to heal and live life only for me. It's been wicked at times, at other times exquisite.*

During my first twenty-something year, I was experiencing euphoria. I was at a top university, was doing well in a vigorous business program, and belonged to a campus ministry. I had huge dreams and even huger confidence that they would come true and possibly change the world.

But I had a secret I kept from most everyone except my closest friends and immediate family. At fourteen I was diagnosed with manic depression. At eighteen, I committed to Christianity. I was taught to rely on God for healing, instead of psychology. I went off my medication in this vain hope.

Fast-forward to age twenty-one. I had not had a major manic episode since I was fourteen and first put in a psych ward. Perhaps I was due. Friends noticed changes in me that final semester of my senior year. Staying up night after night, talking too fast, and attempting to do too much indicated to them I was not myself. I just thought they all seemed so dull, cautious, and complacent. Eventually, I was picked up by the police for trashing our dorm office, taken to the emergency room, and promptly sent to an upscale psych hospital. The one question I had was, "Why do I keep ending up in places like this?" I stayed for a fuzzy sedative-induced week. Once my meds were stabilized, I was released and went home to my parents.

I did manage to complete my degree. At my graduation, as others joyfully cheered, I cried, unsure of what my future could possibly hold. My once solidly promising world was crashing down around me. It was as if I was a beautiful porcelain doll that had fallen from her pedestal and was lying in shattered pieces on the floor.

I am twenty-seven now, and the last six years have been a mix of rehabilitation, discovery, misery, and rebirth. Picking up the pieces of my life and making an inspiring mosaic has proved the most challenging experience of my life. Mentally and emotionally, I was and am like an accident victim who must learn to talk, walk, and live all over again. I've had to create new dreams and invent new modes of surviving and flourishing.

Society's stigma is still very harsh, and rather uneducated, against individuals with a mental illness. So I only talk about it with people who I know I can trust, and who can be supportive encouragers. Some members of my family don't know, while my few friends do. There is shame I feel about the instability that has stood in the way of achievements I wanted to accomplish before age thirty. There is also a certain amount of shame in the sense of not wanting certain people, like employers, to find out.

It's been a long road to even accepting my diagnosis, admitting my need for recovery and treatment, and seeing psychology and medication as a necessary lifeline. I had to realize my inner turmoil was not my fault, but the result of a physiological imbalance in my brain chemistry. The medications correct that imbalance so I am able to work toward my life goals and dreams.

But the medication could not make me love myself. When I see myself solely as my disorder, I've entertained hateful self-talk that I'm ugly or no one would or could ever love me. I've thought of suicide as my only option and planned ways to see it through. I also pursued relationships with men who were bad for me — controlling men, abusive men, married men, and men who had no intention of loving me — just so I could feel loved, or at least delude myself with their overtures.

On the flip side, when I love myself, by talking to myself kindly and choosing to follow my bliss, I don't feel or see myself as mentally ill. I pursue experiences that uplift my heart, like acting and singing, working with disadvantaged children, and spending time with mentors and best friends that are harbors for my soul.

Today I give myself permission to heal and recover mentally and emotionally from years of trying to be "normal." I am still trying to define myself as a twenty-something woman rather than someone with a manic-depressive disorder. I am vastly better off at twenty-seven than I ever was before. I am proof that you can survive destruction in your past and choose strength and wisdom for your future, all the while being beautifully flawed.

Peeling Off Our Labels

When we are diagnosed with a problem, it's human to want to deny it because almost immediately we feel "broken" or "different." Carla tried to fight against her label, but then she realized that to heal and bring peace to her life, she needed to accept it and get on the "same team" with it. She accepted manic depression as something she *has*, not something she *is*. This is critical. By doing so, Carla acknowledges that while manic depression impacts her life, it does not have to take center stage in her life, and it doesn't define who she is. She is discovering ways to lovingly separate herself from it.

We all have the ability to make choices about how we perceive ourselves. When we see ourselves with loving eyes, we encourage our sense of peace and enthusiasm. Whereas when we see ourselves as disorders or as emotional states (such as "anxious"), which carries a sense of hopelessness and stigma, we slip into self-defeating behavior.

One of the most challenging aspects of any label is shame, which cripples our ability to move into acceptance and separation. I remember in middle school, I would white out the word "psychiatrist" on my doctor's excuse notes because I didn't want the volunteer moms in the attendance office to start gossiping. It is unfortunate that our society makes so many assumptions based on a word. We can start releasing any shame we feel by remembering that our disorders are not our fault and are not who we are. It is just something to deal with on this journey through life. And believe me, everyone labels themselves as something, but why not label yourself as something fabulous as well? Add the labels of self-aware, compassionate, funny, insightful, creative, and so on. Start embracing *all* aspects of yourself in your twenties, and imagine the rest of your life free from shame!

A first step in the direction of de-shaming a label is finding a support group for your particular disorder. These days, there are groups for everything, just Google your label. Research several group meetings in your area and try a couple different ones to find the one that is the best fit for you. Being around others who can empathize supports you in freeing yourself from shame. It may in fact be the first time you are in a group where everyone is the same, rather than you being the one who is different. If you cannot find a support group to physically go to, try online support resources and groups. It's incumbent upon you as a twenty-something adult to build a healthy life and not hide behind the shadow of a label. It does not have to brand you.

GIVE YOUR LABEL A NAME

I've found it helpful to give disorders a name, to personify them as a way of separating from them. One of my clients named her ADD "Sue," and she keeps a specific journal that is just for Sue. This gives that part of her a special place to vent, pontificate, and be upset. When my client feels like her ADD is really acting up, she gets out Sue's journal and lets her take over. Sometimes Sue just rambles about nothing, other times she criticizes herself ("I hate this, what is wrong with my brain, I am stupid and can't focus"), and often she throws a pity party ("This is too hard, I can't do it, I should just give up, it's hopeless"). By creating a separate identity for the label, you allow it to become just a "part" of you, instead of a definition of you. My client has reported that this technique is so useful that she even takes the journal into the bathroom at work if she needs to. For so much of her life, she was labeled as ADD, and it seemed to control her life. Now she doesn't have ADD; she has Sue. And she can cope with Sue.

Self-Prescriptions

I asked Carla what types of activities were most healing for her during her recovery and during those moments today when she feels like she is in a funk. She said:

"Creativity has been my second savior! I love to act and sing, dance, play the piano, draw, and make crafts. Creativity has often been the one good thing in my life and the most constant. I've had the opportunity to do commercials and student films and act in plays. I'm still learning to draw and find a lot of satisfaction and peace of mind in doing so. I create crafts for people I love. It all makes me feel useful and brings serenity to my world. Beauty, balance, and harmony somehow come from the madness, and that is tremendously healing."

> "People don't realize that I have a pretty profound learning disability. I've developed coping strategies and focused on my people skills, my ability to communicate with others, and my ability to lead, rather than letting it slow me down or define me."
>
> *Intern, 22, dating, Iowa*

I have to agree. Anything creative and expressive is the best self-prescription for the label blues! Additionally, a self-prescription is empowering. Instead of just "following the doctor's orders" or taking the advice of others, we are choosing the best way to treat ourselves. One of my favorite self-prescriptions is coloring. I always loved coloring books as a kid, and when I feel down, I'll go to the drug store and buy a coloring book and a fancy set of crayons (at least sixty-four colors, and I like the box with the built-in sharpener), and then go home and play with them. Listening to your favorite kind of music is another great form of therapy. Finding ways to express yourself when you feel like "it" is consuming you helps you vent and maintain balance, reinforcing your healthy belief that "it" does not control you.

SENSE ABOUT DOLLARS

Money. We need it, we want it, we like to spend it, and somehow we never seem to have enough of it. In the Manifesto Survey, 60 percent of twenty somethings identified money as the area of life they are most unhappy and stressed out about — even more than love and career issues! What is the number-one thing twenty somethings feel they never learned? Money management. What's ironic is that even though twenty somethings worry about money the most, they still pay more attention to and seek more advice about relationships and career choices. Perhaps the pressure to look like we "have it all" encourages buying into our society's dangerous attitude of "charge it today; worry about it tomorrow." Credit cards are passed out today like candy, making them easier to get than dinner reservations.

Debt is a four-letter word among twenty somethings. They hate having it and often have to shack up with Mom and Dad to climb out of it. In fact, for twenty somethings, "money management" could more accurately be called "debt management." In this section, I don't intend to offer standard "money management" advice — how to balance your checkbook, set a budget, or invest — but you can find great resources for money management at the *Manifesto* website (www.20somethingmanifesto.com). Rather, I want to address that four-letter word: "debt" — why it's important to deal with it (stat!), and how not to let it control your life.

> "The largest difficulty I have faced is learning to deal with the consequences of my own actions, like opening a credit card account and realizing that it's not magic and having to pay high interest rates."
>
> *Customer service representative, 27, engaged, Illinois*

To clarify, I make a distinction between what's sometimes referred to as "good debt" and "bad debt." Your student loan, or any

> "I wish someone would have told me that I should get started right away investing in mutual funds or stock options before starting work in order to allow my money to grow. I was not aware of these types of investment options until recently."
>
> Writer, 30,
> serious relationship, Connecticut

money spent on education, is good debt; it's an investment in yourself that will likely pay itself off a hundred times over. However, I understand it's still money that you owe, and even though it was spent on a good cause, it's most likely causing you a certain degree of stress. That is why it's paramount to exercise healthy spending and saving habits. You don't want to bury that good debt under a steadily growing mountain of I-didn't-feel-like-cooking-and-the-purse-was-on-sale-and-I-really-needed-that-trip-to-Mexico bad debt.

If you are experiencing dangerous debt because of toxic behaviors, like maxing out your credit card and overspending when you're feeling depressed, you must *immediately* take steps to remedy this. Debt is not like wine: it gets worse over time — so don't take your twenty-something debt into your thirties.

"CHARGE IT" by Aaron, 29

DECLARATION: *The consequences of living above my means were not worth the thrills and frills.*

In my early twenties, I was living it up. My lifestyle was styling; my bank account was not. At twenty-four, I was making about thirty grand a year, living in a big city, and had racked up over fifty grand in credit card debt. I had overdrawn my checking account twice. And a savings account? Yeah right, I didn't even think of it. I couldn't even opt in to the 401(k) plan my company offered because I needed every cent I was making. I had student loans I should have been paying back, but I just deferred the payments and looked the other way as the interest rates went up. I couldn't sacrifice fun for practicality — you only live once, right?

So my solution: charge it. Theoretically, I didn't really need cash to participate in all sorts of consumer activities. Gas, food, gym membership, music, parking tickets, travel, and even a $1.41 cup of coffee at Starbucks can go on the plastic. It was way too easy. When one credit card got maxed out, I'd charge it to another. If I ran out of credit cards with available credit, I just opened up new ones. What no one ever bothered hammering in were the consequences that not paying minimum payments and late fees can have on your credit score. I wasn't a total idiot; I knew the bills were coming in and I'd eventually have to pay them "someday." My overconfidence about my money-making potential and the pressure I put upon myself to exude a certain kind of image perpetuated my debt.

> "I didn't expect life to cost so much, and I didn't realize how much responsibility I would end up with as an adult. For a long time I wanted to live wild and free . . . until of course I understood that there was not much future in that direction. Learning real accountability and responsibility was a big step."
>
> *Executive administrator, 26, dating, Tennessee*

My humiliating day of reckoning came when I tried to pay for dinner with a hot date and two of my credit cards were declined. She ended up paying. There was not a second date. Utter embarrassment motivated me to finally open that doomsday drawer. To say I was overwhelmed is an understatement. There were so many different cards; I was so behind I didn't know were to start. So once again, I went back to my comfortable land of denial. Then I started getting calls from collectors — ouch. Eventually, all my accounts were closed.

I was a mess. I didn't want to admit to myself, much less to anyone else, that I was drowning in debt. I couldn't stop thinking about anything other than how to keep my head above water. I finally put my tail between my legs and met with a financial planner — who met me as a favor since he was an older brother of a friend. After about two hours of tough talk, I had a game plan to get myself out of the hole I was in. Some major changes needed to take place. All of a sudden my rock-star lifestyle turned into eating peanut-butter-and-jelly sand-wiches and taking a part-time job to supplement my income. I lived on a cash-only basis so that I knew exactly how much money was coming in and how much was going out.

It took a dateless year and a half to get my finances back to a point where I could consolidate my debt at a lower APR, open another credit card account, and begin to repair my credit history. I'm still not debt free; however, my spending is under control and I am aware of my debt. I have a plan for paying it off and look forward to the day I can be "debt free"!

From "Charge It" to "In Charge of It"

Aaron's story makes clear a few hard truths about debt: one, it's easy to practice fiscal denial. Not only do credit cards make it possible (and tempting) to spend more than you make, but banks and collectors take their time catching up with you; in the meantime, all you have to do is put the bills in a drawer. Two, living on plastic is expensive; fees, charges, penalties, and higher interest rates mean you will pay much, much more for your debt tomorrow than you will today. And three, bad credit stays with you and affects your future (and not just your dating future). Establishing and maintaining good credit is essential for leasing or buying a home or car or getting a loan. Even potential employers may check credit ratings. Check your credit (FICO) score *today*.

To take charge of your charges, I encourage you to follow these simple tips:

- Whenever you open a new credit card account, sign up for online billing and account balance access; set a weekly reminder on your calendar to check all your credit balances.
- Opt in for emails from the credit companies to remind you that your payment is due.

- Always pay your bills on time. Even if you pay only the minimum, pay it on time. Late and/or delinquent payments deflate your credit score. Set a monthly reoccurring reminder on your calendar.
- You never really need more than two credit cards. The more cards you have, the more you'll spend, and the more likely you are to rack up your debt.
- Your credit is your responsibility, so regularly check for unauthorized charges. Get in the habit of viewing your online statement at least once a week, and to protect your identity, shred or tear up credit card offers and statements before throwing them away.
- If you already have a lot of debt, live on a debit-card/cash-only system until you are debt free. If need be, consolidate your credit card debt in one place with a low APR.
- Read the fine print! Credit card companies are allowed to change your finance rates and often have a yearly service fee that they inform you of in minuscule print. Squint your way to becoming a responsible and prepared credit card holder.

THROW A MONEY PARTY

Don't throw a pity party just because you're downscaling your lifestyle to stop drowning in debt — throw a money party instead! You can still have a good time on a budget! A money party isn't the kind of party with Trader Joe's appetizers, plastic cups, and iPod mixes in the background. It's a way to make becoming fiscally fit fun, social, and supportive.

Twenty somethings freely talk about making money, but they rarely discuss money management. I doubt IRAs and credit scores came up over red wine and beer at the last girls' night out or poker party. I further doubt any of your friends know as much about your financial health as they do about your love life. But what if they did? What if you and your friends supported one another in paying off student loans, getting out of debt, saving more, and getting smarter about money? I recommend making a money party a "guys only" or "girls only" night. Why be fiscally sexist? Two reasons: men and women relate to and talk about money in different ways, and money is often considered a very intimate topic.

Here are some tips to get you started:

1. Send out an email to at least three friends telling them of this idea, and ask them each to suggest at least two other people to invite.
2. Set a date, and send out an evite.
3. Pick a financial topic for your first party.
4. Write up a confidentiality agreement that everyone signs, so that you feel comfortable talking openly about finances.
5. *Make it fun!* Serve green food; play a round of Monopoly (Monopoly is still fun, right?).
6. Ask each guest to bring at least one financial tip, piece of advice, or resource to the party.
7. Meet on a regular basis (I suggest bimonthly) and discuss your financial behaviors (spending, saving, budgeting), your financial goals, 401(k)s, IRAs, money market accounts, mutual funds, savings, stock portfolios, flexible spending accounts, and investments.
8. Start a Fiscal Fitness book club and read a book together about money management.

9. Consider inviting a professional financial planner or adviser from your local bank or financial institution to speak to the group. Often advisers will do this for free because you and your friends are potential clients.
10. Collectively brainstorm creative and practical ideas to save and earn money, and capture them on a whiteboard.

Financial Independence

Think all it takes is a lot of money to be financially independent? No, it takes self-control and reasonable expectations.

A twenty-seven-year-old woman writes: "I think some twenty somethings, like me, still feel like children. I have moved back home twice. Even though I make a good salary, I don't want to pay money for rent. Everything is just too expensive. To really begin life and own a house, you have to have two incomes and get married, which is unfair. An educated twenty-something woman with a good job should be able to buy a home for herself."

This woman's comment is laced with both understandable angst and a desire for instant gratification. She has a good job with a good salary, so why should she wait at mom and dad's house for "life to start"? If you can relate to her feelings, consider getting a roommate, paying rent, and leaving never-never land. We all have to save up (and grow up) to afford the lifestyle we desire.

"A friend and I started a personal investment club with five other women, where we learn about investment and our finances and invest our small dues as an exercise to understand the stock market. Making it fun motivated me, and I now have a strong understanding of where I put my money, why I put it there, and what's happening to it when it's invested."

Policy analyst, 26, dating, Washington, D.C.

Becoming financially independent takes some sacrifice. Just because you can't afford a house does not mean you should be living in the one you grew up in. Don't expect to move into a place as nice as your parents' home. And don't expect Mom to keep cooking your meals. Living on peanut-butter-and-jelly sandwiches for a while can be even more satisfying when you are the one buying the groceries, paying rent for the kitchen you eat it in, paying for the electricity that runs the refrigerator, and paying for the water that washes the dishes.

> "I am most proud of living on my own and making it work. Although, it is tough and trying at times, I feel empowered by my financial independence."
>
> Salesperson, 28,
> recovering from a breakup, Virginia

Financial independence means paying your way, not being free from work, debt, and bills. And happiness doesn't require a house or tons of cash in the bank. Take it from this twenty-five-year-old: "I expected that the big house, the Mercedes SL, and the $3,000 bags would make me happy. I have all the superficial things — now what?"

Money buys stuff, not contentment. Financial independence also means not being dependent on money and material things to fulfill you.

13. SHIFT HAPPENS

Let's face it... shit happens. And when it does, one of two things can follow: more shit, or a shift. While it can be fairly obvious when the proverbial "shit happens" in your life, the eventual and important *shift* may be more discreet. Eventually, we'll realize that events, people, or feelings we once considered awful, hurtful, and unpleasant have shifted. The usual Expectation Hangover doesn't arrive, and we're living in a more positive state. Of course it's not easy to go through the shit, but invaluable once we do.

The stories in this chapter are about this shift. They are shining examples of how we can survive any quarter-life crisis and discover wisdom on the other side. They are the stories of people who have discovered that certain clichés are sometimes true, such as:

"Everything happens for a reason," "Expect the unexpected," and "This too shall pass." As you read these stories, allow yourself to simply be inspired and resist the urge to compare your progress to theirs. These folks have arrived on the other side of their twenty-something crises; they've navigated the Twenties Triangle. Don't panic if you're still sailing furiously in the midst of your own. Keep going — you will get there too. I am rooting for you!

"DIVORCE — TAKE TWO" by Heather, 29

DECLARATION: *Life isn't about finding yourself.*
Life is about creating yourself.

At twenty-six, I was staring down divorce number two. That's right, number TWO. It seemed like yesterday when I was eighteen, filled with hope for the future and vowing to be nothing like my parents. But no. Here I was repeating history like some kind of bad, bad sitcom. I was sure I wouldn't recover. The shame was thick and weighed heavily on my shoulders.

The husbands are hardly important. Two marriages and divorces within the span of six years had absolutely nothing to do with the men and absolutely everything to do with me. I couldn't remember loving either. What I do remember is becoming completely consumed in both relationships. My weight whittled down to virtually nothing, and I, once a strong healthy woman, looked like a fragile, ill girl.

It seemed apparent that something was wrong with me. My internal dialogue sounded a bit like this: "You don't deserve to be happy. In fact, you deserve to be completely miserable and surrounded by completely miserable people." And true to that core belief, I was. The people I worked with, hung out with, and married were all the same — miserable. They were going nowhere and neither was I. Only I didn't know this. I was too busy being a victim, obsessing, or replaying every conversation we had, trying to figure out what I had done wrong. It never occurred to me that I might be part of the problem. I never pondered as to why I would bring such draining, energy-sucking people into my life. In fact, I'm almost positive I was addicted to the drama, pain, and misery.

After the divorces, things got worse, not better. In a crisis with another, I'm golden. I can manage, cry, scream, and go to couples counseling with the best of them. With only myself to contend with, I had no clue what to do. I was having feelings that I couldn't identify. I quickly found another emotionally handicapped man to date, but even that was no longer satiating. I was running as fast as I could from myself and into the arms of any crazy who would take me.

But I got tired of running. It was time to face my greatest fear — myself. The first stop and most obvious choice was therapy. It was cathartic for a time, but then something strange happened. I became incredibly tired and bored of telling my same old pathetic childhood story. I was nauseated by my own storyline — a twenty-six-year-old woman with a severely dysfunctional childhood and two divorces under her belt. I had had enough. I figured it was time to move into action.

> "During the most difficult time of my life, I have gone from being an immature child, asking everyone else what I should do with my life, to being able to make my own decisions. I have taken my work and life experiences and have incorporated them into a meaningful job and healthy way of living."
>
> *Graduate student, 27, serious relationship, Delaware*

Through a series of synchronistic events, I discovered Christine, and she supported me in realizing that I could not only learn from my past, but actually change my present and create the future. We focused on what I could do to love myself and create a life that was authentically me.

I then started to do something I hadn't done since leaving husband number two. I started to cry. A lot. I screamed and cursed and beat pillows. I wrote poetry. I slept in. I took naps. I cried some more. I let myself miss him even when it seemed like missing him was just another form of my delusion. I let myself hate my parents and then forgive them for being jackasses who didn't know any better. I started going to poetry readings — even hosting one for a brief time. Most important, I started connecting with myself. I thought about going back to school. Instead, I took a digital photography workshop and went wine tasting — less pressure, more of what I wanted and needed.

A friend of mine gave me a journal that said, "Life isn't about finding yourself. Life is about creating yourself." Those words hit me hard but felt terrific as I realized there was no magic place that I would arrive at to find Heather. I would create who I was step by step. And I could be whoever the hell I wanted to be.

With that, I signed up for a pottery class. I went to a few Toast-masters [public-speaking training] meetings and spoke in front of strangers about my struggle to create myself. I laughed. I dumped the toxic people in my life; quit the job with a nutso, husband-resembling boss. Got rid of the obnoxious, critical roommate who was making my home life stifling. I started receiving monthly massages. I practiced yoga. I wasn't making a lot of new friends, but I was figuring out who and what I liked. When I found something that didn't fit — job, person, or situation — I let it go. I let myself be. Even better, I wasn't thinking, talking, and obsessing over a husband.

The next big step for me was to get incredibly comfortable with being alone. I started out small; lunch at a sushi bar by myself. Then the movies. I had spent marriage number two vehemently opposed to going to the movies alone, as I believed it made the statement that I was a horrible companion, even in a dark room. Turns out that I *love* going to the movies alone. No more violent action flicks or Beavis & Butthead movies — I can watch cheesy romantic comedies to my heart's content. My biggest "me" time adventure was going to a Jerry Seinfeld show by myself, surrounded by a sea of couples. But standing there, dressed up, and laughing out loud, I felt a tinge of something that I was not familiar with … I felt proud. I was living my life. I was being me.

With each independent victory, I felt empowered. I created a vision board filled with everything I wanted for my new life. A Kitchen-Aid mixer, a laptop, an amazing tropical vacation, great friends, a writing career, and beautiful flowers. I placed it in a high-traffic area and walked by it every day.

It's three years later, I'm twenty-nine, and I'm happy to say that almost every single item on my vision board has come to fruition. Most of the items on my board I received as gifts. It is still amazing to me that I was able to create this incredible life.

I'm still living life on my own terms, but things have softened a bit. It's not nearly as important as it was in those early healing days that I do everything alone. I've been fortunate enough to attract a few key people who make my life better and who honor me as an individual. I've even been able to attract a quality man, and we're having a fantastically healthy relationship. I'm still taking what works and tossing what doesn't. I'm finishing my college education, and I'm spending my days doing what I love the most.

It would be trite to thank my husbands for their part in my story. But it would also be remiss not to acknowledge that their presence helped me get where I am today...and I like where I am.

ESCAPE YOUR SCAPEGOATS

If we try to outrun ourselves or the real reasons that we are unhappy, we should really give it up because eventually we all catch up with ourselves. At some point we will look in the mirror and realize that the big bad wolf is looking at us when we are brushing our teeth. Looking to yourself as the *one and only* person who is responsible for your life is one of the hardest, yet most important, responsibilities you have as a human being. Why do I call it a responsibility? Because I think we live in a society that blames way too much. We want to blame parents, peers, lovers, our past, circumstances, society, even the

"I thought by my late twenties I would have a couple of kids. Instead, I was divorced and depressed, and then I had the most fun I've ever had traveling. I made the decision to invest money in myself and my well-being, and so I traveled throughout Africa, experiencing life in a way I never could have before."

*Freelance writer and photographer,
30, divorced and remarried,
British Columbia, Canada*

president for everything we don't like about our lives. True, a lot of twenty somethings didn't hit the jackpot when it comes to parents or life situations; however, as an all grown-up twenty-something person, it's time to look within. Life is not always easy, but we are the only ones with the power to shift it.

Heather learned to stop looking out and to look in. She finally moved to understanding her past instead of blaming it and then re-creating different versions of it. As she realized she was one of those "miserable people" in her life, she detoxed herself. She got support, wrote, cried, talked, and learned to have a relationship with herself. She even came to enjoy being with herself. Remember, the relationship you have with yourself will dictate the types of relationships you have with others.

However, another thing to remember is that we all must follow our own paths to healing. If you find Heather's story inspiring, don't run out and try to repeat everything she did and expect your shift to happen. We only get results if we take things one day at a time and do what fits for us. Heather's self-prescription of journaling and solo movies supported her healing because it came from inside of her.

> "This is *my* life. No one is making choices for me anymore. I am the person in charge of my emotions, my thoughts, and my actions. If I am unhappy, I have no one to blame but myself."
>
> *Police officer, 25, single, Michigan*

One of the most healing things that Heather realized was that her shame about her divorces was suffocating her. Part of my work with Heather was to encourage her to talk to people about her divorces just to prove that they didn't plaster a scarlet letter "D" to her chest. It began to click for her that she no longer had to quarantine herself to the "divorced at twenty-something" island. She could join the rest of us in the land of "breakups, broken hearts, mistakes, and learning experiences." Incessant self-criticism keeps you exactly where you are. Look at your past, learn from it, and move forward, but don't wear it on your chest like a scarlet letter.

Another important aspect of Heather's story is that she actively reconnected with parts of herself that had become lost, or that she'd never explored before. She took classes in digital photography; she went wine tasting. As her self-appreciation grew, it created almost a kind of adrenaline as she kicked into a free-wheeling discovery mode. My advice here is to proceed with caution. Your new lens on your life is, well, new. Give yourself time to adjust, soak it in, and nurture yourself. Like Heather, don't take on huge commitments at first, but try activities that are low stress, inexpensive, and not mentally taxing. A photography class is probably a more appropriate move than graduate school.

> "The last two years have been overshadowed by the culmination of a traumatic family breakup, a relationship breakup, financial trouble, and the struggle to find a job. After years of uncertainty, I decided to investigate possibilities within my interests. After what felt like so much bad luck, things really feel like they have turned a corner."
>
> *Urban planner, 24, single and love it, Manchester, England*

CREATE A VISION BOARD

A vision board is a grown-up arts-and-crafts game. It is a creative expression of all the things in your life you would like to become physical manifestations. Your dreams, hobbies, goals, wishes, and desires are represented visually on your vision board. To create one, get some blank poster board, an art book, or a notebook and collect representations of what you want. Cut out pictures and words from magazines of things that appeal to you — don't worry about why they do. Be artistic about it, and display it someplace where you can see it. A physical representation of the types of things you are drawn to communicates to the Universe what types of things you want. Answers to many of the questions you are asking may lie within the vision board you create. There are no rules in creating a vision board, except that you have to actually believe it is possible for you to manifest what you put on your board!

NO SHIT, NO SHIFT

We don't mind surprises we like. When we meet an intriguing and attractive person, get a raise, or find a great parking spot, our faith in the universe and ourselves is restored! But not all surprises are good. When unexpected shit happens, then what? Is our only choice to lose faith?

We talked about how Expectation Hangovers often make us question the universe, our faith, and even our self-worth. When the unexpected happens, it does test our faith, but this is when we truly learn how to shift our perspectives. Getting to this shift doesn't involve some magical moment, either; achieving it is usually the result of the simple determination to keep moving forward even when we have no evidence we'll be successful. If we let the events of our lives play out, we will soon begin to see the blessing, the lesson, and the light — the coveted "aha" moment. And we appreciate the "aha" even more after going through some shitty experiences.

"Reflecting on my twenties brings to mind how the road map of my life turned out completely differently than I had planned or expected. A negative beginning erupted into the most positive and enriching part of my life so far. Unexpectedly, I discovered that despite my initial resistance to marriage and motherhood, with the start of my family, I had unearthed my temporary calling."

Licensed day-care operator, 30, married, Virginia

"THIS TOO SHALL PASS" by Jenna, 27

DECLARATION: *Be brave, be persistent, and always have faith in yourself, and things will change.*

Okay, I know that sounds like the title of some lame country song, but bear with me. I know how overwhelming it can be to be twenty something, to have your whole life ahead of you. You have accomplished school, getting your first career job, and once you've done all that, it's time to find a "soul mate." I also know how scary it is to realize that there is no guarantee that you are going to find, keep, and love someone. Or worse, love someone and not be loved back. Or even worse than that, love someone, not be loved back, and then find out he is in love and marrying someone else.

Oh yeah, I know. I know because that was me about a year ago. And when I found out, it was like all I had accomplished suddenly did not matter anymore. I felt completely worthless and hopeless. I became very depressed. I could barely eat. I could hardly sleep. I'd wake up at four in the morning with panic attacks. I felt like I was in a bad dream that I couldn't awaken from.

The problem with being depressed is that it's a Catch-22. I knew that I was the only one who could help me, but I was so down that I struggled to find the motivation to do it. But I forced myself to keep trying. I did everything I could get myself to do. I tried going to church. I tried joining the church's twenty-something group. I joined the gym. I tried to go out with my friends more. I joined Match.com. Sometimes, just the trying was excruciating, but I was persistent and patient for lack of any other option.

And guess what? It got better.

I did not find the cure or my answer in any one particular place or in a self-help book. I believe it was the combination of everything I did and the energy that I put out there by doing it that got me back to the land of the living. I managed to meet someone really great, and we started dating. I forced myself to take the last class to get my CPA license, and I got it. I left a job that was making me miserable, and I got a new one that fits me better.

Today, one year past the worst time of my life, I feel like I finally have my life back. I am getting married next year. I love my new job and the city I moved to. If I had known how my life was going to change the way it did, I would not have felt so bad. But as they say, hindsight is 20/20. So, the moral of my story: be brave, be persistent, and always have faith in yourself, and things *will* change. And above all, know that you are not alone.

In order to know what light is, we have to experience dark, right? Similarly, often it's the awful experiences we go through that make us appreciate the good ones even more. How about another analogy? Picture this: You are sitting in a middle coach seat on a crowded, hot airplane next to a crying baby for a nine-hour flight. Here's a very uncomfortable situation we would immediately want to flee. Now imagine sitting in a beautiful living room on a cushy recliner, sipping your favorite drink and watching your favorite television program. Now that's better; we wouldn't mind doing that for hours. But without knowing the feeling of being confined, would we really be able to appreciate the feeling of being totally relaxed? To really appreciate feeling comfortable, we have to experience discomfort. That is just the way it is, and the less we fight it, the fewer rounds we will go in the boxing ring with ourselves.

"EVERYTHING HAPPENS FOR A REASON" by Kim, 28

DECLARATION: *I thought that cliché was just something people say to try to explain the unexplainable.*

A little over a year ago, I quit my job, packed up my apartment, and moved clear across the country to my parents' house for a job that I ultimately didn't get and for a relationship that essentially was over before I left.

It was the darkest time of my life. For months, I had no money, no job, no boyfriend, and no hope that things would get better. I hibernated at my parents' house, avoiding everything and everyone. How could I see anyone in that state of mind? How would I pay to go out? What would I talk about — who won on *The Price Is Right*? Sure, I was lucky that I had a roof over my head, food on the table, and caring parents. But all I saw when I looked in the mirror was a failure. I had failed in my career. I had failed on my own in Los Angeles. And I had failed in my relationship.

My mom used to say that "everything happens for a reason." I hated hearing that. I thought it was just something she'd say to try to explain the unexplainable — something she'd say to comfort me when I didn't get the job I wanted or my date stood me up. But over the past 452 days, I've realized that in actuality, everything does happen for a reason. Damn! She was right.

If it weren't for quitting my job and abruptly leaving LA, I would not have been home when my dad got sick. I would not have met and worked with my career coach, who has awakened my spirit to discover what my purpose is. And without having that cush job to fall back on, I don't know if I would have had the courage to make the career change that I needed to make. The one that gets me psyched to start each day. I would not have met the love of my life and finally realized the meaning of a healthy relationship. But the most important thing that happened during that dark time is that I became the light I had been searching for. I was given the opportunity to discover myself. And I took it. And I will be forever grateful.

I shudder when I remember the person I was. I wish I could go back in time and hug her and tell her that it will get better, that this is one of the best things that will ever happen to her, and that (as much as I hate to say it) everything does happen for a reason!

NO RISK, NO REWARD

I am sure you've heard this advice before — no risk, no reward. It's true, and our twenties are often a great time to test it out. If you're unhappy or frustrated with where you are, there is probably no better time to take a big gamble on something you've always wanted to do but have been too scared to try. I have one golden rule when it comes to taking risks: you cannot care about the outcome.

In other words, withhold your expectations and fears of failure and, as Nike says, "Just do it." Have faith in yourself to pull through whatever obstacles you may face, and don't undermine yourself with thoughts of failure and embarrassment about what could happen. If you take a risk, the reward is often not found in what you achieve. The real reward is how you feel about yourself for having taken the risk, for proving to yourself that you can "just do it" and survive, and maybe even thrive.

"I'VE DONE MORE THAN SURVIVE — I'VE STARTED TO THRIVE"
by Denelle, 29

DECLARATION: *I decided if my life was going to be less than the vision I had imagined, then it was going to be spectacular in the living.*

At twenty-seven, in an attempt to extricate myself from a quarter-life crisis, I left my family, friends, job, home . . . everything that was important and meant security to me and moved three thousand miles to the other side of the country. Why the drastic change? Why would I, the control freak who never does anything without a plan, move to a city I'd never visited, without a job, and to an apartment I'd never seen? The answer is simple: desperation.

When I was younger I'd always had this perfect vision of my life.

I'd graduate from college (with as many letters as possible after my name), go to work at the perfect job that let me travel the world and get married to a guy who was well-educated and successful. We'd have two or three beautiful children, and we would eventually buy a house where we could have all our family together for Christmas and throw fabulous dinner parties with the best guests, food, and entertainment. This perfect vision of mine also included me six inches taller…that should have been my first clue that I was expecting too much.

Cut to reality. I was living at home with my parents, stalling on going back to school for my master's because I couldn't decide what I wanted to do with my life, and working at a job that drove me crazy and offered no room for advancement. And I hadn't dated anyone in years. I suddenly feared that I was closer to becoming that old weird woman who ends up alone with fourteen cats than I was to becoming the perfect woman of my dreams.

> "I moved from a monotonous life in a rural, stagnant population. Because of this change, I was able to 'start over' and build my life on my own terms and 'come to terms' with myself, my goals, and my expectations."
>
> Assistant dean of admissions,
> 26, married, Oregon

I had finally grown up enough to understand that almost no one ends up with their perfect fantasy life. However, I didn't want to be the person who just settled for a mediocre existence. I decided if my life was going to be less than the vision I had imagined, then it was going to be spectacular in the living. And the only way I was going to achieve that was by throwing myself out of the nest, so to speak, and forcing myself to fly. Staying too close to home would only let me remain too dependent upon the safety net and familiar, maybe false, sense of security that had gotten me into this position in the first place.

So I left. I loaded up my car with everything I owned and headed for New York. My first view of my apartment in Brooklyn tested my resolve. In fact, it made me cry. And they weren't tears of joy. At that moment, I began to doubt my life-changing move. I remember thinking, "I haven't even unpacked anything. . . . I can just get back in the car and head in the other direction." Thankfully, pride is a powerful motivator. I couldn't bring myself to throw in the towel before I'd ever even

> "I've really explored other options for myself and realized that I don't have to do what is expected of me in society's eyes. I have been able to learn that there isn't much out there that we cannot achieve, and to shoot for it."
>
> *Teacher, 29, serious relationship, Texas*

spent the night in my new home — and it was a stretch even calling it that.

I found a job almost immediately, which is still amazing to me in a city where I knew absolutely no one. But I used Craigslist, the classified ads, and numerous online job search tools, and sent my résumé to as many places as I could. The best response I received was from placement agencies and headhunters. They were able to set up interviews for me and tried to plug me into positions that fit my skill set.

I had the job but everything else was an uphill battle. Things were still tight financially. The stress of trying to make ends meet was mentally and physically draining. In addition, I was emotionally exhausted. I hadn't made any really close friends since moving to the city. The rest of my emotional support system was thousands of miles away. I was lonely. On more than one occasion all I wanted to do was go home.

Even though I feared I had made a mistake, giving up and going home would be the equivalent of failure. I knew that there were people who thought that I had made a rash and somewhat ignorant decision by making this move — I did not want to prove them right. On some level I was afraid that maybe they were right. Maybe I had taken on more than I could handle.

But if I went back, I'd be going back to my life exactly as it was before, and nothing would be different — no thank you. Even though things were hard, there were also times when things were good. I might have a moment where I was struggling with the loneliness or the fear, but I would suddenly look up and see the Empire State Building and be amazed and thrilled all over again to think about where I was living. I would think about all of the other people who struggled, often in conditions and situations worse than mine, to make it on their own in this city, and I would feel a sense of gratitude to even have the opportunity to have the experiences I was having. The words "What doesn't kill us only makes us stronger" echoed in my mind. It was that certainty that I clung to when I felt completely overwhelmed. The nights I would cry myself to sleep, when I felt like I couldn't be any more alone, I would tell myself over and over again, "You can handle anything that life throws at you. You will survive this."

And I did survive. And more than survive, I've started to thrive.

I've been in New York almost two years now. I have a job that I love and a much better apartment in a neighborhood that is truly home. I have made friends that share common interests, I've started working on my master's degree, and I hope to get a job that allows me to travel the world.

I'm no longer afraid of being alone or uncomfortable with just myself for company. I've learned how to install window air conditioners and entire closet systems by myself. Life today is less about success in the traditional sense of the word, less about how others perceive my success, and more about me being satisfied with my life. I am happy with my choices, even if I'm not making six figures a year and I don't have the fairy-tale prince and castle. I have come to understand that while my independence is precious to me, there are times when I simply can't do things by myself and I need to ask for help, and that there is no shame in doing that. And that really, there is very little I cannot do if I simply put my mind to it and refuse to give up.

Anything I decide to do will be easier now that I have knowledge of how I have succeeded in the past. I will never again allow what I want to accomplish to be limited by my limitations. I have discovered that my potential is greater than I knew, and that opens an entire world of possibilities for the future.

The limitations you believe you have are not real. They are perceived limitations that become excuses for unhappiness or lack of fulfillment. As long as you continue to view them as limitations, you will be limited. Well, duh. So how about changing your perception? See them as motivators, see them as malleable rather than permanent. Or how about this . . . stop seeing them all together!

GETTING COMFORTABLE IN THE UNKNOWN

Here's something to ponder: "You don't know what you don't know." With all the things you are worrying about right now, there is an infinite number of things you don't even know about that may be in your future. We really do not know what is ahead. Our plans can never anticipate everything. The only thing we can be sure of is death, taxes, and traffic whenever we are running late. So what do we do? Practice getting more and more comfortable with ourselves, with our ability to improvise, and with the unknown.

Not sure how? The following story has some great suggestions. I've tried several and had a blast (though personally I prefer Bono over Justin).

"DANCE NAKED" by Tamara, 27

DECLARATION: *The unknown, the unsure — it's the blessing and the curse of my twenty-something experience.*

What I don't know is what I can't worry about, but I have trouble not worrying. And the unsure perpetuates my own insecurities and self-doubt. The unknown — the unsure — it's the blessing and the curse of my twenty-something experience. In college, I went through the motions, the risk taking was controlled, and there was always a safety net. In the "real world," there's rent, concern for job security, and a constant striving to balance conforming with rules and challenging the process.

I've done some things that have helped me deal with the uncertainty about my future, take risks even without a safety net, and calm my own insecurities. I put myself in new situations on a regular basis. Last year I joined a kickball team and didn't know anyone on the team. I go to parties alone, I strike up conversation with someone new at work every month, and I invite new people to lunch. I always show up to whatever it is; even if I really, really, really don't want to. Usually, these are the most rewarding experiences. I've started taking risks even though I don't have a safety net, and I've been amazed at what I can do.

For example, I volunteered to speak about homelessness at a church when my boss couldn't fit it in her schedule. When I arrived, I realized I was the sermon. I stood absolutely terrified in front of two hundred people. But I didn't back down. I did it and learned that I could speak about homelessness passionately and publicly. From then on, I sought out opportunities to get myself in front of groups of people regularly.

I keep asking questions, partially to help make sense of my fears and to gain new insights and perspectives from people who've been there. I look myself in the mirror and really face whatever it is I'm scared about. And finally, and I can't believe I am sharing this, I dance naked in my room — privately of course! This is the best because I have to face myself. I can scrutinize all the things I hate about my body, or I can embrace it — and embracing it feels a lot better. I celebrate me in these moments and often laugh at how ridiculous I look after ten minutes of groovin' to Justin Timberlake! It's private, it's freeing, it's liberating, and just for me.

Believe it or not, all of these things, especially being vulnerable enough to dance naked, have supported me in trusting myself more. I've been able to have faith in the unknown and believe that there is a path I'm on even if the final destination seems unclear. I've learned that I have to listen to my gut. If it tells me to move forward, then I do it. If it tells me, "Hold on a second," then I wait and tell myself, "Be patient." And if it says, "Crank up 'SexyBack' and get your groove on," I listen.

EXPECT THE UNEXPECTED

Why do we cling to our expectations when the unexpected moments in life are what make our lives what they are? It's in the unexpected moments that we discover parts of ourselves we didn't know existed or see parts in other people that surprise us. It's in the unexpected that we often discover what we are passionate about. It's in the unexpected that we learn the lessons we need to learn the most. And it's often in the unexpected that we really learn who we are, what we want, and how to get it.

> "I never expected to be living in Asia. I certainly never thought I'd be married to a Korean man. I expected I would be pretty settled in Canada right now with an okay job, but here I am having an exciting time every day."
>
> Content developer for ESL books, 27, married, Korea

The here and now is all we have. We can't count on what the future will bring, so we must trust that the present is giving us everything we need. Enjoy where you are and who is with you. If you can be in the moment, embrace surprise, and cultivate happiness within yourself, you will do more than survive, you will thrive.

AFTERWORD: SHARE YOUR TWENTY-SOMETHING STORY

Congratulations! You've successfully investigated your Expectation Hangovers, navigated through the questions of the Twenties Triangle, and put together the pieces of your twenty-something puzzle. The twenty somethings who have shared their stories and insights have been your fellow passengers along your journey, and I'm honored to have been your tour guide. But now it's time for you to chart your own course. Where have you been and where are you headed? Don't wait for anything or anyone else to come along to lead you to the pot of gold at the end of your twenty-something rainbow — you are the navigator of your journey!

To review what you've learned so far and to clarify the action steps you now know you are ready to take, I encourage you to write your own "Twenty-Something Manifesto." What is your twenty-something story? What are your "aha" moments? What lessons still challenge you? What blessings are you celebrating?

Writing your own story can itself become a unique journey of self-discovery and personal acknowledgment. It may help you make sense of things or perhaps bring resolution to lingering issues or questions. If you feel inspired after you write your story, I encourage you to share it with others. Sharing your story is incredibly liberating — as I've found out from experience! Send your story to your loved ones, send it to me, start a blog, or join the www.20somethingmanifesto.com community. On this website, I've posted a suggested story structure if your inner writing muse needs a jump start.

My greatest wish for all twenty somethings is for you to realize that you and you alone have the ability to transform your twenty-something experience. As you navigate through the Twenties Triangle, experience and savor all the stages that come when answering its three questions: Who am I? What do I want? and How do I get it? Understand life will continue to come with Expectation Hangovers, so practice treating them. Have faith that every loss, every struggle, and every heartbreak has a lesson and an ending. Look to the *present*, rather than to the future, to discover solutions within yourself, and take one step at a time toward healing. Know that your twenties aren't supposed to be *the* time in your life; they are *a* time in your life. You don't want to peak now, with a good fifty-plus years yet to live, do you? Of course not!

Do you know how I know when I'm in the presence of someone who really "gets it?" Someone who has gotten to a place of contentment and peace with their life? I know it when someone is telling me about the worst thing that ever happened to them with a smile on their face and light in their eyes because they now relate to it as the best thing that ever happened to them. I am grateful that I can now tell my twenty-something story with a smile on my face. Reflecting back, I can summarize that decade as one of the worst and best times of my life so far. Have faith that you too can get to this place of acceptance and tell your own twenty-something story (even while you are still in your twenties!) with a smile on your face.

ACKNOWLEDGMENTS

I did not write this manifesto alone. I am grateful to every one of the twenty somethings who participated in the Manifesto Survey and to the inspiring writers who have made the *Twenty-Something Manifesto* possible.

To New World Library and Georgia Hughes, for another opportunity to write about the twenty-something experience. To Jeff Campbell, whose insightful edits helped shape this book. To Mona Miller, the University of Santa Monica, and my spiritual community, for your support and guidance. To the Sirens Society, being a part of our mission helps me to fulfill mine.

To the people who stand by me as I write my own story: my beloved friends and my incredibly supportive family — Mom, Dad, and Carrie. And to my biggest cheerleader and best proofreader, my husband, Chris — thank you.

CONTRIBUTORS

Each of the stories was written exclusively for this book and generously shared voluntarily by the authors. Many contributors chose to use pseudonyms or to remain nameless. The following contributors have chosen to be acknowledged by first and last name, and some have shared a brief bio or information about what they're up to.

- Brady Akers
- Warren Alexander holds bachelor's degrees in English and business administration from the University of Washington.
- Jessica Bundy is a clothing designer from Ontario. Visit her website at www.houseofsocialgrace.com.
- Denelle Burns lives and works in New York City, where she is pursuing a master's degree in global affairs at New York University.
- Amy Butler

- Laura Cline can be found online at www.claremontgirl.com.
- Lucy Cline
- Lauren A. Davis, MEd, is an academic adviser at Cleveland State University in Cleveland, Ohio.
- Kim Delaney
- Julie Freese works in public relations, event planning, and marketing in New York City.
- Jennifer Froth
- Kaitlin T. Garvey
- Megan Gibbens is a freelance writer for consumer magazines in the United Kingdom. She plans to return to her home country of Australia at some point during her twenties to continue her writing career.
- Alexandra Hynes
- Kate Jackett is twenty-eight years old, lives in upstate New York, and earns a living as a transportation consultant.
- Giscelle Kilayko is a graduating psychology major at York University in Toronto.
- Eileen Korte is an aspiring television writer and graduate of Northwestern University. She currently resides in Los Angeles, California.
- Ann Mathiot lives in Lancaster, Pennsylvania, where she works with special-needs children. For more information or to contact Ann, visit www.myspace.com/annie83.
- Angela McKinster is now twenty-eight years old, married with two stepsons, and working as a procurement consultant in the government contracting arena.
- Elissa Meadow
- Caitlin Petre lives in New York and works at a public interest communications company.
- Lindsey Pollak, a writer and speaker, is the author of *Getting from College to Career: Ninety Things to Do before*

You Join the Real World (HarperCollins, 2007) and writes
a career advice blog at www.lindseypollak.blogspot.com.

- Erin Posanti
- Gretchen Sechrist
- Jeannette Sepulveda
- Heather Strang is a writer and teacher passionate about
  living her most authentic life. Learn more about her at
  www.heatherstrang.com.
- Rebecca Suarez
- Kristin Viola currently resides in San Francisco, where she
  enjoys reading, writing, and making the most of her
  twenty-something experience.
- Anne Walzel
- Kimberly Weisensee, a graduate of Northwestern's Medill
  School of Journalism, specializes in magazine editing.
- Diane Wetzel is a graduate of James Madison University
  and currently resides in northern Virginia.
- Jon Zucker is a songwriter and recording artist who per-
  forms throughout the United States, and whose music has
  appeared in feature films and on television. Please visit
  www.jonzucker.com for more information.

INDEX

A

acceptance, 272, 275–76
  See also self-acceptance
Acceptance Process (exercise), 276–77
accountability, 48, 309
ADD, 300, 305
addictions, 296, 297–99, 300
  See also drinking; drugs; eating dis-
    orders; *specific addiction*
ADHD, 300
adulthood, puberty of, 75
adulthood, transition to, 109–22
  attention shift during, 120–21
  case studies, 111–13, 117–18
  delayed, 24–27
  designating time for, 116
  doing "right" thing and, 118–20
  exercises for, 119–20, 122
  getting sea legs during, 109–10, 114, 115
  self-awareness and, 79–81, 93–94
  taking time during, 114–17
  See also What Do I Want?
"aha" moments, 89–90, 237–38, 266–67, 322

alcohol. *See* drinking
altruism, 234
American Dream, 15
anniversaries, first, 18–19
anti-anxiety drugs, 300
anxiety
  checklists and, 5–6, 108
  coping with, 76
  disorders, 300
  over life ambitions, 107–9, 117–18
  self-awareness and, 64, 66–68, 74–77
  uncertainty and, 107–9, 117–18
apartment, finding, 116, 121
"apprentice" mentality, 262–63
authority figures, dealing with, 172–74

B

Baby Boomers, 15, 16–17
balance
  Expectation Hangover recovery and, 50–51
  finding your stride and, 145–47
  interdependence and, 147

balance (*continued*)
  success as, 263
  work/life, 47, 48, 226, 243–45, 265
bank accounts, 121
behavioral disorders, 291, 300
bipolar disorder, 300
blame, 98–99, 319–21
body image, 59, 76, 293–97
"boomerangers," 27–29
bosses
  impact of, on work environment, 237
  parental memories triggered by, 172,
    173–74
  toxic relationships with, 160–61, 162,
    237, 277, 318
  walking out on, 162, 318
  workaholic, emulating, 242–43
breakups, 82, 198, 206–11, 298–99
Buddha, 276
budgets, 47, 116
bullies, 280–83
burnout, 146
business start-up
  advisory team, 256–57, 262
  "apprentice" mentality, 262–63
  brainstorming/strategizing,
    255–56
  case studies, 258–59
  evaluation, 260, 264–65
  execution, 260, 263–64
  exercises for, 258, 266
  financial difficulties during, 258–59,
    265
  hobbies and, 253
  investing in, 264–65
  keeping full-time job during, 257
  mission statement, 254–55
  Mission Vision Plan, 254–58
  networking, 260, 262–63
  Quarter System, 260–66
  research, 255, 260, 261–62
  scheduling, 264
  self-doubt and, 264
  vision board, 254–55
  work/life balance, 265

C

caffeine, 152
career
  case studies, 244–45, 248–51
  changing, 248–51, 325
  checklists for, 4–5
  Expectation Hangovers and, 33, 231
  hobbies vs., 251–53, 257
  love vs., 223–25
  networking and, 11
  options available, 141–42
  passion and, 232–36, 247–51, 255, 263
  purpose and, 233–34
  risk-taking in, 234, 247–51
  rivalries in, 280–82
  sacrificing for, 240–43
  small steps toward, 41–42
  success stories in, 11
  twenty-something advice on, 266–67
  twenty-something concerns with, 156
  work/life balance, 47, 48, 226,
    243–45, 265
  See also business start-up; jobs
career coaches, 325
case studies
  adulthood, transition to, 111–13,
    117–18
  body image, 295–97
  business start-up, 258–59
  career, 244–45, 248–51
  checklisting, 4–5
  comparisons and regret, 40–41
  credit card debt, 308–10
  dating, 195–96
  divorce, 283–85, 316–19
  drugs, 298–99
  escapism, 25–27
  Expectation Hangover recovery,
    50–51, 53–54
  Expectation Hangovers, 20–21,
    150–51
  friends, 167–68
  How Do I Get What I Want?,
    142–44, 148–49, 150–51

instant gratification, 15–18
invincibility, 22–24
job satisfaction, 237–38, 244–45
love, 186–89, 192–93, 207–8, 214–16,
   218–21, 228–29
marriage, 228–29, 278–79
mental disorders, 301–3
option paralysis, 9–10
overdependency on parents, 28
parents, relationship with, 178–80
self-awareness, stage 1 (basic),
   66–68, 70–71
self-awareness, stage 2 (investigative), 79–81, 84–87
self-awareness, stage 3 (integrated),
   93–94, 97–98, 100–102
the shift, 316–19, 323–25, 326–29
tough stuff, 273–74, 278–79, 280–82,
   283–85, 286–88
toxic relationships, 173–74
What Do I Want?, 111–13, 123–25,
   126–28, 130–31, 133–34
challenges. See tough stuff
checklists, 4–7, 9, 108, 147
Cheesecake Factory paralysis, 7–9,
   141–42, 167
children, 18–19, 79, 226
Clarifying Goals (exercise), 36–37
classes, enrolling in, 171–72
coach, 100, 325
college
   addictions during, 298–99
   bubble of "invincibility" in, 23
   checklisting during, 5
   enjoying, 113–14
   graduation from, 63–64, 110–14
   making friends in, 170
   as preparation for real life, 140–41,
      264
   reality vs., 110
   reviewing experience in (exercise),
      122
   urgent necessities during, 120–21
comfort zone, stepping outside, 172

commitment, 223
Commitment Contract (exercise), 49–50
communication, 222–23
community, 22
comparisons
   with friends, 168–69
   regrets and, 40–41
   self-awareness and, 65–66, 69
   stopping, 42–43, 55, 129
compartmentalization, 145
compassion, 90, 234
consumer culture, 38–39
control, 76–77, 160, 213–17, 280–83
counseling, 100, 148, 216, 275, 285
couples
   exercises for, 222–23
   issues facing, 211–12
   love vs. career, 223–25
   male vs. female relating styles,
      217–22
   marriage and, 225–29
Covey, Stephen, 47–48
Create a Vision Board (exercise), 321–22
creativity, 69, 90, 234, 306, 317–18
credit cards
   debt encurred through, 307, 308–10
   tips for using, 310–11
criticism, 161–62
   See also self-criticism
crushes, 186, 193

D

dating, 195–206
   balance and, 146
   case studies, 195–96, 200–201
   after college graduation, 110
   credit card debt and, 309–10
   as elimination process, 195
   emotional baggage undermining,
      202–3
   exercises for, 205–6
   expectations while, 198, 201
   internet, 201
   male vs. female behaviors, 197–98

dating (*continued*)
  marriage and, 200–202
  relating and, 211–12
  as research, 132–33, 198–200
  "rules" in, 196
  saying yes to, 195–96, 199–200
  self-confidence required for, 193, 203
  the shift and, 323–24
  in Smart-Slacking Game Plan, 116
  soul matches, attracting, 203–6
debt, 270, 291
  case studies, 308–10
  consolidation of, 310
  escapism and, 26
  exercises for, 311–13
  Expectation Hangovers and, 47
  "good" vs. "bad," 307–8
  tips for avoiding/getting out of,
    310–11
decision making
  anxiety/depression caused by, 121
  career choice, 232
  divorce, 284–85
  during Expectation Hangovers, 47
  limitless options and, 7–11
  marriage, 225–29
  potential outcomes of, 130–31
  responsibility for, 320
  self-awareness and anxiety regard-
    ing, 75
  the shift and, 317
  taking time for, 114–17
  See also risk taking; What Do I
    Want?
denial, 24–27, 272, 275, 304, 309
depression, 5–6, 64, 300, 323–24
  See also anxiety
diet, 46–47, 48, 292, 294
difficulties. *See* tough stuff
disappointments, dealing with, 148–49,
  322–25
discrimination, 270, 273–74
dislike, 270, 278–83
divorce, 270

case studies, 283–85, 316–19
  expectations and, 212
  parental, emotional effect of, 187, 190
  second, 316–19
  singlehood after, 318–19
  support system and, 179
Do-It-Yourself Personality Tests (exercise), 132–33
domino effect, 43
dramas, interpersonal, 270
dreams
  Expectation Hangovers and, 39
  resurfacing of, 87
  self-awareness and, 67
  tweaking, 20–21
drinking
  binge, impact on health, 292
  Expectation Hangovers and, 46, 48,
    152
  "invincibility" and, 23
  reducing amount of, 46, 101–2, 152,
    194
  self-awareness and, 76–77, 101–2
  singlehood graduation and, 194
  tough stuff and, 275
drugs, 291
  addiction to, 22, 296, 298–99
  case studies, 298–99
  Expectation Hangovers and, 46
  health impact of, 292
  self-awareness and, 76–77
  self-focus and, 22
  tough stuff and, 275
duality, 66, 90
DUI charges, 300

E

eating disorders, 291, 297–98
  Expectation Hangovers and, 46, 48
  self-awareness and, 76–77, 101
education, continuing, 133
emotions
  in acceptance process, 272, 275, 276
  acknowledging, 175

barriers against, 186–92
buried, 286–89, 297
triggers, 173–76
twenty-something concerns with, 156
entitlement, sense of, 13
entrepreneurship. *See* business start-up
escapism, 24–27
exercise, physical, 46, 117, 146, 293, 294, 295–96, 323
exercises
    Acceptance Process, 276–77
    Clarifying Goals, 36–37
    Commitment Contract, 49–50
    Create a Vision Board, 321–22
    Do-It-Yourself Personality Tests, 132–33
    Expectation Hangover Treatment and Prevention Plan, 54–56
    Expectation Implants, 39–40
    Finding Your Keys, 191–92, 289
    Get Inspired, 12–13
    Give Your Label a Name, 305
    Graduating from Singlehood, 194
    Grat-I-tude, 78–79
    I Am Who I Am, 92
    Identifying Toxic Relationships, 162–63
    Identifying Triggers and Corner Pieces, 176–77
    "I Hate My Job" Survival Kit, 239–40
    Manifest Your Soul Match, 205–6
    Mission Vision Overview, 258
    Past-Performance Review, 122
    Qual-you-ty Time, 82–83
    Quarter Plan Overview, 266
    Relationship 101, 222–23
    Right-Answer Reflex Game, 119–20
    Self-Awareness Continuum Counselor, 104
    Smart-Slacking Game Plan, 115–17
    Throw a Money Party, 311–13
    Walking in a Bully's Shoes, 283
    What's Your Twenty?, 29–30

Expectation Hangovers
    breakups and, 206, 211
    case studies, 150–51
    causes of, 32–33, 110–14, 231
    decision making during, 47
    defined, 19
    examples of, 33–34
    exercises for, 36–37, 39–40
    firsts and, 18–21
    goals vs. expectations, 34–37
    minimizing, 35
    more/better/different and, 109
    others' expectations and, 37–40
    preventing, 55, 59
    relapses, 149–52
    relationships and, 33, 160, 166
    self-awareness and, 59
    self-focus during, 51
    symptoms of, 31–32, 48
Expectation Hangovers, treatment for, 44–56
    acceptance, 44–46, 55
    exercises for, 49–50
    gratitude, 51, 56, 152
    healthy behavior, 46–47, 56, 152
    plan for, 54–56
    proactivity, 47–50, 56
    relapses, 151–52
    selflessness, 51–54, 56
Expectation Hangover Treatment and Prevention Plan (exercise), 54–56
Expectation Implants (exercise), 39–40
expectations
    while dating, 198, 201
    goals vs., 34–37, 127
    of instant gratification, 13–18
    letting go of, 55, 140, 142–44
    male vs. female, 217–22
    of romance, 184
    See also Expectation Hangovers
expectations, of others
    of Baby Boomers, 15
    career choice and, 126–27, 142–44, 248–51

expectations, of others (*continued*)
  divorce and, 212
  doing "right" thing and, 118–20
  Expectation Hangovers and, 37–40
  parental, 161, 181, 187
  self-awareness and, 75–76
  tuning out, 142–44
experience
  experiencing, 113–14
  past, 144–45
  shitty, 322–25

F

failure, fear of, 246, 247
faith, 99–104, 144, 322–24, 334
faking it, 87
family
  marriage and, 226
  as support system members,
    177–78
  toxic relationships, 160, 161, 277
fears
  as chief career obstacle, 247–48, 251
  of doing "wrong" thing, 10–11
  of marriage, 228–29
  of quitting jobs, 232, 244–47
Fear Trifecta, 245–47
finances
  business start-up and, 258–59, 264–65
  Expectation Hangovers and, 33, 151
  identity and, 59
  independence, 313–14
  male vs. female views of, 312
  management of, 307–8
  marriage and, 226
  organizing, 116
  success and, 95–96
  twenty-something concerns with, 156
  See also debt
Finding Your Keys (exercise), 191–92,
  289
firsts, 18–21
forgiveness, 182, 271, 285–88
Frankl, Victor, 34

friends
  acquaintances vs., 171
  being there for, 167–69
  case studies, 167–68
  comparisons with, 40–41, 168–69
  making, 110, 170–72, 328, 329
  marriage and, 226
  purpose and, 233
  toxic, 160–61, 164–67
Friends (TV show), 170
future
  fear of, 247
  intuition and, 135
  planning for, 111–13
  twenty-something obsession with,
    5–6, 43–44
  when/then thinking and, 251

G

Gandhi, Mohandas, 238
gay relationships, 222
Get Inspired (exercise), 12–13
Give Your Label a Name (exercise), 305
goals
  checklists for, 4–7
  clarifying (exercise), 36–37, 55
  commitment to (exercise), 49–50
  exercises for, 29–30
  expectations vs., 34–37, 127
  marriage and, 226
  personalized, 95–96
  small steps toward, 41–42, 55, 85–86,
    94, 142, 143
  time required to reach, 17
  See also How Do I Get What I
    Want?; What Do I Want?
Graduating from Singlehood (exercise),
  194
grass-is-greener mentality, 26–27
gratification
  deferred, 18
  instant, 13–18, 38, 109
gratitude, 51, 56, 77–79, 152, 263
Grat-I-tude (exercise), 78–79

gratitude journal, 43
grief process, 272
group mentality, 25

H

"having it all"
  American Dream and, 15
  body image and, 295
  checklists and, 6
  credit card debt and, 307
  passion and, 232–33
  success not as, 224
  women and, 219, 225
Hawkins, David, 104
headiness, 84–86
health benefits, 240
health insurance, 110, 116, 121
healthy behavior, 152
high school, making friends in, 170
hobbies, career vs., 251–53, 257
home ownership, 18–19, 79, 93–94, 313
How Do I Get What I Want?
  accepting results, 152–54
  balance, 145–47
  case studies, 142–44, 148–49, 150–51
  Expectation Hangover relapses and,
    149–52
  finding your stride, 140–49
  interdependence, 147–49
  internal momentum for, 140–42
  Life IQ, 140, 144–45
  real life as preparation for, 139–40
  "shoulds," tuning out, 140, 142–44
Hulnick, Ron, 103–4

I

I Am Who I Am (exercise), 92
Identifying Toxic Relationships (exercise), 162–63
Identifying Triggers and Corner Pieces
  (exercise), 176–77
identity
  externally-imposed, shedding, 69,
    90, 96
  job as, 59, 93–94, 234

identity crisis, 63, 74
"identity onion," peeling, 59–60
if/then thinking, 194, 248, 251
"I Hate My Job" Survival Kit (exercise),
  239–40
illness, 284–85, 287–88
impatience, 91
income, steady, 93–94
independence
  Expectation Hangovers and, 147
  financial, 313–14
  from parents, 90, 96–99, 177–80
infatuations, romantic, 186
inspiration
  getting (exercise), 12–13
  self-criticism following, 11–12
instant gratification, 13–18, 38, 109
interdependence, 147–49, 329
internal momentum, developing, 140–42
internet dating, 201
interpersonal skills, 11
interviews, 116
intuition, 126, 133–37
investment clubs, 313
invincibility, feelings of, 22–24, 292

J

Jerry Maguire (film), 185
jobs
  anxiety over, 108
  attitude changes toward, 236–39
  changing, 123–25, 128, 324
  exercises for, 239–40
  Expectation Hangovers with, 148–49
  fear of quitting, 232, 244–47
  finding, 253, 328
  first, 18–21, 94, 112–13, 117–18, 121
  health benefits, 240
  identity and, 59, 93–94, 234
  interviews for, 113, 114
  noncareer, 111–13, 115, 116, 142–43
  second, 265, 310
  while starting business, 257
  "window shopping" for, 117

jobs (*continued*)
    work/life balance, 47, 48
    work schedule, 110
    See also business start-up; career; job
        satisfaction
job satisfaction, 232
    attitude changes for, 236–39, 241
    case studies, 237–38, 244–45
    exercises for, 239–40
    respect and, 241–42
    sacrificing and, 240–43
    work/life balance, 243–45
journaling
    as Expectation Hangover remedy, 47
    gratitude, 43
    healing through, 320
    stream-of-consciousness, 289
    toxic relationships, 163, 176–77
justification, 246–47

K

Katrina Relief, 53–54
King, Martin Luther, Jr., 144

L

labels
    behavioral/mental, 291, 300–303
    de-shaming, 304–5
    exercise for, 305
laziness, 46
learning disabilities, 300, 306
Life IQ, 140, 144–45
lifestyle, healthy, 46–47, 56, 292–93
loans, 256, 307–9
love
    breakups, 82, 198, 206–11, 298–99
    career vs., 223–25
    case studies, 186–89, 192–93, 207–8,
        214–16, 218–21, 228–29
    control vs., 213–17
    emotional baggage undermining,
        202–3
    exercises for, 191–92, 205–6, 222–23

first, 18–19
    marriage and, 225–29
    media portrayals of, 183, 184
    passion vs., 212–13
    purpose and, 233
    self-confidence and, 192–93
    soul matches, 183–84, 203–6

M

manic depression, 300–303, 304
Manifesto Survey, 33–34, 156, 292, 293,
    307
Manifest Your Soul Match (exercise),
    205–6
marriage
    case studies, 228–29, 278–79
    deciding on, 225–29
    desire for, 108, 200–202
    deteriorating, 277
    fear of, 93–94
    second, 278–79
    self-awareness and, 79, 93–94
    See also divorce
Match.com, 90, 323
maturity, 149
meditation, 135–37
memories, triggered, 286–89
men
    attitude toward marriage, 225,
        226–27
    dating behavior, 197–98
    as fixers, 217–19, 221
    intuition and, 134
    money as viewed by, 312
    self-appreciation and, 78
    women's romantic expectations of,
        184
mental disorders
    case studies, 301–3
    de-shaming, 304–5
    labels attached to, 291, 300–301
    self-prescription for, 306
Mission Vision Overview (exercise), 258
Mission Vision Plan, 254–58

mistakes, as lessons, 48, 55–56
money. *See* finances
money parties, throwing, 311–13
more/better/different mentality, 55, 69,
    109, 153–54
    See also comparisons
mother-daughter relationships, 180–82
moving, 325, 326, 327–29
music, 306

N

networking, 11, 146, 238, 240, 260
noodle throwing, 123
    See also risk taking
numbness, emotional, 186–92

O

options
    Expectation Hangovers and, 34
    paralysis in face of, 7–11, 141–42, 167
    risk taking with, 123
others
    changing, 279–80
    comparisons with (*see* comparisons)
    expectations of (*see* expectations, of
        others)
overcommitment, 145–47
overeating. *See* eating disorders
overwork, 46, 48, 275

P

parenthood, 79, 93–94, 233
parents
    aging, marriage, and, 226
    Baby Boomers as, 16–17
    blaming, 98–99
    case studies, 173–74, 178–80
    death of, 178–79
    divorce of, 187, 190
    expectations of, 37–38, 161, 181, 187
    "helicopter," 21
    independence from, 90, 96–99,
        177–80

living with, 325
married life of, effect on children,
    228–29
overdependency on, 27–29, 112, 327
as people, 96–98
restructuring relationship with,
    180–82
sick, 325
as support system members, 177–78
toxic relationships, 161, 172–76
passion
    career and, 232–36, 247–51, 255, 263
    defined, 234–35
    hobbies and, 251–53
    love vs., 212–13
    unexpected and, 331–32
past
    deconstructing (exercise), 191–92
    experience, 144–45
    looking back at, 154, 320–21
Past-Performance Review (exercise),
    122
personality tests (exercise), 132–33
Peter Pan Syndrome, 24–27
possessions, Expectation Hangovers and,
    38–39
present moment
    checklists and, 6
    enjoying, 113–14, 118–19, 154
    focus on, Expectation Hangover pre-
        vention and, 47, 55
    meditation for, 135–37
proactivity, 47–50, 56, 180
promotions, first, 18–19, 79
puberty, 75
purpose, passion vs., 233–36

Q

Qual-you-ty Time (exercise), 82–83
"quarter-life crisis," 74, 89–90, 219
Quarter Plan Overview (exercise), 266
Quarter System, 260–66
questions, asking, 73–74, 81–82, 85, 86,
    153–54

R

racism, 273–74
reality, 140–41
reality check, 56
regrets, 5, 40–42
Relationship 101 (exercise), 222–23
relationships
    with authority figures, 172–74
    case studies, 173–74
    changing nature of, 160
    escapism and, 26
    exercises for, 162–63, 176–77
    Expectation Hangovers and, 33, 160,
        166
    identity and, 59
    interdependence and, 147–49
    mother-daughter, 180–82
    need for, 108
    as networking, 11
    restructuring of, 180–82
    risk taking and, 172
    same-sex, 198, 222
    self-awareness and, 76, 82
    toxic, 160–63, 216, 277, 318
    twenty-something concerns with, 156
    See also bosses; couples; family;
        friends; love; marriage; parents
religion, 103, 226, 302, 323
responsibility, 157
    blaming and, 319–21
    financial, 309
    for job satisfaction, 239
    proactivity and, 47–48
    in relationships, 166–67
    self-awareness and, 91
    smart slacking and, 114–15
résumés, 108, 116, 240
Right-Answer Reflex Game (exercise),
    119–20
"right" thing, doing, 10–11, 118–20
risk taking
    breakups and, 208
    career choice and, 234, 247–51

case studies, 123–25, 130–31, 133–34,
    326–29
disappointments resulting from,
    128–29
elimination process with, 125–28, 129
intuition and, 133–37
as noodle throwing, 123
potential outcomes of, 130–31
relationships and, 172
thriving after, 326–29
uncertainty and, 330–31
Robbins, Tom, 282
romance. See love
roommates, 164–66

S

savings, 226
security, financial, 93–94, 151
self-acceptance, 68, 69–71, 85, 86, 169
self-appreciation, 55, 77–79
self-awareness, 59, 106
Self-Awareness Continuum, 60–61
Self-Awareness Continuum Counselor
    (exercise), 104
self-awareness, stage 1 (basic), 63–71
    anxiety/depression caused by, 64,
        66–68
    case studies, 66–68, 70–71
    duality and, 66
    roles and self-definition, 64–68
    in Self-Awareness Continuum, 60, 61
    self-improvement and, 69–71
    transitioning from, 68, 69
self-awareness, stage 2 (investigative),
    73–88
    of adulthood, 79–81
    anxiety/depression caused by, 74–77
    case studies, 79–81, 84–87
    exercises for, 78–79, 82–83
    questioning, 73–74, 81–82, 85
    relationships affected by, 76, 82
    self-appreciation and, 77–79
    in Self-Awareness Continuum, 60, 61

self-trust and, 83–88
transitioning from, 87–88
self-awareness, stage 3 (integrated),
  89–104
  case studies, 93–94, 97–98, 100–102
  characteristics of, 89–90
  exercises for, 92, 104
  independence from parents, 96–99
  personalized success during, 95–96
  in Self-Awareness Continuum, 60, 61
  spirituality and, 99–104
  weaknesses embraced during, 90–93,
    98–99
self-confidence, 192–93, 203, 208, 227,
  278, 297, 322–24
self-criticism, 11–12, 41, 93, 320
self-discovery, 68, 82–83, 116, 133–34,
  325
self-doubt, 202–3, 264
self-focus, 21–24, 51
self-improvement, 69–71
selflessness, 51–54, 56
self-pity, 56
self-reliance, 85–86
Self, spirituality as connection to, 102–4
self-sufficiency, 148–49
self-trust, 83–88
sexuality
  dangerous, 291, 292, 293
  love and, 212–13
sexually-transmitted diseases (STDs),
  293
shift, the
  case studies, 316–19, 323–25, 326–29
  exercises for, 321–22
  responsibility for healing, 319–22
  risk-taking and, 326–29
  wisdom derived from, 315–16
shock, in acceptance process, 272, 275
shopping sprees, 46
shyness, 170–71
sickness, 284–85, 287–88
singlehood
  case studies, 186–89

after divorce, 318–19
emotional numbness and, 186–92
enjoying, 185, 194
exercises for, 191–92, 194
graduation from, 194
as "incomplete," 185–86
insecurity and, 192–93
as protective strategy, 190
self-love and, 186–89
skills, 144
slacking, smart, 111–17
small business loans, 256
Smart-Slacking Game Plan (exercise),
  115–17
social life, 146, 171–72
soul matches, 183–84, 198, 203–6
spirituality, 99–104
structure, need for, 108, 113
student loans, 307–9
success
  balance and, 263
  life satisfaction as, 329
  love vs. career as, 223–25
  personalized, 95–96
Superfriend, being a, 167–68
support groups, 216, 275, 304–5
support system, 147–48, 159–60, 177–78,
  272, 275, 299, 328
  See also family; friends

T

taxes, 110
therapy, 317
Throw a Money Party (exercise), 311–13
tough stuff, 270–89
  acceptance process, 272–77
  case studies, 273–74, 278–79, 280–82,
    283–85, 286–88
  changing others, 279–80
  effects of, 291
  exercises for, 276–77, 283
  forgiveness and, 285–88
  as inspirational experience, 270, 271
travel, 83, 116, 233, 319
triggers, 173–76, 286–89

Trump, Donald, 240
trust, 99, 164–66
    See also self-trust
Twenties Triangle, 58, 106, 152–54, 156,
    334
        See also How Do I Get What I
        Want?; self-awareness *entries*;
        What Do I Want?
20somethingmanifesto.com, 334
twenty-something transitions, 2
    celebrating firsts, 18
    checklisting and, 4–7
    as crises, 3–4
    domino effect in, 43
    escapism and, 24–27
    exercises for, 12–13, 29–30
    Expectation Hangovers and, 18–21
    finding your stride in, 140–49
    inspiration and self-judgment, 11–12
    instant gratification and, 13–18
    online help, 334
    option paralysis, 7–11
    overdependency on parents,
        27–29
    as puzzle, 156–57, 173–74, 231
    self-focus and, 21–24
    sharing, 333–34
    uncertainty and, 58
twenty-something years
    as "in-between stage," 108–9
    leaving, 152–54
    as yellow brick road, 10

U

uncertainty
    anxiety/depression caused by, 107–9,
        117–18
    as blessing, 128, 331–32
    checklists and, 6–7
    faith in, 331
    risk taking and, 330–31
    self-awareness and, 102
    Twenties Triangle and, 58

understanding, in acceptance process,
    272

V

vacations, 194
victimhood, 316–17
vision board, 321–22
volunteer work, 52–54, 69, 116, 146

W

Walking in a Bully's Shoes (exercise),
    283
weaknesses, 26, 90–93, 98–99
wellness, maintaining, 46–47, 56, 292–93
What Do I Want?
    anxiety over, 107–9
    case studies, 111–13, 123–25, 126–28,
        130–31, 133–34
    disappointments, dealing with,
        128–29
    elimination process, 125–28, 129
    exercises for, 132–33
    intuition and, 133–37
    risk taking, 123–37 (*see also* risk tak-
        ing)
    taking time to decide, 114–17
    See also adulthood, transition to;
        How Do I Get What I Want?
"what ifs," 43–44
What's Your Twenty? (exercise), 29–30
when/then thinking, 55, 248, 251
Who Am I? *See* self-awareness *entries*
women
    attitude toward marriage, 225
    and body image, 295
    dating behavior, 107
    as feelers, 217, 219–21
    "having it all" and, 219, 225
    and money, 312
workaholics, 243
work/life balance, 47, 48, 226,
    243–45, 265
worry, 43–44
    See also anxiety

ABOUT THE AUTHOR

Christine Hassler left her successful job as a Hollywood agent at age twenty-five to pursue a life she could be passionate about. Today she is a life coach with a counseling emphasis, specializing in relationships, career, and self-fulfillment. She supports men and women in discovering the answers to the questions, Who Am I? What do I want? and How do I get it?

As a professional speaker, Christine leads seminars and workshops for audiences around the country. She has appeared on the *Today* show, CNN, and PBS as well as various local television and radio shows. Christine is the author of *Twenty Something, Twenty Everything* (New World Library, 2005).

Christine received her undergraduate degree from Northwestern University, and she has trained at the Communication Arts Company. She is currently studying in the graduate program in spiritual psychology at the University of Santa Monica and is a candidate for receiving her master's degree in 2008. Originally from Dallas, Texas, she now lives in Los Angeles with her husband, Chris. To contact Christine or learn more about her workshops, speaking events, or coaching sessions, visit www.christinehassler.com.